The Legacy of
Albion Small

THE HERITAGE OF SOCIOLOGY

A Series Edited by Morris Janowitz

THE LEGACY OF ALBION SMALL

VERNON K. DIBBLE

THE UNIVERSITY OF CHICAGO PRESS

CHICAGO AND LONDON

Vᴇʀɴᴏɴ K. Dɪʙʙʟᴇ is professor of sociology at Wesleyan
University. This is his first book.

Tʜᴇ Uɴɪᴠᴇʀsɪᴛʏ ᴏғ Cʜɪᴄᴀɢᴏ Pʀᴇss, Cʜɪᴄᴀɢᴏ 60637
The University of Chicago Press, Ltd., London

Library of Congress Cataloging in Publication Data

Dibble, Vernon K.
  The legacy of Albion Small.

  (The Heritage of sociology)
  Includes index.
  1. Small, Albion Woodbury, 1854–1926.   2. Sociolo-
gists—Biography.   I. Title.
HM22.U6S484   301'.092'4 [B]   74-16686
ISBN 0-226-14520-4

The adequate record of even the confusions of our forebears may help, not only to clarify those confusions, but to engender a salutary doubt whether we are wholly immune from different but equally great confusions. For though we have more empirical information at our disposal, we have not different or better minds; and it is, after all, the action of the mind upon facts that makes both philosophy and science—and, indeed, largely makes the "facts." Nevertheless, those who do not care for the natural history of man in his most characteristic activity, who have neither curiosity nor patience to follow the workings of other minds proceeding from premises which they do not share, or entangled in what seem to them, and often are, strange confusions, or engaged in speculative enterprises which they may regard as hopeless, ought in fairness to be warned that much of the story which I am to try to tell will be for them without interest.

Arthur O. Lovejoy

Contents

Acknowledgments

MANY PEOPLE AND institutions were of help to me in writing this book. Phyllis Davis, Bettina Hansen, and Dorothy Sanstrom, at times under very trying conditions, typed successive versions of the manuscript. Mark Testa was a conscientious research assistant during the early stages of my writing. Cynthia Cohen, Steven Hoffman, and Pericles Vallianos found several errors in my citations, and helped to prepare the manuscript in many other ways. Ann Turner, of the library of Norwich University, gave indispensable help to a stranger who had no claim on her services or on the facilities of her institution. William Dillon, Michael Durkan, Harold Geisse, Alan Nathanson, and many others at the Wesleyan University library were always available when I needed them. The libraries of Andover-Newton Theological School, the University of Chicago, Colby College, and Johns Hopkins University provided copies of numerous archival sources. Ellis O'Neal, of the Andover-Newton library, was especially helpful in supplying not only documents, but also clues, leads, and fugitive published sources. Nancy Taylor, of Temple Adath Israel, Louisville, Kentucky, went out of her way to find an especially fugitive source. Wesleyan University and the Center for the Study of Social Organization of the University of Chicago gave financial support. I learned a lot from discussions with Phillip Ennis, Ursula Goehre, Morris Janowitz, William Martin, Louis Mink, Thomas Jack Morrione (and from his unpublished masters essay on Albion Small), and Hubert O'Gorman. The department of history at Wesleyan University provided a formal setting in which Neil Coughlan, David Konstan, and David

Swift made useful and sometimes challenging comments on part of
the manuscript. David Konstan later read and commented upon the
entire manuscript with his usual thoroughness, care, and rigor. And
Frances J. Adams, who edited the entire manuscript, synthesized her
scathing comments with disarming charm. I hope these people will
like this product of their time, their labor, and their thought.
    This book is dedicated to E. S. D. and L. C. D.

INTRODUCTION: THE COHERENCE
OF SMALL'S THOUGHT

SHORTLY AFTER ALBION Small's death in 1926, one of his former students described his teacher for the benefit of readers in the second half of the twentieth century.

> Fifty years hence the student who wishes to form a mental picture of the pioneer sociologist, Albion W. Small, should begin by calling up in imagination the ideal of a gentleman.... He should think of a person somewhat below the average height but notably virile and erect, speaking in a rich voice, and bearing himself with assured dignity. He should see him as always attired with the quiet elegance of an ambassador. And when he conceives of the traits which intimate acquaintance would reveal he should think of modesty and magnanimity.

> Earnest as Professor Small has been in the declaration of his ideas, he has also been ready as few scholars are to acknowledge the tentative character of his teaching, free from determination to defend a position once taken because it was identified with himself, hospitable to the ideas of others up to the very end of his active life, and generous in his appreciation of the contributions of other scholars in the field in which he has himself been a contributor.

> To these traits must be added the fact that the fundamental element of his life has always been the ethical interest. He has been interested in scholarship chiefly as a means of solving life's puzzle and bringing to realization the possibilities of good inherent in mankind.[1]

As with many of Small's contemporaries, in sociology and in

other fields, his "ethical interest" accompanied a commitment to "science." He believed that sociology was both a scientific and an ethical discipline. For Small exemplified the transition, in the United States, from moral philosophy to sociology.[2] In this transition the moral concerns of the older discipline carried over to the first generations of sociologists. Small also exemplifies the German transition from history to sociology,[3] and the Germanic components of his thought were also consistent with his "ethical interest." For example, he shared with Gustav Schmoller a belief in the social sciences as ethical disciplines.[4]

Small's intellectual biography combines, possibly to a greater extent than any other sociologist, these two transitions, the American transition from moral philosophy and the German transition from history to sociology. For Small was rooted in a moralistic, American Protestant tradition and also had strong personal and intellectual ties with Germany.[5]

A descendant of old Yankee stock and the son of a Baptist clergyman, Small was born in Buckfield, Maine, in 1854. He graduated from Colby, a Baptist college from which his father had also graduated, in 1876; and from Newton Theological, also Baptist, in 1879. He taught history at Colby from 1881 to 1888, when he took a leave of one year to obtain a Ph.D. in history at Johns Hopkins. Upon his return to Colby in 1889, he became the president of that college.*

At the end of his first year as president, on 10 June 1890, Small reported to the trustees that he had changed the subject matter of one of the standard undergraduate courses of that era, Moral Science. He wrote that "instead of attempting to trace the development of metaphysical philosophy in any portion of history," he had "introduced the class to modern sociological philosophy."[6] That is, he had taught one of the first sociology courses ever given in the United States.[7] For he had been reading sociology—Ward, Spencer, Schäffle, Ratzenhofer, and others—for many years and had become dissatisfied with history.

In 1892 William Rainey Harper (also Baptist), president of the University of Chicago (also Baptist, in Rockefeller's original intent),[8]

---

* An autobiographical letter that Small wrote in 1915 is reprinted in Appendix E.

offered Small the chairmanship of the department of sociology. Small left Colby in 1892 to found, at Chicago, the first department of sociology in the world. He remained at Chicago until his death in 1926. During those years he founded the *American Journal of Sociology*, the first sociological journal in the United States; published many books and dozens of articles; served as president of the American Sociological Society; and brought to his department people such as W. I. Thomas, Robert Park, and Ernest Burgess, who were able to carry out the vision that he had had since the early 1890s. This vision became realized in the 1920s as the "Chicago School of Sociology."[9]

On the German side, after Small graduated from Newton Theological in 1879, he spent two years in Germany, studying at Berlin and Leipzig. His study with economists of the German historical school was a lasting influence on his thought. He returned to the United States with a German bride, the daughter of a Junker general. He kept in contact throughout his life with German scholars, and with their writings. For example, he published Simmel and other Germans in the *American Journal of Sociology*,[10] and was responsible for bringing Ratzenhofer, Sombart, Weber, and other prominent Germans and Austrians to the Saint Louis Exposition of 1905. He wrote a book on the German cameralists.[11] His book on the origins of sociology is devoted exclusively to German thinkers.[12] And his writing often has a Germanic ring, especially on topics remote from his American experience such as his lengthy discussion of "The State" in *General Sociology*.[13]

Small was only one of thousands of American students who studied in Germany during the last decades of the nineteenth century. He was only one of a large number of leading American scholars of his time who had taken that trek in their youth and whose thought bore the imprint of their German education.[14] And he was only one of dozens of clergymen and sons of clergymen among the first generation of American sociologists.[15] But Small seems to be unique in the extent to which he combined and typified both the Germanic transition from history to sociology and the American, low Protestant transition from moral philosophy to sociology.

These dual origins always showed through Small's writings.

Germanic: "The elementary interest of a State ... is the development of its corporate individuality ... [and] in the very nature of
the State, it is uncompromising warfare with everything that
threatens to limit the State-individuality."[16] Religious piety gone
secular: "In all seriousness, then, and with careful weighing of my
words, I register my belief that social science is the holiest sacrament
open to men. It is the holiest because it is the wholest career within
the terms of human life.... The whole circumference of social
science is the indicated field for those 'works' without which the
apostle of 'salvation by faith' declared that faith is dead."[17]

Both the Germanic abstraction and the American, low Protestant
moralizing may seem strange to most American sociologists in the
1970s, to most students of sociology, and to most readers who have
a lay interest in the field. But Small's thought does have an internal
logic that makes sense. And his thought seems also to make sense as
one kind of reaction to, and reflection of, his historical setting.

This book is about both the internal logic and the historical
setting of Small's thought. It will report other facts about Small's
life and career as they seem relevant to the understanding of his
intellectual progression into sociology and to the analysis of his fully
developed sociological thinking. But it is not a biography. It is,
rather, an attempt to analyze, both historically and in terms of inner
logic, the peculiar synthesis of ideas that Small created. And it
attempts to suggest some reasons why this synthesis broke down,
leaving later generations of sociologists in the United States with
only a portion of Small's legacy.

Briefly, Small's synthesis combined a commitment to scientific
methods, as he understood them, with a belief in sociology as an
ethical discipline. It combined a belief that social scientists should
not actively take sides with any one class, party, or interest group
against any other, with a commitment to a reformist politics in
which expertise and knowledge of society had an especially
important place; and with a belief in the distinctive role of social
scientists in the improvement of society. It combined an assertion of
the material bases of human nature and a faith in the universality of
causal processes with a belief in morally responsible, sentient,
volitional selves. And it combined a definition of sociology as the

science of "association" with a definition of sociology as the most general social science, as the science of the total "social process" that drew upon, and subsumed, the more specialized social sciences. This latter definition of sociology, in turn, was linked to Small's view of sociology as a science. For in Small's conception of "objectivity," the more holistic the study of society—the greater the number and variety of points of view it embraced, or the more complete its vision of the total "social process"—the more objective and the more scientific it was.

To say that these beliefs constitute a "synthesis" is to assert that they were not simply juxtaposed in the same head, or in the same corpus of writings. To be sure, there are occasional loose ends, or examples of loose talk, in some of Small's works. But on balance, these diverse ideas hang together coherently.

Only some of these ideas, however, have come down to later generations of sociologists. Notably, most of Small's ideas about "science" seem quite familiar and conventional to sociologists in the second half of the twentieth century. Just as Parsons and other mid-century sociologists often found "convergences" in their field, Small believed that by the turn of the century sociologists were fast converging upon a single science of sociology. He presented a paper on "Some Points of Agreement Among Sociologists" at the first meeting of the American Sociological Society.[18] He believed also that sociology was becoming more objective, that "during the nineteenth century the social sciences were half-consciously engaged in a drive from relatively irresponsible discursiveness toward 'positivity' or 'objectivity' " and that the "American Sociological Movement" was a "lineal continuance" of this drive.[19] He believed that sociology was and should be cumulative; that it should be empirical, and that students of sociology should be trained in empirical research; and that sociology should also be a theoretical, nomothetic discipline, not a purely descriptive one.

In short, Small had a vision of sociology as a science that is quite similar, in its broad outlines at least, to the conceptions of scientific sociology that have prevailed, until recently at least, among later generations of sociologists. For Small, in part through his publications, but probably to a greater extent through his teaching, his appointments of others to the Chicago department, and his administrative work for sociology through the American Sociological Society and the *American Journal of Sociology*, was one important source of these conceptions for later generations.

The next three chapters of this book deal with these more familiar aspects of Small's work, with that portion of his legacy that remained alive. Chapter 2, "The Coming Science of Sociology," spells out Small's vision of convergence and cumulative knowledge in his field. It gives examples of convergence, as Small saw them, and examples of the buoyant optimism—tempered late in Small's life—with which Small viewed the recent past and the immediate future of his field. Chapter 3, "Politics, Pedagogy, and Social Research," traces the steps by which Small progressed, in the 1880s, from history to empirical sociology. It suggests some of the reasons for this progression in Small's experiences as an undergraduate teacher of history and of political economy, and in the political goals that he brought to his undergraduate teaching. Briefly, empirical sociology, more than history or political economy, would help students to become knowledgeable, reformist citizens, who would be neither revolutionary nor complacent with things as they are. Chapter 4, "Objectivity, Theory, and the Unity of Knowledge," examines Small's styles of theorizing, as related to Small's conception of his role in sociology—that of a "methodologist," as he used the term, or "general sociologist"—to his politics, and to his conception of "objectivity." It suggests some reasons why sociological theory, for Small, should be not only general but also holistic, why theory should embrace the total "social process."

Small's insistence upon a holistic sociology, as distinguished both from specialized work in diverse subfields and from latter-day "theories of the middle range," in Merton's phrase, marks one divergence between him and most American sociologists who came after him. This holistic vision, in turn, is closely related to another difference between Small and his successors, his belief that sociology was an ethical discipline and that ethical questions are a special type of scientific question. Briefly, his thinking was as follows. Sociology should be objective. That social science is most objective that is most holistic. Hence, sociology should be holistic, should study the total "social process." But the study of the "social process" involves the study of the ends that are inherent in it. And the study of ends inherent in the "social process" is the study of ethical goals.

Chapter 5, "Professors as Moral Leaders," spells out these links between Small's conception of science, his definition of sociology as the study of the social process, and his belief that sociology was an ethical discipline. It also suggests certain connections between this belief and the historical moment in which Small's sociological thinking developed. For example, it shows the congruence between this belief and the social role of university scholars in Small's day, a role that he wanted to extend to the point of having university-affiliated social science research institutes determine the fate of capitalism itself. This chapter also analyzes the internal logic of Small's thinking about the relation between sociology and ethics. It attempts to show forth the rather distinctive, and internally coherent synthesis in which Small combined cognitive with moral assertions.

A synthesis of scientism and moralism, or the belief that such a synthesis is not possible, depends upon one's understanding of the nature of scientific and of moral statements. Chapter 5 deals with such issues. The synthesis depends also upon certain substantive beliefs about the world. For example, a belief in individual moral responsibility is less congruent with the belief that all human behavior consists of responses to internal and external stimuli, and that the subjective experience of conscious choice is epiphenomenal, than it is with a view of human behavior that attributes a crucial role to some internal mechanism that coordinates diverse stimuli, whether that coordinating mechanism be termed the central nervous system, the self, or the will. Chapter 6, "Human Nature and the Social Process," deals with these issues. Briefly, in order to be both scientistic and moralistic, Small had to be scientistic but not mechanistic. He required a conception of human nature that allowed him to believe both in conscious choice and in the universality of causal processes, both in sentience and in the material bases of human beings. And, as chapter 6 points out, his conception of human nature is important in his sociology because his view of the "social process" is, in some respects, profoundly individualist. The "social process" is the objectification of the subjectivities of human beings in association with one another. Hence, individualized human nature, as it spills over into the "social process," is one major determinant of the nature and direction of that process.

These two chapters, "Professors as Moral Leaders" and "Human Nature and the Social Process," are the most important ones for making the case that Small synthesized, and did not merely juxtapose, ideas that must seem incongruent to many sociologists today. Chapter 7, "The Social Process and Progressive Politics," shows the links, on which Small himself was quite explicit, between this scholarly synthesis and Small's political views. That chapter brings together the connections between Small's politics and the single most central concept in his thought, the concept of "social process." That concept implied, for Small, opposition both to laissez-faire capitalism or Jeffersonian individualism and to socialism; and support for corporate, welfarist capitalism. It implied a kind of reformist politics that relied on the middle class more than on any other, and relied most of all upon the knowledge and expertise of people such as social scientists, who were presumably able to assess all conflicting claims in society and to give all claimants neither more nor less than their just deserts from a more objective point of view than anybody else could attain. Chapter 8, the concluding chapter, reviews and assesses Small's legacy, suggests some historical reasons why his synthesis was not sustained among later generations of sociologists, and asks the question, Is this book about the heritage of sociology or is it antiquarianism?

The answers to that question vary with the changing political and scholarly goals, and the historically relative situations, of sociologists today and in the future. But sociologists of diverse political views and scholarly styles have shown an increasing interest, during the 1960s and early 1970s, in the ethical and political impact of their work.[20] Chapter 8 presents some reasons why many sociologists who cannot accept the details of Small's synthesis will continue to be more concerned than they have been in the past with the relationship between sociology and ethics.

Throughout the book I make frequent use of quotations from Small, including some that are rather lengthy. The lengthy quotations will give readers a better feel for Small's rhetoric and style of thought than paraphrases or summaries could give. I also make frequent use, in quotations and elsewhere, of unpublished sources from the archives of Colby College, Andover-Newton Theological Seminary, Johns Hopkins University, and the University of Chicago. These archival sources are indispensable to the understanding of Small's work. Without them, it would not be possible to see, for example, the steps in his progression from history to sociology; or the full extent of his commitment to empirical research; or certain aspects of his conception of his own work and of himself as a sociologist. The selections reprinted in the appendixes include archival sources as well as excerpts from Small's publications. Selections of both types are elaborations upon, or further evidence for, points made in the text. Hence, the selections do not necessarily reflect Small's own conception, or the conceptions that other authors writing about Small might have, of what was most important or most typical of his work. The choice of selections stems from the analysis of Small that this book presents. A different analysis would have resulted in different choices.

As noted above, many readers may find Small's language and style of thought strange and perhaps difficult to grasp until they have had time to become familiar with his rhetoric and with the way his mind worked. But the themes of the next chapter—sociology is a brand new field; it is underdeveloped, and still has a long way to go; but the diverse strands within it are fast converging into a genuine, fully developed science—are, some seventy years later, still familiar to all sociologists.

2

THE COMING SCIENCE OF
SOCIOLOGY

In one of his first writings in sociology, a printed but unpublished "Outline of Course in Sociology" that he prepared for his sociology course at Colby, Small asked, "Can we have a science of Society?" He answered affirmatively, for, "Life is subject to law." But the science cannot be exact because the "phenomena of society are too complicated, too variable, too indefinite, for precise measurement."[1] In 1894, in the text that he wrote with George Vincent, Small refers to sociology as an "inchoate science" that was "thus far an interrogation of social reality, not a code of matured social doctrines."[2] In 1900, attributing the origin of sociology, in part, to the dissatisfaction of some scholars with the methods of the philosophy of history, Small wrote:

> The implication is not intended that the sociologists have invariably been more scientific than the philosophers of history. On the contrary, they have been, as a rule, equally and sometimes more unscientific. They have, however, undertaken more deliberate attempts to construct plans of research that would conform to the principles of exact science. The consequence is that, while sociology up to date can show comparatively little in the way of absolutely new knowledge about society, it has accumulated a wealth of perception about the value of different portions of knowledge, and about ways in which knowledge of society must be tested and organized. Although these perceptions are not yet coordinated in any system which is generally accepted by sociologists, there is an unformulated consensus about standards of

10

objectivity and correlation which is steadily reducing sociological speculation to the soberness of observational and experimental science.[3]

In his treatise, *General Sociology*, published in 1905, Small claimed, "The sociologists are attempting to develop a general science which will have relations to the special social sciences analogous with the relations of general physics to the special physical sciences, on the one hand, and to the various physical technologies, on the other...."[4] In the same work he wrote:

The fundamental difference between the philosophers of history and the sociologists is that the former hoped to explain human experience by means of logical deductions from speculative premises. The latter know that human experience is to be understood only by inductive investigation of an evolutionary process.[5]

For Small, these assertions of the scientific character of sociology were historical statements about the recent past and visions of hope for the fairly near future. Through all his working years as a sociologist, he was convinced that he was living through the formative period of a science of sociology. And during most of those years, until he became discouraged in the early 1920s, he was quite pleased and optimistic over the pace of the progress which he thought he saw.

TOWARD AGREEMENT AND CUMULATIVE KNOWLEDGE

Small believed that disparate strands of thought in sociology were converging into a single sociological science, and that there was more agreement among sociologists than appeared on the surface. His books, articles, and reviews contain dozens of passing remarks, or longer passages, that express these beliefs. For example:

... except in details which need not concern anyone but the sociological specialist, there is no important difference among sociologists about the substantial matter referred to by the word "social."[6]

> I am not aware that there is a sociologist in the world who accepts Spencer's sociology at its author's appraisal.[7]

> ... consciously or unconsciously, the sociologists have been working upon one sociology. Exaggeration of some single factor in association, or of some single feature in method, does not constitute a special sociology. It contributes, directly or indirectly, positively or negatively, to the development of the one general sociology.[8]

> Among the writers on sociology, I have yet to discover the first one who does not betray by implication and as a necessary postulate, whenever an attempt is made to trace out genetic relations, a belief in all that is essential in the organic concept.[9]

When Small wrote such lines, he meant not simply that he saw, beneath doctrinal disagreements or differences in terminology, a "more radical and general agreement than the disputants imagine."[10] He meant also, and more crucially, that there was not simply change in the direction of more agreement, but cumulative growth.

In *General Sociology* Small attempted to demonstrate cumulative growth. His prize example is the synthesis of Spencer and Schäffle:

> Ever since Spencer wrote, there has been lively debate of the question whether his scheme should be accepted or rejected. The upshot will be neither. It will be assimilated and coordinated. In many arguments the issue has been Spencer *versus* somebody else. It has been assumed that it was a question of exclusion. The only social theorist who needs be excluded by conceding some value to Spencer's scheme would have to be one who denies the fundamentals of association.[11]

As Small saw it, one of Spencer's central contributions was the concept of "structure," whose "essential idea ... is parts of a whole at rest in relation to each other."[12] Schäffle, in turn, contributed the concept of "function." But, Small contended, "Spencer, in spite of himself, tended to seek the meaning of social structure in structure" while Schäffle tended "to see the meaning of social functions in function, rather than in causal and consequent conditions in the persons functioning."[13] Small concluded that it is necessary to make a "transition from [these] two partial views of social reality to the most comprehensive view at present possible."[14] He spelled out his argument as follows:

> We have thus taken brief account of the two conceptions which have been prominent in the history of sociological theory: the conception of social structure, and that of social functions. These concepts have been, in turn, centers for ambitious sociological systems. Those systems are no longer regarded as serious competitors for leadership in social theory. They have served their day, and social theorists cannot be fully equipped without thinking through the problems which those systems confronted and tried to solve. The clue idea in each of those systems is not, and never can be, obsolete. The concepts "social structure" and "social function," or some substitute which we cannot imagine, will always be indispensable in analysis of the social reality.... The work of testing these ideas, as embodied in sociological systems, has trained thinkers to carry analysis farther, and to propose more adequate programs of social interpretation. We are now at a point from which we may with advantage approach the most searching scheme of social analysis that has thus far been proposed.[15]

Small's belief that the sociologists of his day were converging upon a single sociology included more than his perception of cumulative growth and synthesis of ideas. There was also methodological progress. He defined the "thesis" of *General Sociology* as the contention that "The central line in the path of methodological progress, from Spencer to Ratzenhofer, is marked by gradual shifting of effort from analogical representation of social structures to real analysis of social processes."[16] And late in his career, in *Origins of Sociology*, he argued at length "the main thesis that during the nineteenth century the social sciences were half consciously engaged in a drive from relatively irresponsible discursiveness toward 'positivity' or 'objectivity,'" and that "the American Sociological movement" was one "lineal continuance" of this drive.[17]

Small's optimistic belief in progress toward the science of sociology was summed up in a paper he presented to the first convention of the American Sociological Society, "Points of Agreement Among Sociologists."[18] Small's "points of agreement" were highly general— "We agree that the primary task of sociology is to discover and to formulate the laws of those processes of human association which differ, either in degree or in kind, from processes that occur in antecedent orders in the scale of evolution";[19] "We are agreed that the structural or static phase of social occurrences is a sort of mirage";[20] "We are agreed that our distinctive center of attention and our principle synthesis is personality."[21] Not a single point of agreement stated a substantive conclusion. Despite the highly general nature of his discussion, Small did find one basic disagreement among sociologists. There was disagreement between the materialist or biologically oriented sociologists who believed that "society has been produced chiefly by the same forces that have produced the flora and fauna of the earth" and the more psychologically oriented sociologists, himself included, who believed that "society has been produced ... chiefly by forces by virtue of which society is something essentially different from flora and fauna."[22] But Small attempted to place this disagreeement in the context of a division of labor within the field; and he proclaimed the hope that this division of labor would, in the end, result in the single science of sociology.

Very few men are likely to be equally capable of the highest efficiency in physical and psychical research.... Some men may be able to do very little first-hand investigation either of physical or psychical elements, yet they may do good work in verifying estimates of the proportions of those elements in typical situations. Provided men of these types are working within hailing distance of one another, and are keeping tab on one another's performances, it is in the interest of the economy of effort that each type shall work upon its specific clue to the limit. Let the men who believe that language, and art, and science, and politics, and love, and religion, are merely the finished products of the same forces which have reached an equilibrium in the forms of matter that are apparent to our senses—let them work away upon their hypothesis, until all the evidence within reach is brought to the support of their theorem. Let the men who believe that mind rather than matter determines the phenomena peculiar to human society—let them also summon the evidence and display it for all it is worth. Let the men who are attorneys neither for physics nor for psychics continue to hold the balance between the opposing claims, and to find a place in the reckoning for each new factor, or power of a factor which either of the other types has overlooked or underrated. Instead of causing schism among us, that definite grouping and method will turn out to be in the interest of ultimate agreement.[23]

Viewing the disagreement between adherents of physical forces and adherents of psychical forces in this light, Small was able to summarize his paper with the announcement that "the sociologists are fairly well agreed about their point of view."[24] That news was momentous to Small. For:

Anyone who has looked below the surface of the history of science knows that when a group of scientists have gone that far they have potentially solved their major problems. Whatever else sociology is, we all see that it is important, first of all simply as a point of view. We have taken possession of our standing ground, and we shall now proceed at our leisure to move the world.[25]

Small frequently disparaged the actual accomplishments of sociology. "Judged by results, sociology up to date has comparatively little to say for itself."[26] And "up to date" could refer not only to 1900, when these words were published, but to any date throughout Small's life. But his faith in the future was great.

One of Small's reasons for wanting an authoritative social science was to counter the influence of amateur theorists of social doctrines, and of the "agitators," especially leftist agitators, whom he scorned. A unified science, as distinct from a discipline that included two or many sociologies, would tend to keep Marxism and other bodies of belief that the agitators disseminated from achieving legitimacy in academic sociology.[27] Small seems to have had few worries on this score. He was sustained by his analogies to the natural sciences (there are not two biologies or two chemistries); by the late-nineteenth century conception of universities as havens of free inquiry[28] (as against the more traditional American conception of colleges which are abodes of institutionalized truth)[29]; and by the conventional liberal belief that a free marketplace of ideas is valuable, not because it allows irreconcilable cultural traditions backed by unequal political or economic strength to co-exist, but because free discussion makes for ever greater increments of truth. Small was confident that a unitary science of sociology, increasingly scientific and increasingly unified, was on the way.

A Touch of Disillusionment

Late in his life, after announcing for more than thirty years that great things were in store (though they had not yet arrived), Small became more discouraged than he had been about the actual accomplishments of sociology and of the other social sciences. And he became less optimistic than he had been about the prospects of the science of sociology and about its potential contribution to the welfare of humanity. In *Origins of Sociology* he wrote that in the United States

> ... a few scholars a generation ago became dissatisfied with the way things were going among the different social sciences. After fretting fruitlessly for a while, they decided to create a science of their own. They advertised that they were going to furnish the world with a science that would correct the errors of the older and futile social sciences. [A note here in the original text.] They would substitute a social science as it should be, capable of explaining all about society, including principles and rules for guiding society in the future to a speedy perfection. They adopted the name "sociology" and I am frank to admit that they accepted it as a compliment when, after a few years, European scholars began to refer to "sociology" as the "American Science."[30]

In the note to the first half of this passage, Small wrote, "I was one of them, and this way of putting it is a humble confession." But the humble confession, and the touch of satire in Small's description of the great hopes for a science of sociology that his generation of sociologists had entertained, did not entail any change in Small's view of the scientific nature of sociology. As in earlier years, Small found analogies between sociology and the natural sciences. For example, "In one respect, sociology is to the older divisions of social science what the use of the spectroscope is to chemistry, or blood analysis to physiology. That is, it is the addition of a certain technique by means of which phenomena partially investigated by other techniques may be still further investigated."[31]

Fifteen years before, Small had claimed for sociology the status of the general social science, analogous in its relations to the specialized social sciences to "the relations of general physics to the special physical sciences ... and to the various physical technologies." And this general science was going to "move the world." To call sociology a "technique," like spectroscopy, was to make less ambitious claims. But this more modest sociology was no less scientific than the grandiose sociology had been. As noted above, the entire work in which Small's humble confession appears argues "the main thesis" that during the nineteenth century the social sciences became increasingly objective and that American sociology was one "lineal continuance" of that trend.[32] Small became less optimistic about the accomplishments and prospects of the social sciences. But he did not change his views about their scientific character.

SMALL'S CONCEPTION OF "SCIENCE"

It is not sufficient, however, simply to note that Small believed in "science" and that sociology was becoming "scientific." For his conception of what a science of sociology would be differs from the conceptions of scientific sociology that prevailed, until quite recently at least, among later generations of American sociologists. Some elements in his conception of a scientific sociology would seem quite sound and quite familiar to the most scientistic sociologist of a later generation. Small's views about (a) observation and induction, (b) general conceptualizations, and (c) predictability, and to a somewhat lesser extent his conception of (d) objectivity, are quite consistent with textbook notions of "science." His belief that sociology, *as a social science*, is in part an evaluative, ethical discipline—that "the ultimate problem on the side of *pure science* is: What is worth doing?"[33]—differs considerably from conventional beliefs about value-free social science.

In Small's mind, the diverse elements in his conception of scientific sociology formed a coherent package. *An Introduction to the Study of Society*, the textbook published in 1894, summarizes a chapter on the three branches of sociology as follows:

> Sociology is thus the organization of all the material furnished by the positive study of society. Sociology is, first, Descriptive— coordinated facts of society as it is; second, Statical—the ideal which right reason discloses of society as it ought to be; third, Dynamic—[investigation of] the available resources for changing the actual into the ideal.[34]

In later writings, Small changed both the number of generic divisions within sociology and the terms he used to name them. In "Points of Agreement Among Sociologists," and elsewhere, he writes of "The Three dimensions of Sociology, cognitive, ethical, and constructive."[35] And in some contexts he referred to types of questions, instead of branches or dimensions of sociology. In *General Sociology*, for example, Small lists the four generic questions that sociologists face.

> The general *genetic* question about all [human] association is: Through what course of differentiation did these activities come into existence? This question demands the researches of all species of historical science. The general *statical* question about associations is: What forms and qualities of forces, in what proportions, maintain social structures in equilibrium? ... The general *dynamic* question about societies is: What influences operate, and in accordance with what formulas, to change the equilibrium or type of societary status? The general *teleological* question about association is: What ends or systems of ends are indicated by the foregoing exhibits of human resources? What is the apparent goal toward which human cooperation tends, and toward which it may be directed? This a question of valuations, to be answered in accordance with logical and psychological principles which have a competence of their own in sociology, but always dependent upon recognition of principles of knowledge involved in the antecedent stages of analysis and synthesis.[36]

Whatever the variations in terminology, however, Small always held to a view of "science" in which empirical investigations had ethical consequences, and ethical judgments rested upon empirical investigation. My analysis of this view of social science, and of its internal coherence, will require examination of Small's views of the nature of ethical judgments and of his theory of value. It will lead still further, into the ways in which he experienced his role as a university professor, and in which he envisioned the social position of social science in modern societies. That topic, in turn, will lead back to his politics; and to a superficially quite different topic, his strikingly innovative ideas about the organization of team research in the social sciences, complete with university-affiliated research institutes and grants from foundations. I turn first, however, to those elements in his conception of "science" that are most consistent with the textbook conceptions, to Small's view of sociology as an observational, inductive discipline, and to some of the factors in Small's background as an educator that contributed to the development of these views.

3

POLITICS, PEDAGOGY, AND
SOCIAL RESEARCH

INTRODUCTION

The textbook, *An Introduction to the Study of Society*, which Small and Vincent published in 1894, asserts that the "method of credible Sociology must be the method of observation and induction...."[1] It seems appropriate that Small made one of his earliest assertions of the empirical character of sociology in a text. For Small's experience as an undergraduate teacher was one of the factors that pushed him into sociology and that made him view sociology as an empirical discipline. That pedagogical experience, and the development toward empirical sociology that came out of it, were also colored by Small's political views.

Briefly, the logic of Small's development through the 1880s was as follows. Colleges should educate students to become intelligent, informed citizens who are neither radicals nor reactionaries. Empirical social science has an inherent tendency to make centrist, reformist citizens out of college students. For the observation of actual social conditions both prevents complacency and instructs students in the complexities of society which utopians leave out of view. In Small's judgment, neither history nor political economy was doing this job. Hence, empirical sociology and the training of students in empirical research.

SOCIAL RESEARCH AS PEDAGOGY

Throughout this development, Small was first of all an educator. His first major work in sociology, *An Introduction to the*

Study of Society, was that of an educational innovator. Small denied that that book was a text. It was, rather, a "laboratory guide," which the authors hoped would be judged "not as a supposed contribution to sociological knowledge, but as a proffered help in the training of beginners." And just as Small often found analogies between sociology and the natural sciences, the authors compared their sociology text with laboratory guides in biology.

> Together with a judicious teacher, who is at liberty to do more than hear recitations, the book should serve a purpose in Sociology analogous with that aimed at by Parker's *Elementary Biology*, or by Huxley's *Practical Biology*.[2]

Small and Vincent attempted to make their text into a training manual by listing "Subjects for Investigation" at the end of each chapter and, most of all, by a lengthy "Natural History of a Society." This section, written by Vincent,[3] was a fictional history of a midwestern city from the first settlement by a single farm family, through "The Rural Group" and "The Village," to "The Town and City." The purpose of this section was:

> (1) to exhibit qualitatively, not quantitatively, the various factors of social life as they appear at different stages of social organization; (2) to illustrate the tendency toward integration, specialization, and interdependence of parts which characterize a growing society; and chiefly (3) to suggest to the student a method of observation, which seeks to gain a conspectus of all social activities in their interrelations, not to scrutinize separately one department of life.[4]

In their advice to instructors using their text, the authors note that since their work is supposed to be a training manual, it will not be used "to best purpose unless students use the principles of analysis and synthesis illustrated in the text for investigation of corresponding conditions within the range of their own observation."[5] Hence,

> The ideal use of the method would result in an account of the history and present conditions of the town in which the study is being pursued, following the model of Book II [i.e., the fictional natural history of a city] and carrying out the details of social

structure under the categories [e.g., "The Functions of the Family," "Phenomena of Authority," "Morality and Law"] indicated by Books III, IV, and V.

A year after this text was published, one of the earliest community studies in American sociology, a study of Galesburg, Illinois, was carried out, according to its subtitle, "After the Method of Small and Vincent."[6] By 1896, at the latest, Small's concern that students investigate "conditions within the range of their own observation" was brought home to Chicago. He referred in that year to "the vast sociological laboratory which the city of Chicago constitutes."[7] And a number of Ph.D. dissertations, such as "A Study of the Stock Yards Community at Chicago, as a Typical Example of the Bearing of Modern Industry upon Democracy" (1901), by graduate students in sociology at Chicago during the early years of the department's existence were in the spirit of the "local inquiries" that Small and Vincent had proposed in 1894.

The seeds of the later "Chicago School" were already there by the middle of the 1890s. They might have germinated more fully and more quickly than they did, if Small had got everything out of President Harper that he was pressing for. As early as 1894, in the same letter to Harper in which he recommended the appointments to the department of W. I. Thomas, George Vincent, and others, Small recommended the appointment of a statistician for one quarter, and he argued the need for a longer appointment than that. He explained, "This course in the planning of statistical investigation of social conditions would expand the courses already offered in such a way as to greatly increase their value."[8] A month later, Small urged upon Harper, at greater length, the need for statistics in a department of sociology.* He defended himself from the charge that he was stepping into the preserve of the department of political economy, and added the argument that "It is important that an expert statistician should work in cooperation with Dr. Henderson and myself in carrying out plans of investigation directly tributary to our lines of study."[9] But he did not get his statistician. And five years later, still pressing the issue in 1899, Small complained to Har-

---

* The letter referred to here is reprinted in Appendix A.

per that there was "a crying need for a specialist in statistics and the University has never felt able to pay the salary that would secure the properly equipped man."[10]

THE BACKGROUND OF SMALL'S BELIEF IN EMPIRICAL SOCIOLOGY

Small's co-authorship of a "laboratory guide" for students of sociology and, more generally, his definition of sociology as an observational, inductive science, stem in part from his experiences and opinions as an educator during the period of considerable change and reform in undergraduate education that he lived through—as student, college teacher, and college president—from 1872, when he entered Colby, through 1892, when he left the presidency of Colby to found the department of sociology at Chicago. These pedagogical opinions, in turn, were colored by his politics, and by his view of the kind of citizens required in a democratic society.

An Introduction to the Study of Society embodies a pedagogical philosophy. It contains pedagogical injunctions both to students and to their instructors. Small and Vincent believed that "it would be useless or worse to experiment with this method," that is, to have students use their book as a guide to their own observations of social phenomena, "unless the instructor has some time for independent observation and reflection."[11] That is, the instructor had to be not only a teacher, but something of a scholar and researcher as well. This opinion seems appropriate to Albion Small, the first member of the faculty of Colby College in the history of that institution to hold a Ph.D.[12] It reflects the general trend of that period away from academicians who were exclusively college teachers to teachers who were scholars as well. The authors also had advice to scholar-teachers who would use this text about their behavior in the classroom, and about the educational policies of their colleges: unless he "is at liberty to do more than hear recitations," their book will not serve as a "laboratory guide."[13]

"Hearing recitations" refers to the way in which virtually all college classes in the United States were conducted until lecture courses and laboratory courses were introduced after the Civil War.

As a student at Colby between 1872 and 1876, Small witnessed the introduction of these and of other reforms to his alma mater.

The president of Colby at that time was the Reverend Henry E. Robins.[14] He was a Baptist clergyman, as most of his predecessors had been. He had firm beliefs about the Christian character of Colby, and about the necessity for all genuine education to be religious education. During his presidency, from 1873 to 1882, he reasserted Colby's Baptist tradition.

But Robins also introduced a number of secular reforms. He took the first steps toward electives, and the term "elective" first appears in the Colby catalogue for 1874-75. He introduced the distinction between lecture courses and recitation courses. As Small noted some forty years later, it was under Robins's presidency that, for the first time in Colby's history—and against the disapproval of some members of the faculty—an instructor in the natural sciences actually performed experiments in front of a class.[15] And more generally, according to Small's later reminiscences, there was a new spirit at Colby under the presidency of Henry Robins.[16]

We have no basis for tracing the precise consequences of this undergraduate experience on Small's later thinking as an educator, and as a sociologist. His reminiscences forty years later do not necessarily prove that he was attuned to all of these innovations at the time; and if he was, these reminiscences do not document any continuing influence throughout the intervening years. We do know, however, that Small, too, became an educational innovator. If he had never become a sociologist, or had never left Colby for Chicago, he would have had at least a minor, but permanent place in the history of higher education in the United States.

Small's innovations include both curricular and administrative policies. During Small's third year as professor of history at Colby, 1883-84, he taught the first course in political economy ever given at that school. Other members of the faculty objected to this daring, and most disreputable act. Small complained, in his annual report at the end of the year:

> I may say that the faculty have weighty contentious scruples about tolerating such an encroachment of a nineteenth-century study upon the exclusive antiquities of our curriculum, and that

unless these objections can be so far over-ruled that a place more in accordance with a modern estimate of Political Economy assigned to it, I shall not think it worth while to try to teach the science another year.[17]

Six years later, having returned from a year at Johns Hopkins where he obtained his Ph.D., and having become president of the college, Small taught what he mistakenly thought was the first sociology course at any American college.[18] In administrative matters, President Small had to handle a controversy over coeducation (among other problems, the women were winning too many prizes), and he was apparently the first college president ever to come up with the idea of coordinate colleges as the solution to this controversy.[19] After he went to Chicago he continued his interest in pedagogy and in educational reform. He corresponded with Harper on matters of general educational policy, as when he urged Harper to relent on the stringency of the Latin requirement.[20] He developed doubts about the value of sociology in the undergraduate curriculum, in part because he felt that the field was not sufficiently well developed for the usual sort of instructor to pass on to undergraduates.[21] In 1896 he presented a paper on "the pedagogical philosophy with which my sociology allies itself" to a meeting of the National Educational Association.[22] In 1897, his Chicago colleague, John Dewey, included that paper in his book, "My Pedagogical Creed."[23] In later years, Small served as a dean at Chicago and continued to publish papers and deliver addresses on a variety of general policy issues in higher education.[24]

The "laboratory guide" of 1894, in short, was the work of two professional pedagogues who had turned to sociology—Albion Small, former college president who remained a theorist of education; and George Vincent, the vice chancellor of the Chautauqua System of Education when the book was published, who received his Ph.D. in sociology at Chicago two years later, taught sociology there for many years, published a book called *The Social Mind and Education*,[25] and later became president of the University of Minnesota.[26] For Small, at least, the definition of sociology as an observational and inductive science, and the attempt to write a training manual instead of an ordinary text, were culminations of some ten years of experience with, and innovative thought about, undergraduate education.

While professor of history, and later president at Colby, Small held that "the College is not designated for professional but for general training." He was unhappy, both with the degree of specialism—"landing the larger part of our strength to the making of all the students Philologists, ... lawyers, or Chemists, or Engineers"—and with the dull and unscientific nature, as he saw it, of the teaching that took place there. For example:

> We are teaching a cut-and-dried Philology, by a method persistently unscientific, and allowing such instruction to take the place of study of the growth of the human mind. We are doing with Homer, and Sophocles, and Plato and Tacitus very much what the Harvard Law School would be doing if it used the Constitution of the United States simply as an exercise book in English grammar.[27]

It is important to note the nature of this charge. In disagreements over educational policies at American colleges today, a belief in general, liberal education does not usually go along with a belief in scientific training: and a belief in more specialized training tends to go along with a more scientistic orientation. In contrast, Small's charge was that the teaching at Colby, in his day, was too specialized and too unscientific. He wanted just the opposite package—a more general, liberal education for citizenship, with a more scientific orientation.

POLITICS AND EDUCATIONAL PHILOSOPHY

It is necessary to put this package into the context of Small's political beliefs. For those beliefs colored Small's conception of the kinds of citizens that a scientific but liberal education was supposed to produce. Small, like most of the founders of American sociology (and with the major exception of William Graham Sumner), was opposed both to Marxian theory and socialist politics, and to laissez-faire. Small waged recurrent campaigns against socialist or revolutionary politics. His report to the president and trustees of Colby University in 1888 announced that "no single period of History contains more timely lessons ... than the period of the French Revolution." For "Nearly every socialistic expedient, which is today prescribed for the ills of society, was tried and found wanting between the years 1789 and 1795." "The history of these failures is the most impressive commentary on the schemes of American socialists."[28] More than thirty years later, in the columns of the *American Journal of Sociology*, he denounced Lenin's "fantasies" and announced that the Soviet Union's New Economic Policy was "Lenin's confession of the failure of his experiment."[29]

On the other hand, he believed in "volitional social progress."[30] He was sympathetic to what he called "the social movement."[31] He cared about, and often wrote about, the economic insecurity of workers.[32] He proposed various reforms for governmental regulation of business.[33] He was, more or less, a "progressive," as that term was used during the decade or so before World War I. At a time when positivistic social science, especially in evolutionary versions, was often associated with "ameliorative drift,"[34] that is, with political quietism and laissez-faire economics, Small welcomed Lester Ward's *Dynamic Sociology* for, among other things, its "startling assertion that positivism is not necessarily indifferentism, nor Manchesterism, nor fatalism."[35]

In Small's own mind, these political beliefs required a certain kind of citizenry, which required a certain kind of education. In 1889, in an address to a meeting of the American Institute of Instruction, Small said:

> Volitional social progress in democracies is conditioned upon popular insight into the facts of social relations. Democracies must be capable of distinguishing the accidental in social order from the essential; the conventional from the structural; the organized from the organic; the artificial from the natural; the legal from the just; the actual from the possible. Democracies must attain wisdom in social diagnosis ...
>
> The proximate end, at least of democratic education is, to popularize knowledge of these structural and functional phenomena of society, and of the truths which these phenomena contain.[36]

Small's concern was that the citizen who mistook "the accidental" for "the essential" would oppose all social reform. And the citizen who saw everything as "accidental" or "organized" and nothing as "essential" or "organic" would listen to the "agitators" and go off in support of some "socialistic expedient" that the French Revolution had long since proven to be a failure. Social science would teach them the difference, and would teach them both that "the organized" is subject to "volitional progress" and that "the organic" must remain. This theme was more explicit in Small's mind (or at least in his writing) six years later, in 1895. In a letter to President Harper, he stated "some of the reasons why a journal of sociology is demanded of the University of Chicago."* Among many other arguments, Small held that a journal of sociology was "needed both to exert restraint upon utopian social effort and to encourage and direct well advised attempts at social cooperation."[37]

From History to Sociology

During the first few years of Small's teaching at Colby, the study of history, in Small's broad conception of that field, was supposed to do this job of training citizens. As he saw the purposes of his history courses in 1882, "the students must be taught to recognize the more obvious and general laws which historical evolution illustrates" and they should "be exercised in gathering evidence for themselves, and in deducing from it definite and legitimate conclusions." Good citizens, broadly educated but exposed to scientific procedures would result. For:

> On the one hand, the materials gathered by historical research so broaden the view as to rescue all other thinking from provincialism; and on the other hand, the habit of mind induced by training in scientific historical processes is precisely the habit which every man of affairs must sooner or later acquire in order to estimate rightly the forces that modify the society in which he moves, and the probable effect of proposed measures, policies, and institutions.[38]

In a slightly different version the following year, Small wrote

---

* This letter is reprinted in Appendix B.

that "the aim" of "the department of History . . . is to secure on the part of the student not only a familiarity with the leading facts of the period investigated, and with the elementary principles of historical reasoning, but particularly such facility of induction that he can apply the teachings of history in the interpretation of current events." For he "kept in view the definite end of making this department contribute . . . to the fitness of the students for the discharge of the obligations of citizenship."[39]

Undergraduate students of history, "gathering evidence for themselves" and developing a "facility of induction" would become good citizens, in the sense in which Small's politics required that they be. When Small wrote this way about training in history, he really knew what he was talking about. Or, at the very least, he discovered a few years later. Throughout his career, Small rarely gathered evidence for himself. He rarely attempted to draw "definite and legitimate conclusions" from a close reading of data of any sort. But his Johns Hopkins dissertation, *The Beginnings of American Nationality: The Constitutional Relations Between the Continental Congress and the Colonies and States*[40] (which he completed in 1889 under Herbert Baxter Adams, Richard Ely, and Woodrow Wilson) includes some very close and careful readings of numerous historical sources. From his scrutiny of the sources, he drew conclusions about the early constitutional history of the United States that differed considerably from the interpretations that had previously prevailed. But by the time Small was doing this research, he had become disappointed in history as the vehicle for the scientific, but liberal education of future citizens. In 1885 he decided that the effort during the preceding academic year had been a failure. He complained that the students in history

. . . have recognized in the record of Greek and Roman life no living issues, no social questions still unsettled, no interplay of moral forces identical with the motives and motors of our modern life. They have been burying themselves in archeology. They have found in the literatures of Greece and Rome nothing but philological museums.[41]

An alternative vehicle might have been political economy,

especially the ethically and historically oriented brand of political economy which Small had absorbed from Schmoller and others in Germany. But Small apparently saw that field, or at least his Colby courses in the field, as having less grandiose potential than he had seen in history. It is clear that many years later, in *Adam Smith and Modern Sociology* (1907), Small saw the function of economists as "more nearly analogous with that of the engineer than with that of the legislator, while the sociologist has a brief for other interests, over and above the technological, which the legislator is bound to consider."[42] For, in Small's view, in Adam Smith, "Political Economy . . . was the technology of a practical art which was strictly responsible to a moral philosophy that correlated all human activities." But political economy after Smith, "lost its sense of connection with the large moral process, and became the mystery of the craft of the capitalizer." Sociology, instead, took up Smith's "conception of the subordinate relationship of all specific activities within an inclusive moral system . . ."[43]

Small's description of his course in political economy, in 1884, is strikingly similar to this later assessment of the field. He described the course in more narrow terms than he described his history courses at the same time. And he made clear that political economy was subordinate to ethics and to history (as it was later to be subordinate to sociology).[44]

In the meantime, paralleling his developing thought about undergraduate curricula, Small had been doing a lot of reading. In the 1880s he became, in the words of one biographer, "an indefatigable but disappointed reader of the 'philosophy of history.'" As for research historians, Small concluded during this time that they "were not really finding out what mattered most, but were largely occupied with trivialities that would be gossip if they pertained to yesterday or the day before." He became disturbed by the fact that "painstaking research" led to futile and inconclusive results, and he came to believe that in historical research "the permanent tendencies in human affairs, the inner methods of causation that determine the destinies of men and nations were not being revealed."[45] The philosophers of history did not do what Small wanted his undergraduate students to do—"be exercised in gathering evidence for themselves." And the historians who researched minute historical issues lacked other traits that Small wanted in his students—"recognize the more obvious and general laws which historical evolution illustrates" and have "such facility of induction that he can apply the teaching of history in the interpretation of current events."

History should have been the vehicle, but historians were as bad as Colby undergraduates. Political economy was a subordinate discipline with limited ends. It was not supposed to reveal "the permanent tendencies" and "the inner methods of causation that determine the destinies of men and nations." But Small had also been reading sociology. He had apparently read Spencer, Comte, and Schäffle while still in Germany (1879–81);[46] had read Ratzenhofer by 1890, at the latest, and probably some years before;[47] and had read Ward's *Dynamic Sociology* sometime before going to Johns Hopkins in 1888.[48] It was Ward who really hit him.

Years later, at the time of Ward's death, Small recalled the impact that *Dynamic Sociology* had had upon him.

I cannot precisely date my discovery of *Dynamic Sociology*, but its meaning for me was crucial, and I was aware at once that it had leveled barriers to an advanced state in my mental growth. I had been occupying a chair of history and economics for a number of years. So far as I had developed a "method," it was under heavy bonds to speculation, rather than intelligently objective. I had given an undue proportion of attention to the philosophers of history, but both they and the historians proper had lost their grip on my credulity. Two things kept recurring in my thoughts, first, that there must be some sort of correlation between human occurrences, and second, that the clues to that correlation must be found by checking up cause and effect between human occurrences themselves, not in some a priori. I had read both of Comte's major works, but had been more impressed by their absurdities in detail than by the saving remnant of wisdom.... I had read everything that Spencer had published, but the elements in his method that afterward seemed to me most useful failed to find me at first. The sight of the title *Dynamic Sociology* instantly acted as a reagent to crystallize elements that had been incoherent in my mind.... I was aware of feeling as the alchemists might have felt two or three centuries earlier if they had stumbled upon the "philosophers' stone." At the same time the book never seemed to me a solution, but rather a wonderfully expressive symbolic guide to the path in which solutions might be found.[49]

If Small's year on leave at Johns Hopkins had any effect at all on his interest in Ward, it could only have reinforced that interest. For *Dynamic Sociology* was read at Johns Hopkins, and Ward visited the campus when Small was there.[50] In any case, during the few years after Small returned from Johns Hopkins to Colby, he moved fairly quickly from history to sociology. In 1889 he was still emphasizing history, and pushing sociology alongside of it. He had hoped on his return to Colby to be able to teach sociology during the academic year, 1889-90, within the framework of his courses in history.[51] Then, he suddenly became president, in July 1889, after the resignation of the incumbent. He was therefore able to teach sociology, but within the framework of the course in moral philosophy,[52] a course that presidents of American colleges throughout most of the nineteenth century had traditionally taught to seniors.[53] In February 1892 he accepted Harper's offer at Chicago.[54] By that time, he had settled on the three main branches of sociology, as they appeared in *Introduction to the Study of Society*. In a syllabus he prepared for his sociology course at Colby, the course had three parts, "Descriptive Sociology—The actual society of the past and present, the world *as it is*"; "Statical Sociology—The *world as it ought to be*"; and "Dynamic Sociology—The methods available for causing approximation of the ideal, the *world in process of betterment*."[55] And by that time, the pedagogue who in 1882 taught history because "the students must be taught to recognize the ... general laws which historical evolution illustrates" thought instead that "Sociology ... [not history] deals with general characteristics of social phenomena and outlines the principles of social development."[56]

The pedagogical package of the early 1880s, built around the study of history, reappeared in 1894, built around sociology, in *Introduction to the Study of Society*. It was a "laboratory guide," not a text, for Small's students in the early 1880s were supposed to "be exercised in gathering evidence for themselves." Students who used it were supposed to make observations of their own communities under general, conceptual categories, just as Small's history students at Colby were supposed to develop a "facility of induction" which allowed them to think in terms of the general issues under which Greece and Rome could provide lessons for the present. And just as Small's students in the early 1880s were supposed to study history and political economy in order to become good citizens of the kind that Small's politics required, Small and Vincent in 1894 ended their book by "urging competent teachers to lead capable students beyond the point at which the book stops" by proposing "once more the scholarly ideal—not investigation as a substitute for civic service, but investigation as both promise and performance for civic duty."[57] But, they went on, "The right of free thought does not involve the competence of every man to think every order of thought," and "Sociology cannot be brought within the comprehension of everybody." The blessed elite of "scientific students of society," who can understand "wide and involved" social relations, "ought to oppose with all their power the many mischievous tendencies to construct mountainous social philosophies out of molehills of social knowledge." On the other hand:

> This is not to urge that sociologists should be reactionaries. There is little likelihood that men who personally observe actual social conditions, according to the method which we propose, instead of speculating about them in the study, will want to fold their hands and let social evil work out its own salvation. In the interest of larger and truer knowledge, and better social cooperation in the future, it is, nevertheless, necessary to distinguish very clearly between provisional action prompted by sympathy, and the discovery of social principles attested by science.[58]

In short, the logic and the chronology of Small's development through the 1880s took him from history, via political economy, to sociology. But his political and educational goals remained the same throughout. Students should be educated to become good citizens. Good citizens are intelligent and informed about their society. They can distinguish "the organized" from "the organic." They are, therefore, neither radicals nor reactionaries, neither revolutionaries nor believers in laissez-faire. Empirical social science, in which observations are inductively generalized to larger issues, acquired in the context of an education which is both scientific and non-specialized, has an inherent tendency to make centrist, reformist citizens out of students. Observation of actual social conditions both militates against political complacency and instructs students in the complexities of the social process, complexities which utopians and amateurs and agitators leave out of view. Hence, social science should be empirical, but should place specific observations into larger, more general contexts. History, in Small's view, was not doing this job. Some of it was careful research on trivia; some of it, the philosophy of history, was a priori speculation. Political economy did only part of the job, since it had lost its feel for the larger moral context of all specific activities. Therefore, sociology. And sociology must be, among other things, an empirical science.

4

OBJECTIVITY, THEORY, AND
THE UNITY OF KNOWLEDGE

INTRODUCTION

Small preached empiricism much more often than he practiced it. In most of his works he was a theorist. To a large extent, he was a speculative theorist. But he really believed in his empiricist preachings.

The discrepancy between Small's empirical doctrines and his speculative practice was resolved in his own conception of himself as a sociologist. He was a "methodologist," as he used that term, or "general sociologist." In that status he could urge others to be careful about factual observations, to avoid deductive systems, not to generalize beyond their data, and to keep a sense for the raw observation of phenomena, independently of their theoretical schemes. His sense for raw observation, in turn, attuned him to the central fact, as he saw it, of "complexity" in social phenomena. His notion of "complexity," in turn, was related to his conception of "objectivity." That conception, in part, was that the more holistic a work of social science, the greater the number and variety of points of view it embraces, the more objective it is. This holistic notion of objectivity, coupled with a nonfictionalist view of science, required that theory in sociology be globalistic and all-encompassing, as distinct, say, from a series of "middle-range" theories. Despite this requirement, however, there was also room in Small's thinking for holistic diagnoses of concrete, historical situations, and for a style of theorizing that does turn out, after all, to be somewhat similar to "theories of the middle-range." As in all of Small's work, these ideas are related to his political views.

EMPIRICAL DOCTRINE AND NONEMPIRICAL PRACTICE

Throughout his career in sociology, Small preached empiricism. The "laboratory guide" of 1894 asserted that the "method of credible sociology must be the method of observation and induction ..." Thirty years later *Origins of Sociology* asserted that "credible philosophy or psychology must be essentially positive or inductive more than it is speculative."[1]

Small frequently carried on this campaign for empiricism in his numerous book reviews in the *American Journal of Sociology*. In these reviews, "inductive" was a word of praise and "deductive" was a castigation. For example, Giddings's *Principles of Sociology* uses "assertion and deduction in place of demonstration." "The structure of the main argument," though not all of the details, is in the spirit "of pre-Cartesian speculation, rather than of post-Darwinian science."[2] The "radical vice of the method" in Giddings's *Theory of Socialization* "is the haste to abbreviate the process of collecting, criticizing, and organizing evidence, and eagerness to get conjectures accepted as principles while there is justification merely for supposition."[3]

Small was more insistent on giving special attention to factual observations than were some of his contemporaries in sociology. His friend, Lester Ward, objected to his division of sociology into the three branches, Descriptive, Static, and Dynamic. Ward argued, "There is properly no division of descriptive sociology. That which might be so designated is only the work of the collector."[4] Small agreed in principle with Ward's objections. But he answered that, at a time (i.e., 1895) when "men old and young who are dealing with sociology are so unpracticed in the necessary methods"; "are prone to interpret when they have a right only to observe"; and "are with such difficulty convinced that the basis of their alleged inductions is insufficient," reasons of "prudence" dictate a separate branch of descriptive sociology.[5] That "distinct division" is "devoted to the collection and description of facts."[6] Small the pedagogue urged that a special label for the purely empirical division of sociology was "extremely important, both in research and teaching ... and, especially with immature students."[7]

More than prudence and pedagogy, however, stood behind Small's defense of a separate, purely descriptive branch of sociology. He gave up the terminology of descriptive, static, and dynamic sociology.[8] But he always had a notion, probably the legacy of his training and experience in historical research, of raw observation of the facts, of observations which are not yet classified under theoretical concepts. Not only observations of isolated facts, but also very general, summarizing observations may be pre-theoretical. Observations of "things that we see in human associations in general with such insight as we are able to bring to bear upon them now" (i.e., "such insight" as distinguished from well-developed theories) are "the data of sociology, and with these data sociology must begin to do its peculiar work."[9] Hence, Small took issue in his book reviews with sociologists such as Giddings and Tarde, who, in his view, tried to fit all observations under conceptual schemes that were too pat, too neat, and too simple.[10] Late in his life he was still describing a certain book as one which would "satisfy no one . . . who cannot repress his demand for proof that reality runs in accordance with its scheme."[11]

In contrast to this doctrinal empiricism, most of Small's own work was not empirical. The data of Small's intellectual histories, such as *The Cameralists* and *Origins of Sociology*, consisted of the books and articles of other people. Except in that sense, very few of his writings could be called "inductive." Very few, with the major exception of his Ph.D. dissertation, were marked by "the process of collecting, criticizing, and organizing evidence."

Small was quite capable, when he wanted to be, of close attention to factual detail, both in the qualitative, archival research of his dissertation and in the reading of quantitative data. In 1899 he reviewed at length a textbook of sociology which was written "With Special Reference to American Conditions."[12] This text included many quantitative data, from censuses and from other sources, on the population, the labor force, wage rates, and other aspects of American society during the decades prior to its publication. With apologies for stepping outside his field of competence, but with competent scrutiny of the data and of their sources, Small demolished many of the author's conclusions. Among other things, he pointed out that certain supposed changes in American society that the author described were simply the artifacts of incomparable census categories.

In the 1890s, Small apparently intended to do more work with quantitative data than he ever actually did. One of his grounds for arguing that the department of sociology at Chicago should hire a statistician was his need for the help of a statistician in research that he was planning to do.[13] Small did not develop in that direction. But he did have a clear conception of his role, of the place of his own work in sociology and of its relation to empirical research. In a latter-day vocabulary, he would have been called a "theorist," or a "grand theorist." He called himself a "methodologist" or "general sociologist."

SMALL'S CONCEPTION OF HIS PLACE IN SOCIOLOGY

Small conceived of himself as a "general sociologist" fairly early in his career. For example, that conception of himself permeates the content, as well as the title, of *General Sociology*, which was published in 1905. But probably the most fully developed expression of this self-conception was in a talk that Small gave sometime in 1924, shortly before his retirement, to the graduate students of the Chicago sociology department's Society for Social Research. In that talk he defined himself, in relation to empirical researchers.*

If I may trust my own impressions—in the absence of precise statistics—the largest number of genuine research sociologists are at work upon problems of the *survey* type. Next in number come the *social psychologists*. Then, among the also-rans, are the few, among whom I belong, the methodologists or general sociologists.[14]

Somewhat later in this talk, the "general sociologist" expressed his wish that he had been a researcher as well.

I wish I could do a skilled laborer's part of the work that the social surveyors are doing. I can't. I'm not equipped for it. I'm painfully aware of it....

* This talk, "Some Researches into Research," is reprinted in Appendix F.

Again I protest that I would give all my old boots and I would buy new ones for a lot of barefoot youngsters if I could thereby fit myself to make a contribution to social psychology. I know I can't, and again I enthusiastically applaud those who can.[15]

Small also confessed to "seasons of depression" over the prospect "that your generation will not go my way, but will go its own way"; and to "keen sorrow over indications that your generation will not build directly upon the work of my generation, any more than my generation built directly upon the work of Lester F. Ward."[16] But in the end, telling the students that they too would in time be superseded, just as he had been, he remained "confident ... that the best is still in the future."[17]

That future, however, would always include a place within sociology's division of labor for Small and for his type, the "general sociologist." Though they look like "archaeological specimens, in comparison with the up-to-date social surveyors and social psychologists, yet the general theorists ... will continue to be necessary, although in relatively small numbers." Arguing that "there is nothing so misleading as a fact"; that "at its best research is an abortion, even if it actually finds out things, unless it links itself up with a technique and a philosophy which put the discovered things together so that they will yield the most meaning,"[18] Small argued that, in addition to various types of researchers:

... it will someday be an indispensable division of labor for ... [another] group to supplement the work of all the others by carrying on the methodological [i.e., theoretical] researches in demand for correlating the findings of ... investigations ... so as to discover ways and degrees in which they may supplement one another, ways and degrees in which they challenge one another, location of gaps which criticism will detect between the results arrived at by the several groups, and so as to project the next kinds of research needed to complete objective interpretation ...[19]

In short, sociology was supposed to be an empirical science in which observations are generalized into theory, which in turn is supposed to guide further research. In this respect, and in others, Small's ideas about generalization in sociology are quite consistent, in broad outline, with the conceptions that prevailed among later generations of sociologists. Small had no command of the techniques necessary to design research to test hypotheses, or of the technical logic of theory building. He thought more discursively than technically about the construction of theories in social science. But in broad outlines, there seems to be nothing in his talk to the graduate students in Chicago that is offensive to the spirit of, for example, Merton's writings over twenty years later on the relations between theory and research.[20]

Looking closer, however, there are certain peculiarities in Small's view of empirical work in sociology, of sociological theory, and of the relations between the two. One of the jobs of the "methodologist" was "to project the next kinds of research needed to complete objective interpretation...." And Small's conception of "objectivity" is fairly distinctive. It is crucial to the understanding of his style of theorizing in sociology.

SMALL'S CONCEPTION OF OBJECTIVITY

In some contexts, Small used the term "objective" in the everyday sense of "unbiased." Thus, defending the University of Chicago against the charge of taking the tainted money of Mr. Rockefeller and of the Standard Oil Corporation, and turning his analogies between natural science and social science to political use, Small asserted that, at the University of Chicago, "We study trusts just as objectively as our botanists study flowers or our zoologists animals."[21]

In other contexts, "objectivity" is a characteristic, not of the opinions or of the state of mind of a professor at the University of Chicago. It is, rather, a characteristic of the procedures that investigators in the social sciences use. The first several chapters of *Origins of Sociology* trace, step by step, the contributions of each of a number of German historians during the nineteenth century to increasing objectivity in the social sciences. For example, Niebuhr (1776–1837) established the "necessity of subjecting alleged historical evidence to the severest scrutiny."[22] Von Ranke (1795–1886) made contributions which "may be reduced to the formula: Verify by authentic documents, preferably official documents."[23]

Small distinguished these procedural contributions—"contributions primarily to the methodology or technique of the sciences, in the first instance, history, concerned with the interpretations of human experience"—from substantive contributions to increasing objectivity—"contributions to conceptions of the essential content of human experience."[24] To say that contributions of the substantive type aided the development of objectivity in the social sciences is to say that objectivity in social science advanced when social scientists adopted certain substantive beliefs about the nature of society. "Objectivity" in this sense is quite different both from the absence of subjective bias and from the careful use of reliable techniques of investigation.

Small singles out Savigny (1774–1861) and Eichhorn (1781–1854) as two great contributors to "objectivity" in this substantive sense. Savigny and the historical school of jurisprudence emphasized continuity in history. "It is a mark of objectivity in social science to treat each object of attention as an incident in a causal series of human experiences reaching back into the impenetrable beginnings of the human career."[25] This statement appears to be procedural. It is about the way in which an objective investigator treats "each object of attention," as distinct from a substantive statement about the nature of those objects. But Small goes on. He moves from the idea of "continuity" to the idea of causal sequences; and from the idea of causal sequences to the assertion that causal sequences in human history work themselves out gradualistically; and hence, back to the idea of continuity.

Thanks, in part, to Savigny and his school, "Little by little the conclusion gathered the force of demonstration in social science that ... *gradualism* rather than *catastrophism* is the universal manner of social cause and effect."[26] Social science became more objective when there was established a certain belief which most conservatives share with most liberals; which proponents of ameliorative drift share with statist reformers; which all sorts of people share with all sorts of others, except with revolutionaries: the belief in "the inevitability of gradualism."

A second contribution to the development of objectivity, in the sense of "conceptions of the essential content of human experience," was that of Eichhorn. Small summarizes this contribution by the terms "complexity" and "multiplicity of factors."[27] A legal historian, Eichhorn "was setting an example in trying to tell the story of German legal history more objectively by presenting it in its connection with German political history." From political history he was drawn even further afield. He began to see, in Small's words, that "An objective history must be an account of all the different influences which entered into the life of a people, of the ways in which these influences worked, and of the relative effect which each from time to time had upon the total conditions of that people."[28] He began to see that societies are very complex, and that any one part of a society, such as the legal system, is affected by all other parts of that society. In this sense of "objectivity," the more holistic a work of social science, the greater the "multiplicity of factors" in its analysis of any social phenomenon, the more objective it is. The link, in Small's view, between this component of "objectivity" and objectivity in the sense in which professors at the University of Chicago who studied trusts were said to be objective, even though the University took money from Standard Oil, comes out in the following passage.

It had been the well-nigh invariable custom, from the beginning of historical writing, for the historians to be mouthpieces for the interests represented by either rulers, or warriors, or lawyers, or priests. These writers had, accordingly, as a rule, set down merely those groups and series of occurrences which attracted their attention from the standpoint of the respective group interests. Now comes Eichhorn with a partial proclamation of the message which the sociologists have later tried to expand and publish, viz.: You cannot tell all that was true about the things that chiefly interest rulers, or warriors, or lawyers, or priests without telling at the same time many other things of primary interest to many other sorts and conditions of men; and without telling also how these different kinds of occurrences reciprocally conditioned one another.[29]

In short, simplicity in social sciences is identified with perspectivalism, in a sense similar to Mannheim. "Complexity," or the catching up in a work of social science of a "multiplicity of factors," is identified with the overcoming of limited perspectives.

"The Scope of Sociology," published some twenty-five years before *Origins of Sociology*, had included this component of Small's conception of "objectivity." In Small's conception of sociology, as expressed in that article, it was the peculiar mission of sociology to be more objective, in this sense, than any of the other social sciences. Sociology, in his view, was both the science of human association (or of social interaction, in a latter-day vocabulary) and the general science of society, drawing upon the other, more specialized social sciences. Sociology was "the combining, organizing, correlating, integrating stage in the process of knowing human society." Hence, "through the processes of sociology knowledge of society first begins to approach objective reality," as compared with "disintegrated and consequently fictitious substitutes for reality," and with "the fragments of reality [which] are brought to sociology by [more specialized] sciences or experiences that deal with those fragments . . ."[30]

In some contexts, this conception of objectivity had the consequence of placing the sociologist who would be objective between, or above, all the contending social classes or political movements in society. Sociologists stood between all of the "rulers, or warriors, or lawyers, or priests," and were ostensibly allied with none. Or, at least, that was the position that Small liked to see himself occupying, and the position that he urged on other social scientists. He was always placing himself in the middle, between somebody and somebody else.

> The argument is that, as in the case of [conceptions of institutions of] property, so in the case of other social institutions, referee work by scholars is in demand.[31]

> Most men tend either so to venerate the past that they are not free, or so to disregard the past that they are not sane.[32]

> Condemnation of czarism does not justify Leninism. The trustees of a certain university may have been arbitrary, but professors who suffered from them may have been unduly provocative. Judge Gary may be wrong, but it does not follow that the I.W.W. is right. It may have been unjust, impolitic and unenlightened to exclude the socialist members from the New York legislature; but Debs may nevertheless have deserved his imprisonment, and

all the agitators who were convicted by due process of law may have deserved deportation.[33]

OBJECTIVITY AND SMALL'S CONCEPTION OF SCIENCE

But this conception of objectivity was not simply a political gimmick that fitted well with Small's centrist politics. It also fitted well with other ideas about science in general and about sociology in particular that, in some respects, are closer—paradoxically so—to certain Marxian conceptions of science than they are to the prevailing practices in American sociology of the decades after Small. This conception of objectivity had consequences, for—or, at least, fitted appropriately with—Small's style of theorizing in sociology.

Briefly, Small's conception of general theory in sociology was that the "final interpretation of human experience is not to be found in abstractions from experience but in composition of abstractions into a reflection of the totality of experience."[34] The idea linking Small's conception of objectivity with his style of theorizing is this "objectivist" view of science, as distinct from any kind of a "fictionalist" view. Small's general intellectual stance was fairly well set by 1890, or so, when he was thirty-five years old. To be sure, he changed through the years. He had less grandiose visions of sociology in his old age than he had had around the turn of the century. But the fictionalism of the late nineteenth and early twentieth centuries, as in the works of scientists and philosophers such as Mach, Vaihinger, and Poincaré, seems never to have touched him. He believed that, "'science' is a relative term." "Science as we know it . . . is imperfect, approximate, fragmentary, provisional, and tentative." In "an absolute sense," however, "science is a completely objective representation of the totality of phenomena, in all their relations." Hence, "science in its utmost perfection would be all reality as it is reflected in omniscient mind."[35] The conception is far removed from fictionalist notions.

Now, four ideas which we have seen thus far—(a) the notion of raw observation, (b) the notion of "complexity," (c) the sense of "objectivity" in which social science is objective to the extent to which it overcomes limited perspectives by incorporating the "multiplicity of factors" into its analyses of social phenomena, and (d) Small's nonfictionalist, objectivistic view of science—seem related in the following way to (e) Small's style of theorizing in sociology. First, if there is such a thing as raw observation of social phenomena, "with such insight as we are able to bring to bear upon them," but uncoded under theoretical categories, then that raw observation can reveal, among other "things that we see in human association in general," the general fact of "complexity" and "multiplicity of factors" in social phenomena. Second, raw observation reveals a "complexity" that is so basic that objective understanding of any single phenomenon, the overcoming of limited perspectives, is possible only to the extent that a social science incorporates the "multiplicity of factors" into its analyses of any phenomenon. Third, science does not consist of fictionalist models, and it does not consist of studying single classes of phenomena, abstracted out of their context. Science, ideally, "is a completely objective representation [not a series of workable models] of the totality of phenomena, in all their relations." But we have already noted that objective social science incorporates the "multiplicity of factors." Hence it follows, fourth, that sociology, in order to be objective, should not aim at "theories of the middle-range," in Merton's phrase, or at a series of more or less self-contained theories of diverse aspects of society. Sociology must aim at theories that catch up all the complexity and multiplicity which raw observation reveals.

It is curious that Small, who spent decades in campaigns against socialism and against radicalism of any sort, and who denounced Lenin's "fantasies," should have a view of science in general and of social science in particular that in many respects is rather similar to Marxian, including Leninist, views. His objectivistic view of science is closer to Lenin's view than to those of Mach and of other fictionalists whom Lenin attacked.[36] His belief that the question, "What is worth doing?" is a question in pure science is closer to the Marxian view that social science should be objective, but not objectivistic (except in the epistemological sense) than it is to the conventions about value-free science that have been fairly dominant in American sociology since Small's generation passed away. And his belief that objective social science is holistic social science is closer to Marxism than it is to the specialization among American sociologists who came after Small—a specialization resulting in theories of small groups, of formal organizations, of stratification, of kinship systems, and of other classes of phenomena, abstracted from their context, which never come together into Small's holistic "composition of abstractions into a reflection of the totality of experience."

THE ONENESS OF KNOWLEDGE AND THREE STYLES OF THEORIZING

Small was headed toward this ideal of a totalistic social science before he made the transition from history to sociology. In the 1880s he had wanted history to be the totalizing and the generalizing social science. He had even gone so far as to assert that "all college study should be historical study" (though he called this phrase an "obviously hyperbolical formula").[37] These early beliefs foreshadow his later insistence upon "the oneness of knowledge" about social phenomena in the 1890s and later, when he attributed to sociologists, not to historians, the instinct for the oneness of knowledge, and called it their greatest strength.[38]

In Small's works, the "oneness of knowledge" took on diverse forms. The phrase had, in effect, at least three different meanings, entirely apart from the union of empirical and ethical knowledge. Considering only empirical knowledge, the "oneness of knowledge" could mean, first, the use of "general sociology" as a guide to the diagnostic analysis of specific historical situations in all of their multivariate complexity. Second, it could mean general theories characterized by multivariate complexity. Third, it could mean something slightly different. It could mean the development— independently, in some degree, of full-fledged theories that catch up all the "multiplicity of factors"—of concepts that reveal the underlying similarity of apparently disparate phenomena.

These three meanings are not mutually exclusive. They are not incompatible in any way. Small's striving for a totalistic sociology worked itself out in different ways, in different contexts, which had different formal characteristics.

First, Small defined "sociological insight"—and he seems in this context really to have meant "insight," as distinct from "knowledge," or "theory"—as the ability "first, to make out the several interests actually operative in a given social situation; second, to calculate the relative force of the many interest-factors in reaction with each other in given concrete situations."[39] "General sociology" was "a preparation for judging a concrete combination of interests," just as a physician's general training prepared him "for diagnosis of new cases which will occur in his practice" even though "he may never meet precisely the same combinations of conditions and symptoms which he had considered in the course of his preparatory training . . ."[40]

Small went on to exemplify what he meant by supposing that "we are dealing with the practical problems of law-enforcement in a particular town in a state which has a prohibiton law."* Some people treat such situations as if they were simple affairs, "the law on the one side, and its violation on the other." But Small catalogued an impressive variety of "interests" to show that both the law and its violation "are expressions of highly complex mixtures of interests" and that neither "precisely represents the actual balance of interests in the community." Behind the law, there might be a pure moral interest; and a political interest in currying favor with certain voters; and a business interest in getting the trade of prohibitionists; and a number of others. Behind the violations of the law there might be a "willingness to profit by the physical and moral ruin of others"; and an interest in personal freedom which may vary "from hopeless moral perversity to highly developed moral refinement"; and a number of others, apart from the sheer "interest in satisfying the drink appetite."[41]

Small uses this illustration in support of the general point that "our knowledge of sociology, i.e., our systematized knowledge of the human process, will be measured by the extent of our ability to interpret all human society in terms of its effective interests."[42] But the interpretation of "all human society" in this context, refers to diagnostic analyses of particular situations, aided by "general sociology," and not to general theories. Sociologists are supposed to

---

* The passage in question is included in Appendix D, pp. 180–83.

be able to dope out the multivariate complexity of concrete situations. In this example, which is characteristic, sociologists simply find the presence or absence, and the relative strength, of various operative factors. For Small apparently never had a clear conception of the idea of associations between variables.

Second, Small's striving toward a totalistic sociology sometimes took the form, not of attempts to diagnose the full complexity of concrete situations, but of attempts to state general theories—or, more usually, in his actual practice, programmatic steps toward general theories—which would catch up the same sort of mutivariate complexity that Small urged sociologists to look for in their analyses of specific situations. One example of this attempt at multivariate grand theory is *General Sociology*, which chapter 6 will examine in some detail. Another, more circumscribed example is Small's paper "The Methodology of the Social Problem,"[43] a paper whose title would be more accurately rendered as "The Methodology of the Problem of the Meaning of 'The Social.' "

One of the issues in "the social problem," thus defined, was the "discovery of the general laws of interrelationship between human individuals and human institutions."[44] Using the six-fold classification of basic human wishes or "interests" that Small held to (with modifications) throughout his career—"interests" in (a) health, (b) wealth, (c) sociability, (d) knowledge, (e) beauty, and (f) rightness; and taking over de Greef's classification of institutions—(g) economic, (h) genetic, (e) artistic, (j) scientific, (k) moral, (l) judicial, and (m) political, Small then specified the problem as that of "discovering the general laws of interrelationship between the individual element in society, represented in terms of desire by the product a b c d e f and the institutional element, represented collectively by the product g h i j k l m." He then presented a cubic figure to portray graphically "this general task of sociology."[45] After respecifying the problem once again, in terms of the cubic figure, and using the vocabulary of geometry, Small went on to call for these four steps toward "the progressive solution" of this problem.

1. Extension of the method of positive observation to all classes of societary phenomena which have not been adequately observed.
2. Discovery of the relations between such of these phenomena

as have been abstractly interpreted, i.e., in abstraction from the containing reality.

3. Extension of the method of abstract interpretation to other homogeneous groups and series of phenomena.

4. The highest possible generalizations of societary facts, by qualitative or quantitative explanation of all reactions between individuals and groups, which can be seen to fix or to modify either individual or social types.[46]

In short, Small wanted the "highest possible generalizations," based on observations of "all classes of societary phenomena," and including "the relations between such of these [classes of] phenomena" which existing theories have interpreted "in abstraction from the containing reality," i.e., from phenomena of other classes.

Probably most sociologists, seventy years later, would view this style of theorizing as sterile. For one thing, as in so many passages throughout Small's works, there is no genuinely substantive content in this programmatic discussion. Having announced that sociologists should discover "the general laws of interrelationship between human individuals and human institutions" (which might mean many different things), Small does not attempt actually to discover one such law. Instead, he goes on to restate the problem in various ways, and to discuss the style, rather than the substance, of next steps in the development of grand theory.

But this impression of sterility is not completely justified. The call for, and the hypothetical example of empirical "local inquiries" in *Introduction to the Study of Society* inspired one of the earliest community studies ever published in the United States. And Small's geometrical portrayal of the "interrelationship between human individuals and human institutions" inspired the first attempt at mathematical models ever published in the *American Journal of Sociology*, which probably means that it was the first ever published anywhere in the history of American sociology, or of sociology in any country.[47]

A student in one of Small's seminars, Amy Hewes, remarked that the symbolism of the Riemann surface could express more fully the basic idea of Small's cubic figure. Small encouraged her to work on her idea, and the result was published in 1899.[48] In her words:

The object to be accomplished in introducing the Riemann surface is to convey graphically an idea of the kind of classification which must be made of the different social values (a problem now confronting sociologists) in order that, given any of the human institutions in forms of thought, of personal action, of expression, or of cooperation, we may be able to show corresponding to each, in meaning terms, the variable desires, both in past and present, so that the interdependence of each and all may be made obvious, and the direction indicated in which any unknown value is to be looked for; just as the discovery of the element argon was predicted from Mendelejeff's chart by the law of the periodic functions of atomic weights.[49]

Unlike the community studies that Small, and that Small and Vincent inspired, this attempt at mathematical models was stillborn. In the case of Amy Hewes, herself, neither her Chicago dissertation of 1903 nor the one paper that she later published in the *AJS* continued her work along this line.[50] Nor, so far as the record shows, did any other graduate students in sociology at Chicago take it up.[51] But Hewes's article does suggest that, relative to the time and to the social-scientific climate in which Small worked, some of his attempts at theorizing, of the kind that seems sterile and without content today, had more potential impact on sociology than was ever realized. Perhaps the intellectual potential was there, but without the institutional supports that community studies enjoyed, such as a wider audience among the technically untrained, a link to the concerns of settlement houses and social reformers, and the ideological impact of "community" as against a concept such as "class" that indicates a more divided society.

The "oneness of knowledge" has still a third meaning. In some contexts, Small's style of generalizing was rather different from the style of "The Methodology of the Social Problem." That paper was a program for highly general and highly multivariate theory. In this style, sociologists were supposed to catch up in their general theories all the complexity that they were supposed to catch up in their diagnostic analyses of specific situations. Small praised Amy Hewes for trying "to make the fact of *complexity* in all social reactions more evident."[52] On other occasions, however, Small was less insistent that "general sociology" be a theory of all the interconnections between everything and everything else. He was probably not aware of having different styles of theorizing in different contexts. But he did come a bit closer, sometimes, to a notion of more circumscribed "theories of the middle-range." For example:

The sociologist looks out on the same world of people that other students of social sciences confront, but he looks with a differentiation of interest that focalizes his attention in a distinctive way. . . . The ethnologist, for instance, wants to know the facts of racial association. The sociologist says: "Perhaps we assume too much when we start with the presumption that the profoundest truths about racial association are to be discovered by studying racial associations alone. It may be that some of the peculiarities that we find in racial associations, and which we regard as attributes of race, are incidents of geographical, or political, or vocational, or cultural, or sexual, or merely personal association. It may be that some of the things which we attribute to race occur in mobs made up of an indiscriminate mixture of races. There are innumerable sorts of association in which there is action and reaction of individuals with very marked results. Consequently we need to investigate associations of all orders, if we are to be sure that things which we attribute to membership of one association are not equally or more characteristic of other associations. It is by this extension of view alone that we shall be able to trace the ultimate and fundamental relationships between individuals.

The sociologist has taken up the clue that certain principles of regularity run through all human associations, and he wants to find out what these principles are . . . [e.g.,] the ethnologist discovers that one human association is what it is because of other associations with which it is in contact. The church historian discovers that religious associations have been molded by political associations, and the political historians tell us that governmental associations in one state have been modified by contact with governmental associations in another state. Here is the fact of interdependence. The sociologist says: This is not an isolated phenomenon. Wherever there are human associations there are interdependences among the units, and between the association itself and other associations. This fact of interdependence must be understood, then, in its full significance, if we are to comprehend the conditions and laws of human association in their widest and deepest scope.[53]

In this style of generalization, Small is calling on sociologists to subsume apparently divergent phenomena—phenomena in such different systems of interaction as those based on race, or vocation, or gender, or geography—under the same set of concepts, in order to reveal universal attributes of "association," i.e., of social interaction. This is not a call for the theory of everything. It is a call for general concepts (such as "interdependence"), and for general questions (e.g., "Do associations take on varying qualities with varying numerousness of the associated individuals?"),[54] which sociologists could develop *seriatim*.

One of the aims of such generalizations is "to schedule all the traits common to associations of men." In this style, too, lists or schedules of "the things that we see in human associations in general . . . are merely some of the data of sociology." Sociologists are supposed to go on to ask, "What more intimate laws are contained in these data?" But this style, unlike the style illustrated above, does not force the sociologist to deal, from the very beginning, with all of the "individual elements," all of the "institutional elements," and all of the logically possible connections between them. Lists or schedules of traits are steps along the way. It is possible, in this style, to "sit down at the beginning of a journey."[55] That journey, however, is toward "the composition of abstractions into a reflection of the totality of experience." Hence, although this style of theorizing allows more room for middle-range theories than the other style seen above, it represents no compromise with Small's view that, in order to be objective, social science cannot be the science of rulers, or of warriors, or of lawyers, or of priests. It must be superperspectival, and must incorporate all the complexity which raw observation reveals.

5

PROFESSORS AS MORAL LEADERS: SOCIOLOGY AND ETHICS

ETHICS AND SOCIOLOGY: AN OVERVIEW

Small's conception of objectivity and his call for a holistic science of society were closely related to his conception of the ways in which the sociological perspective implies a theory of ethics, and of the ways in which ethics depends upon sociology. In his holistic doctrine, "No sociological perspective is correct unless it turns out at least to have a place for the angle of vision which belongs to people at different posts in the social process."[1] And, "A science of the human whole is necessary ... its parts, its processes, its purposes ... before we can have anything better than dogmatic pseudo-science of fragments falsely held apart from the whole."[2] He sometimes asserted this doctrine in the context of his case for the ethical significance of sociology, and he attributed religious qualities to the holistic sociological perspective, to social science, and to scholarship in general.

When we get a view of the world such as is commanded from the sociological outlook, it turns out to be the theater of a plan of salvation more sublime than the imagination of religious creed-maker ever conceived. The potencies which God has put in men are finding themselves in human experience. This is the drama of life.... [3]

Sociology is really assuming the same prophetic role in social science which tradition credits to Moses in the training of his nation, when he sounded the keynote, "Hear, O Israel! The Lord our God is one Lord." Or the role of the rallying cry of Islam,

"There is but one God and Mahomet is his prophet." Or the role of all unitheists.... Or the role of those modern psychologists who saved us from that mental philosophy which turned the human mind into a department store with devices for opening and closing impenetrable partitions between the divisions of intellect, sensibility, and will. Sociology is like each of these unifying alternatives in the one particular that it is proclaiming the elementary truth of the unity of the social reality, and the consequent unity of all the divisions of science that may be invented as machineries for understanding that reality.[4]

In all seriousness, then, and with careful weighing of my words, I register my belief that social science is the holiest sacrament open to men. It is the holiest because it is the wholest career within the terms of human life.... The whole circumference of social science is the indicated field for these "works" without which the apostle of "salvation by faith" declared that faith is dead.[5]

The first commandment with promise for graduate schools is: Remember the research ideal, to keep it holy![6]

Small's conception of objectivity in the sense of holistic social science, as contrasted with the "pseudo-science of fragments" that had prevailed until sociology sounded its unitheistic keynote, paralleled his conception of "a paramount standard of right," as contrasted with the diverse and contradictory moralities which prevail in urban, industrial society. In a passage entitled "The Ethical Poverty of Society," which is quite similar to Durkheim's analysis of the ways in which the division of labor in modern societies weakens the *conscience collective*, Small envisaged a "universal ethical standard to which one class may appeal against another class and get a verdict which the defeated litigant feels bound to accept." He contrasted that ideal with the prevailing "confusion," in which "there is one code of professional ethics for the lawyer, another for the doctor, another for the editor, another for the employer, another for the employee, another for the teacher, and another for the minister."[7] Just as the special social sciences should be coordinated into holistic social science, so too should the differing moralities which the division of labor and which class conflict engender be coordinated under "a paramount standard of right." It was the mission of university scholars in general, and of sociology in particular, to identify and to create the paramount standards.

Small's views about the relationship between sociology and ethics were not all of one piece. His various statements of this relationship had divergent emphases, and he sometimes seems to bring scientific and ethical issues together by the method of playing fast and loose with language. But one coherent strain of thought in his paper, "The Significance of Sociology for Ethics," is as follows, stated very briefly, and in a preliminary way.

First, an empirical examination of the psychology of the ethical judgments that people actually make in ordinary life, as distinct from an abstract theory of ethics, reveals certain characteristics of such judgments. For example, they are always telic, always made with some end in view. They are always made with reference to something about the human condition. They are never made on the basis of any single, ultimate criterion of value. Moral theorists who posit an ultimate criterion do not in fact make their judgments that way, any more than anyone else does.

Second, an empirical examination of the sociology of value judgments, of their operation within the "social process," reveals further characteristics. At this point, Small's ontology comes into play—his conception of ends and purposes as being not simply the subjective intentions of persons, but as inhering objectively in external reality. He believed that the delineation of purposes is an inherent part of the objective description of any phenomenon, including "the social process."

The concept of "social process"—"a theater of a plan of salvation"—had implications for Small that are summed up in the biblical idea that he often paraphrased and sometimes quoted—that we are members of one body, or (in Ephesians 5:25), " . . . we are members one of another." The concept implied that every person "is an intersection of all the groupings which human beings form in the pursuit of all the ends of life, and all the ends of life are epitomized in . . . [every] man's character."[8] It implied, further, that every last person on earth "carries in himself the evidence that all the phases of human association are ceaselessly working together in a process which binds each man to every man, which makes each man both a finished product of one stage of social production, and the raw material of another."[9]

Now, the "social process," or "human process," or "human association" has "a definite content, a work which it is always doing and which . . . it must always continue to do" so long as the process continues to exist. That "essential work . . . is a rhythmical process of progression in developing, harmonizing, and satisfying the interests partially latent in persons." The following chapter examines the concept of "interests" in considerable detail. For present purposes, it suffices to say that these latent "interests" are the six basic wishes of human beings. Hence, "Human association is a constant reaction of individuals, operating in functional groups, and procuring larger aggregates and juster proportions of health, wealth, sociability, knowledge, beauty, and rightness satisfactions."[10] This is the end, or these are the ends of the social process. And the delineation of these ends is an integral part of the objective description of that process.

Leaving out, for the present, the next few steps in this strand of thought, Small moves forward to the conclusion, on the basis of his empirical examination of the nature of moral judgments, that "the ultimate end which gives value to all conduct . . . [is] the social process" itself, and its inherent, built-in goals. For, "We have no other real measure to apply in a theory of conduct-value."[11] He calls this system of ethics "telecism." Telecism is a relativistic theory of ethics, although Small sometimes speaks of "ultimate ends." It is relativistic because human beings are not gods. They are even lower than the angels. They are fallible. They cannot know ultimate ends, but only the interminably working goals of the social process. Hence, phrases such as "the best that we can know about what is worth doing," or "we have no other real measure to apply," recur throughout Small's writings on ethics, and on the relationship between sociology and ethics.

It is important to note that Small does not argue that it is possible to infer the Ought from observing the Is. Nor is he saying, simply, that social science provides the empirical content for ethics, insofar as ethics has an empirical content. He is arguing that a social-scientific study of what ethical judgments actually consist of sets the boundaries, within which any ethical theory must operate; and that ethical theorists who step outside these boundaries—for example, by setting up an absolute criterion such as "pleasure" or "the will of God"—are only kidding themselves. "Pleasure" turns out to be pleasure as Herbert Spencer experiences it. The "will of God" turns out to be the will of God as fallible people at Geneva, Rome, or Massachusetts Bay interpret it.[12]

Small argues further that sociology provides the concrete content to ethical forms. Precisely because the social process maximizes a variety of values, no abstract system of ethics—no Kantian categorical imperative or clear-cut ethics of duty—can apply unambiguously to any specific situation. It is necessary to dope out the widest possible range of consequences, within the social process, of any given conduct—say, complying with a local prohibition ordinance, or supporting your local bootlegger. It is necessary to see which alternative promotes, on balance, more of the goals inherent in the social process. No abstract theory of ethics can do that job. Nor can any "pseudo-science of fragments." Only an objective, in the sense of a holistic social science can perform that task.

These, then, are two rather different relations between sociology and ethics (although Small did not emphasize, and perhaps was not fully aware of, the difference). First, empirical psychology and sociology reveal the only ethical standards that fallible human beings can possibly perceive. Second, given those criteria—the goals inherent in the social process—holistic social science can provide the concrete knowledge that is necessary in order to apply these criteria to specific situations.

It is possible to understand Small's views on the ethical significance of sociology, and of all university scholarship, in two quite different, but complementary ways. First, they can be understood historically, with reference to Small's intellectual and personal biography, and to the intellectual and social environments in which he grew up, and in which he worked as a mature scholar. One point in this regard is obvious: in Small's day, the notion of "pure" science, or of scholarship for scholarship's sake, was not so strongly institutionalized as it later came to be. All science, and especially social science, was of course supposed to serve humanity. As Lester Ward had put it:

> The real object of science is to benefit man. A science which fails to do this, however agreeable its study, is lifeless. Sociology, which of all sciences should benefit man most, is in danger of falling into the class of polite amusements, or dead sciences. It is the object of this work [*Dynamic Sociology*] to point out a method by which the breath of life may be breathed into its nostrils.[13]

This chapter will consider other historical and biographical factors that seem relevant to the understanding of Small's views on the ethical significance of sociology. Briefly, these views represent, in part, the reaction of a small-town boy from New England, with a strongly religious background, to a more secular, urban, industrial capitalist society. They reflect, in part, Small's religiousness. And they were congruent with the social position of a university scholar, as defined around the turn of the century, and as distinct from other types of intellectuals and scholars that appeared both earlier and later in American history.

Second, Small's views about sociology as an ethical science can be understood in terms of their internal logic. On what assumptions, with what intellectual methods, given what conception of ethical and of scientific statements, and perhaps with what ambiguities of language that allowed him to move back and forth between descriptive and ethical statements, could Small construct an internally plausible case for the ethical significance of sociology?

RELIGION AND DARWINISM: A COMPARISON OF SMALL AND E. A. ROSS

Turning first to the historical setting, R. Jackson Wilson has interpreted the works of a number of Small's contemporaries— Charles S. Pierce and Josiah Royce in philosophy, James Mark Baldwin and G. Stanley Hall in psychology, and E. A. Ross in sociology—as quests for community, in response to the double challenge of Darwinian evolutionism and industrialization.[14] For example, Ross developed his theory of "social control" because, although a progressive in politics, he believed that after Darwin it was no longer possible to maintain the presumption that nature had fitted human beings for social life, much less for progress and improvement in social life. In Wilson's words:

> In the eighteenth century, as Ross viewed it, this presumption had been based on the idea that men had an innate sense of right and wrong, a "set of commandments etched in the soul." The discovery of other cultures with varying standards of morality had dealt a stunning blow to such a simple account. Moralists had then tried to fill the resultant vacuum, especially after Kant, with the assertion that the "soul" was at least endowed with a generalized "sense of *oughtness*," a conscience. But Darwin had demonstrated the emptiness of the idea of conscience, and the search had then begun for a theory of man's morality and fitness for society that would take instinct and emotion fully into account.[15]

In urban society, especially, in Ross's view, natural sociable instincts fail to sustain social order. Only the process of social control, which he identified and studied, could explain morality and order in human society.

Unlike Ross, Small never had to wrestle with Darwinism. Some of the differences between these two sociologists are quite suggestive. As an undergraduate at Coe College, a Presbyterian school in Cedar Rapids, Iowa, Ross attended church regularly, went to prayer meetings, and wrote an oration in which he attacked the "scoffers," that is, atheists and agnostics who "would abolish the moral law implanted in men's conscience but would furnish no new code of rules for human guidance."[16] A few years later he read Darwin and Spencer. A few years after that, by the beginning of the 1890s, the shock had set in. Ross abolished the moral law implanted in the human conscience, and instituted social control in its place.

Small, too, came from a strong religious background. Unlike Ross, he had never been a conservative, or fundamentalist Protestant and (also unlike Ross) he never repudiated his religious heritage.[17] For example, he gave up his belief in the Devil while still a youth, causing a friend to label him an atheist.[18] And Darwinism came with less shock value to liberal Protestants than to fundamentalists.[19]

What is more, Small's brand of Protestant individualism apparently served to weaken the connections, as he saw them, between science and religion. Though a prolific writer in sociology, Small published relatively few sermons or other writings of a specifically religious nature. The archival sources that shed light on the character of his religiousness are also quite scanty. But the available sources do suggest quite strongly that Small's views of religion tended to establish science and religion as different realms of human experience, to which different forms of knowledge appertain. Hence, there could be no simple, and certainly no wholesale transfer of ideas from one realm to the other, and no troublesome intrusion of science into religion.

For example, in a sermon titled "Christ Comforting His Disciples,"[20] published in 1891, Small develops an answer to the question that Judas (not Iscariot) asks of Jesus in John XIV, "Lord, how is it that you will manifest yourself to us and not to the world?" Small answers that disclosure, or revelation, "is at least a double process" that depends in part upon the receptivity of the individual person to whom the revelation is made. Further, "different objects of knowledge manifest or disclose themselves through diverse channels of apprehension." The three "channels" are the senses, reason, and "the revelation of the affections." And "Each kind of truth has its own channel and method of getting at the mind." Hence, while it is fair to demand explanations and demonstrations of spiritual truths, the demonstration "must be to a capacity appropriate to this special kind of truth."

The capacity required for the reception of spiritual truth is quite different from that required for scientific truth. No truth, whether scientific or spiritual, "has ... been revealed to us unless we have experienced the emotions which it is fitted to arouse." Small seems to say, however, that in the case of scientific truth, experimental training and practice provide sufficient experience for arousing the appropriate emotions.

> Any of us may read accounts of what is seen by the astronomers who are using the Lick telescope, but only they who have gazed through the splendid glass, to resolve nebulae into clusters of hitherto undistinguished worlds, have known experimentally, have

personally received the revelation of these hitherto unknown worlds. To one who does not possess it already, words cannot convey any experimental knowledge. They simply name our ideas. Any new knowledge which they seem to give is simply a rearrangement of ideas previously in the mind.... Words are simply the power to turn the kaleidescope of our experience. If we lack the experiences, words cannot give them.[21]

With spiritual revelations, in contrast, training and practice in looking through a splendid scientific instrument is not enough. "God is all about us and within." He is all the time manifesting himself. But only some persons are receptive to this manifestation. For Jesus answers Judas's question by saying, "*If a man love me*, he will keep my words; and my Father will love him, and we will come unto him." Describing a familiar experiment in high school physics proving that air is the medium that transmits sound, Small explains that in the answer of Jesus to Judas, "love is the medium, that condition of the heart, within which alone the manifestations of the divine presence and of divine truth can transmute themselves into revelation."[22]

Science, in Small's view, was a public and a social enterprise. Public, scientific discourse, in which all persons who have acquired the requisite training and practice can participate, would result in a unitary science of society. Receptivity to divine revelation was less public or social. It depended upon the individual experience of love, upon the state of a person's "affections." Scientific truth emerges from public discourse within the community of scholars. Apprehending the truths of divine revelation depends upon a person's individual receptivity to them: and only after people have received these truths do they join the community of believers.

The organization of that community, the church, also had functions which differed considerably from the organization of the community of scholars, the university. The central missions of the university, according to Small, were "standardizing social measures of value" and "the discovery of new values." The function of the church, in contrast, is not "discovery and justification of ultimate standards of value." That is the job of the university. The church's task is the "maintenance of influences that impress the importance and authority of ultimate standards, and that exert constant moral pressure towards practical application of the standards."[23] Both in Small's epistemology of revelation, as distinct from his epistemology of science, and in his conceptions of the proper functions of the university and of the church, he established science and religion as different realms of experience.

These views did not mean, of course, that there was no transfer of ideas between the two realms. But most of the transfer, in Small's thought, went from religion to social science, rather than the other way around. For example, in a sermon published in 1915 entitled "The Life," Small states the basis in the Bible, and in the life of Jesus, for the concept of "function," as used both in the natural and in the social sciences.[24] But he was quite caustic about attempts to import Christianity wholesale into social science; or to substitute Christian doctrine for scientific procedure, and label the result "Christian sociology." Late in his life, he described one such attempt, a work called *Towards a Christian Sociology*, as "the sort of book that makes the judicious grieve."

> It proceeds from the level of intelligence which does not know that it is precisely as muddled to talk about "a Christian sociology" as "a Christian chemistry" or "a Christian mathematics .... [This book] is another case of the illusion that a genuinely Christian attitude toward truth and obligation in general is sufficient qualification for solution of all social problems. A Christian attitude no more makes a social than an electrical engineer.[25]

Believing that science and religion were different realms, to which different theories of knowledge apply; that there can be only a limited transfer of ideas from one realm to the other; and taking social scientific ideas from religion more than he took religious ideas from science, Small did not confront a Darwinian challenge.

Ross and Small differed in still other ways that seem helpful in explaining why Ross was, and Small was not, confronted with this challenge. Small was older than Ross. He was born five years before, and Ross was born seven years after, the publication of *On the Origin of the Species* in 1858. He was already teaching at Colby before Ross began his studies at Coe. He had more time to become set in his way, intellectually, before the Darwinian challenge became widespread.

INNOVATION FROM A TRADITIONALIST BASE: A COMPARISON OF SMALL AND ROSS

Probably more significant, however, were the differences between these two in the extent to which each moved into new intellectual experiences from a traditionalist base. Both Small and Ross read Spencer and Ward in the 1880s, and Ward strongly influenced both. Both traveled and studied in Germany. Both received degrees from Johns Hopkins after coming back from Germany. Both moved into these new intellectual worlds from origins in small-town, Protestant society. But Small was more deeply rooted in that society than Ross was.

Ross, according to Wilson, had a "potent lack of geographical and familial identity."[26] His parents had moved about quite frequently, and died while he was still very young. The bright, talented young Ross was a misfit in the town where he lived with his foster parents. Though something of a campus leader at Coe, late in life he expressed his turning away from his background by describing that college as a "tight little intellectual world ... bounded by Presbyterianism, Republicanism, protectionism, and capitalism."[27] In contrast, Small, late in his life wrote nostalgic reminiscences of his college days for the *Colby Alumnus*.[28]

More generally, though often an innovator, Small was an innovator from a traditionalist base. He was deeply rooted in the traditions of his family (which had been in Maine since 1632), of his region, of his religious denomination, and of two of the schools at which he studied, Colby and Newton Theological. He was the first member of the Colby faculty to hold a Ph.D., the first to teach political economy, and the first to teach sociology. He was the first, or one of the first, college presidents to devise a plan of coordinate colleges for men and women. He founded the first department of sociology in the world and the first journal of sociology in the United States. But other firsts which Small could claim represent his rootedness in his family, his schools, and his denomination.

He was the first president of Colby who was an alumnus, and the first president who was a son of an alumnus, of that school. His inaugural address as president of Colby was on "The Mission of the Denominational College."[29] In other respects, he was not the first, but only one of many people whose lives and careers took them through the same sequence of institutional setttings.

At the time of his death, Small was one of 260 graduates of Colby who had gone on to study at Newton; one of twelve graduates of Newton who had taught at Colby; and one of the six of this number who had been presidents of Colby. He was at that time, one of ten Newton graduates who taught at the University of Chicago, that other Baptist institution which also, like Newton, received money from John D. Rockefeller.[30] He was one of three members of the Colby faculty who went to Chicago, of whom two, Small and the New Testament scholar Shailer Mathews, had graduated from Newton and published in the *American Journal of Sociology*. He was a Republican, who sometimes endorsed his party's candidates at the request of party leaders; but who on one occasion told them he was voting Prohibitionist instead, and who reaffirmed his commitment to Prohibition on his deathbed.[31]

As an innovator from a traditionalist base, Small described his relativistic, nontheological theory of ethics as providing new support for old moral verities. And there was nothing Darwinian about the new support or the old verities. Small never completely embraced the evolutionary model of sociology. His concept of the "social process," which he used both in temporal and in nontemporal ways, was, in effect, his substitute for the concept of "evolution." In Small's thought, the concept of "social process," provided the bridge between descriptive and ethical science. It was the new support for the old verities that he summed up in the slogan, "Live and help live."

Knowledge, Virtue, and the Social Mission of Universities

How to live and help live was, in large measure, an intellectual or a scientific problem, not simply or primarily a problem of external social control or of internal residues of socialization and control. The concepts of social control and of internalization of norms were never central in Small's sociology. For, in his view, the "interest" in rightness—along with the "interests" in health, wealth, sociability, knowledge and beauty—was one of the six basic and universal wishes of all human beings. Or, at least, as seen in the following chapter, the "interest" in rightness was almost as basic and universal as the other five. Darwin or no, relativism or no, Small retained the traditional conception—not of the young Ross's "moral law implanted in man's conscience," since the innate desire for rightness has variable content—but, at least, of a generalized sense of moral oughtness lodged in every human soul as God or nature created it. Given that generalized sense, sociologists and other scholars could tell people who naturally desire to do right what specific things were morally right in their historically relative situations. Ye shall know the truth of social science, and the truth shall make you right.

This association between virtue and knowledge, and most especially with holistic social-science knowledge, was not unique to Small. For example, Charles Horton Cooley, in 1909, noted the growing place of history, economics, political science, and sociology in American universities; the "multiplication ... of government bureaus ... whose main function is to collect, arrange, and disseminate social knowledge"; and "the number of books and periodicals seriously devoted to these subjects." He concluded, "There is ... nothing more certain or more hopeful than the advance in the larger self-knowledge of mankind." One consequence of this advance in social-scientific knowledge would be an "organic" idealism quite similar to Small's own ethical position. Cooley's organic idealists subordinate "each particular ideal ... to a system of ideals based on a large perception of fact." Idealists in Cooley's view, were learning that they have to understand "the whole to which all contribute" and that, to be "effective" they need "a sense for the complication, the interdependence, and inertia of human conditions."[32]

This association between virtue and knowledge was not unique to Small, because it was inherent in the role of the university scholar in Small's day, as Small and many of his academic contemporaries experienced and defined that role. By 1890, American history had seen a number of different types of intellectuals, who had had differing relationships to the institutions of American society, and to the centers of powers—from intellectuals in power, such as Hamilton, Madison and Jefferson, to the transcendentalists, who had no institutionalized position whatsoever.[33] But the most persistent types had been the clergymen and the college teachers, two careers that, as with virtually all college presidents, were often combined in the same person. Few clergymen and few college teachers were specialized scholars, and with the exception of a handful of great evangelists, few operated on a national scale. They were moral leaders, or would-be moral leaders, of local constituencies. And their moral leadership was limited not only geographically, to a single parish or a single campus, but by denominational boundaries as well. Baptist teachers at Colby in, say, 1840, could not be the moral leaders of Congregationalist students at Bowdoin.

Then, with the founding of universities, and of graduate education during the last decades of the nineteenth century, a new type emerged, university scholars who were affiliated with academic disciplines, who both taught and did research and scholarship. The emergence of university scholars, however, did not entail the end of the conception of the intellectual as a moral leader. University scholars (or many of them) did not pursue scholarship for its own sake. The ideological conception of the university as a seat of disinterested learning was a later, twentieth-century idea. Instead, American universities, around the turn of the century, were institutional bases from which the university scholars could exercise their moral leadership on a national scale.

Columbia, Stanford, Wisconsin, Harvard, Chicago, or Johns Hopkins commanded more national attention, among educated followers or potential followers of the moral leaders on their campuses, than most of the older colleges ever had. And they were free of sectarian ties that tended to limit the moral leadership of the older type of college teacher to the adherents of only one denomination. The intellectual as moral leader could hope for a larger, more diffuse audience than ever before.

For example, Thorstein Veblen exposed the foibles of his time. E. A. Ross was a muckraker. Franklin Giddings wrote editorials as a member of the staff of the *Independent*, published popular lectures, and wrote a book attacking occultism in which the final chapter is entitled, "The Present Duty of the Intellectually Honest and Unafraid."[34] The economist, Richard T. Ely, advised workers not to drink, to refrain from violence, to eschew "the slavery of party politics," to "cast aside envy, one of your most treacherous foes," and to "Elevate, organize, wait." For "Christ and all christly people are with you for the right."[35] The psychologist, James Mark Baldwin, went from the ministry to experimental psychology, to cosmic theorizing. After decades as a professor, in Wilson's words, "he was making the same pronouncements he had been trained to make at Union Seminary," and he "was still a kind of a minister."[36]

In Small's case, it is not necessary for historians to attribute a ministerial flavor to his academic career. He made that attribution himself. Small was never ordained,[37] and he never held a pastorate. Fairly late in his career, apparently in 1915, in response to the item, "Call to Ministry" on a questionnaire sent to Newton alumni, Small wrote:

> At the close of my college course, I felt that I should be a Jonah if I did not put myself in training for the ministry, but I have grown more certain every year that my ministry has been more acceptable than it could have been in a pastorate.[38]

Small's conception of the mission of a university was consistent with the social definition of university scholars as moral leaders. In a Phi Beta Kappa address of 1906, entitled "The Social Value of the Academic Career,"* he asserted, "first that *the university has the function of standardizing social measures of value*" and, further, "that *the cardinal function of the university is more than the standardizing of values; it is the discovery of new values.*"[39] The university was "only one among many centers in which mental action is developed to high degrees of precision and power." Academic careers have social value, "not because of superiority in mental discipline, but in spite of certain inferiorities in that respect."[40]

Universities are distinct, and superior, in a very different way.

---

*This address is reprinted below in Appendix D.

They are not concerned with the diverse practical problems of daily life which the division of labor imposes on nonacademic people—"How can I accomplish the day's task? . . . How may I win my case? How may I cure my patient? How may I make my profits? How may I promote my special scheme?" In contrast to problems such as these:

> . . . the university systematically directs the mind away from vulgar centers of attention. It thereby enlarges the range of interests with reference to which judgments of value are formed. By so doing, the university discredits provincial standards of value, and proposes standards which do justice to all the interests of life.[41]

In this conception, universities are not ivory towers, in which scholars pursue disinterested learning. On the contrary, "in the degree in which wisdom instead of impulse controls social policy, the attitude of society will be represented . . . not by the question, How may we confine the demands of the university within the narrowest limits? but, How may we make the university the most effective instrument of social service?" The "social service" of the university, however, is not (or should not be) service to any particular interest in society. The university does not stand outside society. But it stands outside any single, "provincial" interest. "The university is a sort of board of arbitration, sitting in judgment upon the claims of conflicting human interests,"[42] and by taking this stance it "brings to consciousness the implicit demand of society for a common standard of value."[43]

For Small, this conception of a university was not a remote ideal. He thought that he was describing the actual position of American universities, or, at the very least, the position toward which they were tending. In *The Meaning of Social Science* (1910) he identified numerous academicians who were performing the kind of "social service" that university scholars were supposed to perform.

> In Wisconsin, for instance, Professors McCarthy, Meyer, and Reinsch have been giving academic men a new vision of their opportunities by their services to the state in connection with the administration of railroads, and in preparation of legislative bills on many subjects. In our own [University of Chicago] faculty

Professors Freund, Henderson, and Merriam not only have proposed valuations but they have been initiators of constructive action in the city council, in the legislature, and in many business concerns. They have turned knowledge that has been derived from all men's experience to immediate practical use. They have modified our actual dealings with the criminal and the dependent. They have changed standards and conduct with reference to occupational diseases. They have contributed to a solution of the labor question by promoting industrial insurance. They have done much to make the city government more efficient and more honest. Professors Tufts and Mead have done similar work in connection with the City Club, and Professor Jordan also in promoting public hygiene.[44]

RESEARCH INSTITUTES AND THE MISSION OF UNIVERSITIES

In the same book, Small also had more extravagant dreams of institutionalizing morally virtuous knowledge and knowledgeable moral virtue. This book is in part a call for organized, inter-disciplinary team research in the social sciences. Small envisaged what would happen if the social scientists in a university "should deliberately resolve themselves into an institute for investigation in social science."[45] He foresaw a brilliant future. "Some American university and perhaps in no very distant future, will seize this opportunity" and "will at once leap into a position of leader-ship...."[46] Once the first foundation, maybe Mr. Carnegie himself, supported the institute, the second would not lag behind. And "some of my hearers will live to see co-operative research in social science on a scale which will amount to more progress in method and in value of results than came with Niebuhr's processes of sifting fact from fancy in Roman tradition."[47]

The institute that Small envisaged would engage not only in cooperative, interdisciplinary research. If knowledge is associated with virtue, if social-scientific knowledge "has a moral backing which amounts to a sight draft upon the cooperation of right-minded men," then what better paramount tribunal to stand above the ethical confusion of contemporary society than the institute itself? It would decide ultimate criteria of value—insofar as Small's relativistic ethics allowed for ultimate criteria—and it would decide whether capitalism itself is to survive. Concerning questions such as "Should a tendency toward centralization of the control of capital or toward decentralization be encouraged in the United States today?" Small "squarely face[s] the ... question ..., desired by whom?" And, "without a blush," he writes, "*Desired ... by the consensus of our Institute of social science!*"[48] For, "The last available measure of desirability in human affairs is the best wisdom of men that can be applied.... "[49] But the wisdom of any single person is partial, and is likely to embrace only some of the "interests" inherent in the total social process. Hence:

> The most reliable criterion of human values which science can propose would be the consensus of councils of scientists representing the largest possible variety of human interests, and cooperation to reduce their special judgments to a scale which would render their due to each of the interests in the total calculation.[50]

Small's vision of a moral elite of academicians, who would behave as Cooley's organic idealists were supposed to, becomes more grandiose as the lectures that became *The Meaning of Social Science* proceed. The first proposal was for an institute on a single campus. In the final lecture on "The Future of Social Science," he envisages an international chain of institutes. Similarly, he proceeds from the assertion that social-scientific knowledge "has a moral backing," to the assertion that a consensus of scientists provides "the most reliable criterion of human values which science can propose" for the disposition of particular issues of public policy, to the assertion that his institute would be more competent than any other body to decide the fate of an entire civilization.

> Who shall pass upon this question? Who shall determine whether or not there is a case against our capitalistic civilization? Who shall decide whether we are moving toward the apotheosis of wealth or the apotheosis of men? Shall we leave it to the *ex-parte* judgment of capitalistic interests, or shall we refer it to the most judicial commission of inquiry which it would be possible to establish? Could a more competent commission be proposed than such an institute of social science as we have imagined, or ultimately

a chain of such institutes correcting one another in all the civilized nations?[51]

In this vision, the university scholar as moral leader has gone beyond the parochial boundaries of the college teacher, and has found not simply a national constituency, but an international one as well. For, quoting William Rainey Harper's address on "The University and Democracy," the university is a prophet who will "formulate the thinking which will make the earth a paradise": and "The university is . . . a priest" whose future motto will be, "*Service for mankind, wherever mankind is, whether within scholastic walls or without these walls and in the world. . . .*"[52]

The point is not simply that Small was very optimistic about the future, and not simply that he believed that the thinking going on in universities, rather than economic and political struggle, would indeed "make earth a paradise." Optimism, faith in education, and a belief in progress not requiring basic social conflicts were quite common in nineteenth-century America. The point is, rather, the widely shared definition of the social role of a university scholar, and of the social mission of a university, which Small accepted and propounded. In this conception the distance or removal of university scholars from any particular interest, or movement, or class, or party in their society, made it possible to fuse supposedly objective, disinterested scholarship, with moral leadership, from a supposed stance above any particular interest. Professors, and especially professors of sociology who had a holistic perspective on the divergent "interests" in the total "social process," could provide moral leadership to the whole society.

SMALL'S DEFINITION OF THE ETHICAL PROBLEM

Small pushed this definition of the academician's role further than most of his contemporaries. In fusing sociology and ethics, however, he was only doing the job of an academic sociologist, as he and his contemporary academics defined it. But the particular content of that fusion, the call for paramount standards of right above the ethical confusion of contemporary society, was not given in the definition of the social role alone. The combination of distance from, or relative noninvolvement in any single movement or interest with moral leadership for the whole society might incline university scholars to this general stance. But the role does not define the moral problem that the moral leader is supposed to solve.

That problem, for Small, was not that we are all sinful—children of God, but sinful; or that the spirit is willing but the flesh is weak; or that society is becoming secularized, or that social change has caused the older moral verities to go out of date. As is characteristic of much of American Protestantism, Small had little sense for sin, in a theological meaning of the term. It is not even clear that he saw the flesh as weak. For the innate desire for rightness was one of the six basic, human "interests" on a par, or almost on a par, with the desire for wealth. And as seen in the following chapter, Small rejected the Pauline view of human nature in which spirit and flesh are at war. Small did not bemoan secularization. He insisted that his own field, sociology, be secular. And he proclaimed his belief in the old moral verities, resting on new supports which he built for them in the doctrine of telecism.

The problem was a sociological one—"sociological" that is, if one uses the word to refer to the study of social phenomena and if one also accepts Durkheim's equation (in some contexts) of the concept "social" with the concept "moral."[53] The problem was the ethical pluralism that Small saw as moral chaos, the rich variety Small called "ethical poverty." Later generations of centrist, reformist social scientists in the United States have applauded cultural diversity in the name of "democratic pluralism." They call for unity on procedures whose maintenance allows for substantive diversity. Small, in contrast, believed that the division of labor had destroyed the ethical unity of society. His procedural concern was for a "paramount tribunal" that would provide substantive consensus.

This stance seems to be, in part, the reaction of a small-town boy from New England, rooted in his past, to urban, industrial, capitalist society. In rural and in small-town America, and in frontier society, relatively few people were specialists in one line of work, to the exclusion of everything else. Even professionals were often farmers as well. Second, any ordinary person could perform labor that was useful to others, not because all had specialized training to make themselves useful, but simply because someone might be more clever at felling trees, or shoeing horses, or quilting, than someone else; and because any pair of strong hands is useful at a barn raising, and any pair of legs can tramp through the woods to gather sap. Third, and most crucial, people in more specialized occupations, such as physicians, clergymen, or farriers met needs that almost anybody in town might have. There were few occupations—such as account executive in an advertising agency, market researcher, or jet engine mechanic—whose practitioners serve only certain others, in only certain lines of work.

There was always cultural diversity and there was always economic and political conflict in rural America—the well-educated, pro-New York settlers on the west bank of the Connecticut River versus the holders of New Hampshire grants, speculators, and untutored Green Mountain Boy settlers, in southwestern Vermont; or the Federalist Congregationalists at Bowdoin versus the Jeffersonian Baptists at Colby. But within small local communities, at least, if not between them, each person, whether in a specialized occupation or not, was more useful to a higher percentage of all the others—if only for sociability, rather than for work—than can ever be the case in larger settlements with more specialized demands for skills. And it is the specialized or unspecialized demand, not the specialized or unspecialized offerings, which counts. This is the germ of truth in the nostalgic image of the morally unified society of rural America.

By the closing decades of the nineteenth century, when only vestiges of that society were left, many scholars looked back and found in the past their ideal community. Small was among them, though he did not idealize the past as much as Stanley Hall, for example, did.[54] The fictionalized history of a city in *An Introduction to the Study of Society*, intended as a model for students to follow in studying their own towns, does report ethnic and other conflicts in "the rural group" and in "the village." But Small and Vincent saw more moral unity in rural than in urban America. In the village, there was "a group spirit or loyalty to the ... community on the part of its citizens, which goes far to hold them in a unified whole."[55] In the city, "The differences in wealth, intelligence, customs, and ideas ... result in groupings, some of which give coherence to the whole society, while others tend to exaggerate antagonisms and separation."[56] It was this historical standard—however real or imagined the greater moral unity of rural than of urban America—which defined the moral problem that, in Small's view, university scholars as moral leaders were supposed to solve.

This standard defines the ethical diversity that Small perceived in his society as "moral chaos," and set for universities the social mission of discovering new values and of "standardizing social measures of value." They were to be the proponents and the guardians of the paramount standards of right to which all conflicting classes, parties, interests, and points of view would defer. Sociology, more than any other discipline, was suited for this task. For sociology was the most objective—that is, holistic—social science. It was therefore more capable than any other of discovering the paramount standards that would gain general assent. The next two sections of this chapter analyze the way in which, in the internal logic of Small's thought, sociology was going to carry out this modest task.

Small's Internal Logic

Small was certain that there was a close connection between sociology and ethics. But he had no single, and no simple, view of that connection. Isolated passages, considered out of context, from a single paper, "The Significance of Sociology for Ethics," suggest rather different conceptions. Small begins this paper by stating that it "will sketch the argument in support of the following propositions":

1. Every ethical system with a concrete content virtually presupposes a sociology.
2. There can be no generally accepted ethical standards until we have a generally accepted sociology.[57]

This formulation, and variations such as, "Ethics must consist of empty forms until sociology can indicate the substance to which the forms apply,"[58] suggest that Small is arguing only that sociology will supply the empirical content of ethics, insofar as ethics has empirical content. But purely ethical questions are not in the province of an empirical science. For example, if ethics decrees that it is wrong to kill human beings except to prevent further killing, then social scientists might study whether or not the capital punishment of murderers prevents further killing. Once science had provided "the substance" to the "empty form" of the phrase, "except to prevent further killing," moralists would take it from there, drawing their own conclusions about the morality of capital punishment by deductions from premises which include both ethical norms and social-scientific findings. But the science itself would remain strictly empirical.

Other formulations are quite different. In the same paper Small wrote, "The ultimate problem on the side of pure science is: *What is worth doing? The ultimate practical problem is: How may the thing worth doing be done?*"[59] In this formulation, questions of moral worth are, themselves, scientific questions.

Other passages suggest still different emphases. Echoing the words of Lester Ward, published some twenty years before, but with more moralistic overtones, Small wrote:

> Science is sterile unless it contributes at last to knowledge of what is worth doing.... Sociology would have no sufficient reason for existence if it did not contribute at last to knowledge of what is worth doing. As it is hardly worthwhile to challenge the traditional concession of the whole field of conduct-valuation to ethics, we may frankly rank sociology as tributory to ethics. The ultimate value of sociology as a pure science will be its use as an index and a test and a measure of what is worth doing.[60]

This passage is consistent with the formulation of the significance of sociology for ethics in terms of empirical "substance" and ethical "forms," but with an added emphasis on a view of the proper social mission of science. It would be consistent with the view that (1) the content of science is "value-free," since scientific questions are, in principle, different from value questions; but that (2) for extrascientific reasons, science as a social institution may not be an ivory tower: it must serve human, ethical goals. Elsewhere, however, Small writes that "sociologists believe that a positive philosophy of society may be built up which will indicate the value of each detail of life."[61] In this formulation, once again, the content of a "positive," that is, of an empirical, philosophy includes statements of value.

Small sometimes wrote as if he were saying that ethical statements are an intrinsic part of the science of sociology, even though, in some contexts, he also makes quite clear the distinction between empirical knowledge and moral valuation.

> ...we may claim to have learned to distinguish very sharply between that knowledge of sentient activity which traces the causal series from condition and stimulus to that discharge of motor energy which we call the act: and, on the other hand, that quite different order of knowledge which consists in the valuation of the act itself. Thus we may have the psychology of the taboo, of the suttee, of play, of war, of social distinctions, of institutional charity, of partisanship, of patriotism, of religion. Analysis of the activities so classified may be, and in proportion as it is perfectly abstracted it is, as independent of ethical valuation of them as physiological and pathological examinations of the effects of a blow, a stab, or a gun-shot wound are of judgments about the morality of homicide.[62]

In short, I will show a coherent internal logic to Small's views about the ethical significance of sociology. But any attempt to force everything he wrote on that subject into a single, internally consistent scheme would be foredoomed to error. Whatever his variations in argument or emphasis, however, it is clear that Albion Small's sociology was not "value-free."

That statement can have many diverse meanings, because the notion of "value-free social science" means many different things. In some contexts, that notion refers to norms that define the social roles of social scientists. For example, they should not compromise their social definition as scientists by going in for political activism. Or they should clearly separate their roles as citizens from their roles as scientists by, for example, publishing their scholarship and their political opinions in different journals or in different books. Or they should not exploit their authority in classrooms to press their political or ethical opinions on students.

In other contexts, the notion of "value-free social science" refers to the content of the science, not to the social roles of scientists. One version of this general category of conceptions of "value-free social science" is, shall we say, the linguistic version. For present purposes, in order to contrast the internal logic of Small's conception of sociology as an ethical science with a "value-free" sociology, this version is the most relevant.

In its most simple form, the linguistic version of value-free social science distinguishes sharply between certain generic types of statements to which language (or, rather, *a* language with which the social scientist is conversant) lends itself. There are descriptive statements, such as, "I am digging potatoes." There are evaluative statements, such as, "It is good to dig potatoes." There are normative statements, such as, "You, too, should dig potatoes." And there are emotive statements, such as, "Wow, I really dig these potatoes!"

Some theories of ethics claim that evaluative and normative statements are really emotive statements in disguise. But such issues need not concern us here. The point is, first, that in the linguistic version of "value-free social science," science consists of descriptive statements. A science includes statements of many different kinds, from statements reporting observations of specific, time-bound phenomena to highly general theories stating laws of interrelation between phenomena, without reference to time and place; from a simple description of a single phenomenon, made in ordinary language, to complex statements in mathematical or symbolic-logical notation. But they are all descriptive, as distinct from evaluative, normative, or emotive statements. And the point is, second, that there is no way, in the linguistic version of "value-free social science," to derive or to infer evaluative and normative statements from descriptive statements alone. From the empirical observation that digging potatoes enhances the strength of certain muscles, it follows that "You *should* dig potatoes" only if one inserts into the argument some nonempirical premise, such as a norm that "You should do things to develop your muscles."

Now, if there is really no way to move from descriptive statements to evaluative and normative ones, then the inclusion of such nonempirical statements in a work of social science neither adds to, nor detracts from, that work's scientific quality and scientific content. Either they are simply juxtaposed to, since they cannot possibly follow from, the descriptive statements; or they follow from the descriptive statements, but only by virtue of additional, extra-scientific premises inserted into the argument. Or they seem to follow from the descriptive statements, but only by virtue of unclarity and ambiguity in language, such as using the term "function" sometimes in a purely descriptive sense and sometimes in a sense implying moral teleology, without distinguishing clearly between the two senses. In all three cases—simple juxtaposition of evaluative and normative statements to descriptive ones, the inclusion of nonempirical premises to make such statements follow from the descriptive ones, or ambiguity of language—the inclusion of nonscientific content has no consequences whatsoever, in a formal sense, for the scientific content, if any. But in all three cases there is likely to be interference with the process of scientific communication—noise and static in the scientific discourse. Hence, since science requires clarity of communication between scientists, it were well to leave out the normative and evaluative content, or at least to consign it to a separate chapter, or a different publication.

It seems possible to read many passages in Small's works in the light of this analysis, and to analyze away the connections he thought he saw between sociology and ethics. It seems possible to expose these supposed connections as imperfect logic or linguistic confusion. For example, in a passage in *General Sociology*, Small defines "the general *genetic* question," "the general *statical* question," "the general *dynamic* question," and "the general *teleological* question" about societies.[63] Briefly paraphrased, the first three of these questions are as follows. Through what historical processes did contemporary social structures come about? What forces maintain them in their current equilibrium? And, What forces work to change that equilibrium? With "the general teleological question," an additional, apparently nonempirical element enters in. That question is:

> What ends or system of ends are indicated by the foregoing exhibits of human resources? What is the apparent goal toward

which human cooperation tends, and toward which it may be directed?[64]

Small goes on to note, "This is a question of valuations ... " The answers depend upon knowledge that results from answers to questions of the first three types, but the evaluative question is also "to be answered in accordance with logical and psychological principles which have a competence of their own in sociology ... "[65]

In this passage, Small appears to progress from empirical to nonempirical issues by using a purely descriptive term and then, in the next sentence, slipping in some other term that sounds like a synonym of the first, but is not, because it has value connotations. He writes first of "ends," which might be a purely empirical notion. Then he writes of a "goal." A "goal toward which human cooperation tends" might also be a purely empirical notion, especially within the terms of a social science which is more thoroughgoingly evolutionary than Small's sociology ever was. "Ends" and "goal" might be synonymous. But with a goal "toward which human co-operation ... may be directed," a note of social engineering toward some desirable goal slips in. In the next sentence Small writes that questions about goals are evaluative questions. "Ends," understood as an empirical concept, is not synonymous with "goal" after all. The apparently easy logical progression from empirical to evaluative issues depends upon slippery writing and linguistic ambiguity.

Similarly, in "The Life," a sermon published in 1915, Small was able to state the biblical basis for the scientific concept of "function" by going from ethical language, to descriptive language, and then back to ethical language once again.

Jesus was ... full of the spirit of discovery as to what *is* healthy and health-giving.... More life and better life was his aim, and he was ready to scrap former rules of life whenever he found them hindering more than they promoted the particular expansion of life then due. When he lifted the law of the Sabbath to its higher moral plane, in the revolutionary proclamation, "The Sabbath was made for man, not man for the Sabbath," he at the same time set the pace for exploration of a whole higher moral realm. Every rule and every institution is made for man, not man for the rule or the institution. This was virtually the discovery which has lately been rediscovered in the physical world, and by stimulation from physical science it has assumed the place of master-key in human science. The most crucial scientific conception today is that of function. Everything physical or moral is first stated and then appraised in a system of cause and effect with everything else. This is a functional world. The indicated business of this world is to function as efficiently as possible toward the most important purpose which human insight can discover for the world—*a steady output of men and women of progressively higher quality.*[66]

In this passage, Small slips from the ethically proper "function" of rules and institutions, to "function" in a scientific sense of effect within a system; and from effects to "purpose" in the sense of moral goals. A proponent of the linguistic version of "value-free social science" could charge that in this passage, too, Small merely juxtaposes scientific and moral concepts. He only seems to unify them. And he can seem to unify them only because of his loose use of language.

Reading Small in this way is clearly quite inadequate, however, to the purpose of understanding what he was doing, and what he thought he was doing, when he wrote about the ethical significance of sociology. Such readings are inadequate both philosophically and historically. The kind of attention I have thus far given to Small's language is inadequate philosophically, because many terms in a language might be descriptive, given one set of ontological assumptions, and nondescriptive, given some other set of assumptions. For example, in a nominalist context, Small's concept of the goal of the entire "social process" could not be an empirical one. But in some other context, this concept might well be empirical. Such readings are also inadequate historically. For, looking upon Small's conceptions of the relation between sociology and ethics as historical data, it is necessary, first of all, to understand these data in their own terms, as Small saw them. Only then is it possible to understand them in the terms of some other mode of analysis as well. What was Small getting at, as he saw his own work? And how did he think he could get at it?

First of all, Small's goal, like Durkheim's, was to overcome the ethical pluralism—the rich variety which he called "ethical poverty"—of the society of his time. He wanted to arrive at "the only ethics that promises to gain general assent."[67] This formulation is important. He did not aim at some kind of logical, or theological, or philosophical proof of a system of ethics. He aimed for "general assent." The assent of the generality of people in ordinary life, presently divided among themselves by their divergent, fragmentary perspectives on ethics, not the assent of moral theorists who might accept a formal theory as valid, were to be the ultimate tests of the success or failure of Small's system of ethics.

The Reverend Dr. Small was worried about the flock. He was a Baptist. Baptist divines enjoy authority not by virtue of superior theological training (as with Presbyterians, for example), and not by virtue of priestly prerogatives which allow them alone to exercise sacraments that are central to the institution of the church (as with Catholics or High Anglicans). Like Methodists, their authority is based upon their ability to invoke responses in their congregations. And appeals to the experience of the flock are more likely to invoke response, perhaps leading even to general assent, than purely formal demonstrations.

Hence, given Small's goal, his point of departure had to be empirical. He begins by examining the experience of the flock, that is, the characteristics of the "practical judgments of conduct within the actual life-process" which "are the raw material of the only ethics that promises to gain general assent."

> These judgments enlarged, criticized, and systematized are the best that we can know about what is worth doing. They are the real appraisals of conduct, which are the only credible indexes of the concrete content fit to fill the categories of formal ethics.[68]

Small begins his examination of actual value judgments by turning first to what he calls "the psychological form of moral judgments."[69] In his view, psychology and sociology were closely related. He distinguished the subject matter of the two fields as follows:

> Human life is a plexus of relationships which we may formulate technically as the interplay of psychophysical mechanisms that

are installed in the individuals. Those phases of human activity to which the concept "ethical" is applicable have to be analyzed at last in terms of this psycho-physical mechanism, and of the conditions in which it operates. Indeed, for our purposes we may define psychology and sociology by the same formula, merely shifting the emphasis to indicate the peculiar problems of each. Psychology is the science of the *mechanism* of the social process. Sociology is the science of the mechanism of the *social process.*[70]

The "psychological form of moral judgments" is, then, the characteristics of judgments as made, and experienced, by individual persons. The "task which sociology attempts to perform in setting in order the content of those social conditions which furnish the concrete problems of ethical judgment"[71] is the task of analyzing individual judgments within the context of "association," including that full range of "association" comprising the total "social process."

Small finds, or asserts, five psychological characteristics of actual moral judgments. First, "all moral judgments are telic in form." People do not always analyze their own judgments in this way. But moral judgments "are invariably appraisals of things as good or bad because they are believed to make or not make for things supposed to be good." They are always "implied estimates of the usefulness of the actions concerned with reference to ends contemplated as desirable." This "psychological fact ... is not affected by any theory that we may hold about the ultimate sanction of moral distinctions."[72] Theorists who set up absolute criteria of judgment operate, in fact, relativistically. They apply the absolute criterion "by shifting adjustments to concrete situations" in which different ends are temporarily considered as both unproblematic and morally desirable, making other elements in the situations susceptible to moral appraisal in the light of the unproblematic ends.[73]

Second, "The act of judging a thing or an act good or bad is beyond our control."[74] It is involuntary, spontaneous, and not dependent upon the will. Theoretical standards of good or bad, in contrast, are variable, derived, and stem from diverse historical experiences. Jonathan Edwards had stern doctrines of good and evil, but "his working standard permitted him to conduct himself with reference to intoxicating liquors in a way in which the working standards of his successors today forbid." The Continental Congress raised money by a lottery, while a century later the Congress of the United States pronounced lotteries immoral. The standards have varied over time. But the judgments made, both in the earlier times and in the later, were "immediate" and "inexorable." Each person has more or less vague standards. These standards vary. But the "classification of objects or acts as good or bad ... occurs spontaneously whenever particulars become objects of attention."[75]

Third, "The highest thinkable good is a variable condition." For every good that human beings can think of "is a relation to sentient persons in adjustment with situations." Perhaps "some intelligence beyond our knowledge" may be able to conceive of "terminated activity." But such a concept "is repugnant to us," who "conceive of ourselves as conscious, as active, as having feelings, as reacting upon our conditions, as thereby changing the conditions, and consequently as requiring new adjustments to the altered conditions."[76] Though some definitions of the highest good, such as heaven or nirvana, are static, "the implications of all our conceptions of good are dynamic." Small does not spell out why "nirvana" has dynamic implications. He simply rests his assertion that all conceptions of good are variable on the experience that people supposedly have of the process of life. Life is a process. Hence, the only good that humans can conceive is "the good of adjustment," the individual good that is "motion in conformity with the stage in the process in which he belongs" and the societal good, which is "the good fit to assure advance toward the next stage."[77]

Fourth, "the only intelligible measure of good is human condition." For while standards of good and bad are "indefinitely variable," we are "psychologically compelled" to use standards "in which the objects judged are related to the condition of the persons judging." There have to be "some grounds upon which human feelings can find footing."[78]

Fifth, "the existing body of perceptions about human facts and possibilities must fix the limits of our working judgments of the highest good." Existing conceptions of the nature and aims of life limit and determine conceptions of the good. For example, if maximum economic productivity is central to one's conception of civilization, then one will tend to look upon "mind, conscience, aesthetic sensibility, family, school, church, state, solely as related to economic ends. . . ." Hence:

> . . . we must learn the virtue which is in the psychological necessity of employing relative standards of ethical value. We must learn to determine that relative standard which involves the nearest approach to absoluteness which our intelligence can achieve.[79]

These, then are Small's five—in principle, if not in fact, empirical—observations about the psychology of ethical judgments. Such judgments are telic; are spontaneous and involuntary; cannot be made with reference to a static conception of the highest good; are made always with reference to human conditions; and are limited by existing conceptions of the facts, of the potentials, and of the aims of human life.

From these observations or assertions Small draws certain conclusions for the theory of ethics. The method by which he draws these conclusions is seen, for example, in the statement that because existing perceptions of human life limit conceptions of the highest good, we must "accordingly . . . learn the virtue which is in the psychological necessity of employing relative standards of ethical value." This transformation of necessity into virtue is inherent in Small's empirical approach to ethics, and is basic to the intellectual methods by which he fuses sociology and ethics.

Small's goal was an ethics that commands general assent. In order to reach that goal, he starts from actual human experience and asserts empirical generalizations about that experience. One of these assertions, that judgments of particulars are spontaneous and involuntary, unlike historically changeable, and arguable, standards and theories of ethics, serves to dissociate his subject matter—actual judgments—from general theories. The other four assertions about the psychology of ethical judgments all serve to limit, in various ways, the content and the range of variation that general theories of ethics can possibly take on, if they are to have any real relationship to actual human experience and to the ethical judgments that human beings actually make. For example, a theory of ethics that makes obedience to the will of God the highest good, or makes the highest good static, or defines the highest good in some completely nonhuman way, could not possibly describe what actual judgments really are. Such a theory, therefore, could not possibly direct or guide those judgments. Only those theories that accurately describe the general characteristics of the moral life of human beings can possibly gain general assent. Only those theories, therefore, can possibly direct that moral life by adding to the general characteristics the particular moral content appropriate in given, historically changeable situations.

Thus far, however, we have seen only Small's first steps toward such a theory. He proceeds from his five assertions about the psychology, to his analysis of the sociology of ethical judgments. That is, he places the "physical individual . . . described . . . by the physical sciences" and the "sentient individual . . . described by psychology" into the context of "association." Now, moving, at this point, only slightly away from "psychology," Small asserts that individuals in association with one another, in addition to being physical organisms and sentient persons are also "a group of moving interests"; and that these "interests," or "motives" are "the main-springs of the individual's activities" and "the connecting link between the detached persons and the social combination which completes the individual's life."[80]

In Small's vocabulary, a "sentient individual" considered in isolation is the bearer of "the mental process," while persons considered in the context of human association are bearers of "interests." The distinction is that "the mental process" is individualized and subjective, while the notion of "interests," as Small uses it, includes not only the notion of "motive," but also the notion of goals to be realized externally, out there, in the process of association. The concept of "interests" also includes the notion of responses to objective stimuli encountered in that process. Despite the infinite variability of specific desires, goals or motives in human life, it is possible to classify them all under a limited number of rubrics.

These reduce to six sorts of subjective interests, or responses to six sorts of objective stimuli. Every human individual is a more or less highly differentiated demand for satisfactions which may be generalized as *health, wealth, sociability, knowledge, beauty,* and *rightness*. These six factors are logically and psychologically reducible to a much lower unity, but they remain the most valid and significant elements for sociological description. Every known phase of association, from the clutchings of the first man-child after food at the dugs of its dam, to the latest diplomatic effort toward a United States of Europe, has been a fermentation of these rudimentary interests. We have no content for life, thus far, outside of satisfactions of these demands. Human beings are organized requisitions for health, wealth, sociability, knowledge, beauty and rightness. Human life is instinctive and then delibera-tive effort to meet these requisitions.[81]

People pursue these six "interests" in the social process. And the concept of "social process," in Small's view, implies a holistic view of all the connections between any one person and all other persons in the world. Quoting some lines in Longfellow's "Ship of State," "Humanity with all its fears, With all its hopes of future years, Is hanging breathless on thy fate,"[82] Small goes on:

That is, this man, typical of all men, carries in himself the evidence that all the phases of human association are ceaselessly working together in a process which binds each man to every man, which makes each man both a finished product of one stage of social production, and the raw material of another. Accordingly, the sociologists confront the task of making out the different groupings of persons, and of detecting their interrelations, in such a way that the content of the whole life-process will appear, both in kind and in proportion, in the interrelations of their activities.

Or, attempting to make the same point in more vivid language, Small writes:

Individual life, when reduced to its very lowest terms, is still social life. . . . We live and move and have our being, not wholly in ourselves, but chiefly in each other. . . . Yes, even the physical composition of our body is a social affair. The baby born yester-day, and nursing now at its mother's breast, is getting, not the food of nature, but the food of society. All the sciences and arts of civilization are the caterers that serve his innocent meal. The mother's milk was distilled from the tonics of the apothecary, the compounds of the manufacturing chemist, and the artificial supplies of the grocer. It contains some of the disease germs of the town and some of the microbes from the dairy in the country. It is a chemically and mechanically different fluid from that which fills the breast of the savage, or even the rural, mother. The child's tissues begin to organize society into themselves long before its birth. In so doing they merely fall into line with the universal order of reciprocity within the whole range of association.[83]

At this point in Small's argument his telicist ontology comes into play. Such characterizations of "the social process" as I have quoted thus far are only incomplete descriptions of what that process is. In addition:

A further essential of real description of anything is reference of that thing to the end which it is presumed to serve. Suppose, for instance, that I am trying to describe a given chair, but have no idea of the service it was designed to perform. I distinguish certain upright columns and certain cross-bars, then a horizontal plane woven out of straw, then some connections with columns higher than the former, and some further cross-bars connecting the before-mentioned bars; but I have not described anything. I have simply made a catalogue of some unrelated items arbitrarily connected by a common name. But presently I get the idea of a device for the support of the human body in a semi-recumbent position. Then I can give some sort of an account of the relation of these pieces of wood and straw to the process that is to be performed, and the thing begins to have reality. Nothing is ever described properly unless it is described with reference to the end which it is supposed to be fitted to serve. This is conspicuously the case with the fact of human association. Can we get such a view of association as a whole that we may see all around it, and along toward the outcome of it, and may thus describe the details and the incidents of it in the light of its ultimate purpose? If the question means, "Can we find an absolute terminal for the social process, and can we describe association as a finished affair?" the answer is emphatically *no*. Or does the question mean, "Can we discover a definite content of the social process, a work which it is always doing, and which in the nature of the case, as far as we can see, it must always continue to do as long as the process persists?" If this is the question, the answer is emphatically *yes. . . . Human association is a constant reaction of individuals, operating in functional groups, and procuring larger aggregates and juster proportions of health, wealth, sociability, knowledge, beauty,* and *rightness satisfactions.*[84]

The idea that the complete description of a thing includes the description of its purpose does not seem to have any specific philosophical source in Small's thought. This idea does not seem to be Small's version of Aristotelianism, or of Hegelianism, or of any particular school of thought in philosophy. He does not refer to philosophical sources when he asserts this idea. But he sometimes does invoke religious imagery in this connection, and when he describes "the social process." For example, the world, when seen "from the sociological outlook" is "the theater of a plan of salvation." And the concept of "social process" means, "We live and move and have our being not wholly in ourselves, but chiefly in each other." His telicist ontology seems, then, to stem not from any specific philosophical doctrine, but from a more diffuse belief in much of traditional Protestantism, the belief that everything in the universe—every life and every death, every bird and every tree, and every stone—has a reason and a purpose within God's master purpose for the world and for humanity. This idea is quite common in many Protestant hymns. For example:

God moves in a mysterious way, His wonders to perform:
He plants His footsteps in the sea, And rides upon the storm.
. . .
His purposes will ripen fast, Unfolding every hour.
The bud may have a bitter taste, But sweet will be the flower.

The spacious firmament on high, With all the blue ethereal sky,
And spangled heav'ns, a shining frame, Their great Original
  proclaim:
Th' unwearied sun, from day to day, Does his Creator's power
  display,
And publishes to every land The work of an almighty hand.

Soon as the evening shades prevail, The moon takes up the
  wondrous tale
And nightly, to the listening earth, Repeats the story of her birth;
While all the stars that round her burn, And all the planets in
  their turn,
Confirm the tidings as they roll, And spread the truth from pole
  to pole.

Through all His mighty works Amazing Wisdom shines;
Subdues the pow'rs of hell, Confounds their dark designs,
Strong is his arm, and shall fulfill His great decrees and sovereign
  will.

It may not be our lot to wield, The sickle in the ripened field:
Nor ours to hear on summer eves, The reaper's song among the
  sheaves

Yet where our duty's task is wrought, In unison with God's
  great tho't,
The near and future blend in one, And what-so-e'er is willed, is
  done.

And ours the grateful service whence, Comes, day by day, the
  recompense:
The hope, the trust, the purpose stayed, The fountain, and the
  noon-day shade.[85]

The telic view of the world and of human experience that these
lines express is quite similar to Small's telic ontology in general, and
to his attempts, in particular, to state the "ends inherent in human
association." As he understands it, his assertion that "association is
a constant reaction of individuals ... procuring larger aggregates
and juster proportions" of the six basic interests is a purely
descriptive statement, not an evaluative one. Immediately after
reaching this conclusion, he writes:

It is in point to repeat that our discussion all bears at last
upon the significance of sociology for ethics. At present we are
considering the *descriptive* value of sociology.[86]

Even the phrase "juster proportions [of the six interests]" is, within Small's terms, a descriptive one. For as seen in the chapter that follows, justice is the balance of interests. Hence, this seemingly nondescriptive phrase is identical to "balanced proportions." Each of the six basic "interests" strives for realization. The realization of all requires a balance between them. Hence, to say that justice, i.e., balance, is a goal inherent in the social process is, in Small's terms, to make a purely descriptive statement.

Turning to the next step in Small's argument (or to a rational reconstruction of that step), note that if a purely descriptive statement about a phenomenon includes assertions about that phenomenon's purpose, then the purely descriptive statement includes within itself a criterion for evaluating the phenomenon in question. If a description of a chair includes the purpose of a chair, then the description also implies the evaluation that the chair is a bad chair if it falls apart when people try to sit on it. That logic is not quaint, or bizarre, or peculiar to Small. Precisely the same logic permeates Lon Fuller's influential philosophy of law. Fuller's description of the phenomenon, "law," includes the law's purpose, subjecting human conduct to the governance of rules. Given this purpose, it follows that ex post facto laws, or internally contradictory laws, or other laws that cannot possibly subject human conduct to the governance of rules, are bad laws.[87] For when phenomena are described telically, some descriptive and some evaluative statements may be fused, or may be used interchangeably.

Small's logic is similar to Fuller's, or to the logic of any ordinary person who descriptively evaluates (or evaluatively describes) a chair as bad, because it is impossible to sit upon it without crashing through to the floor. First, his five empirical assertions about the psychology of ethical judgments set the boundaries within which any theory of ethics must fall—if it is to be based on real human experience, if it hopes to command general assent, and if it is not to consist of a series of illusions about the real nature of ethical judgments. Among other things, such a theory must be telicist and it must use standards which refer not to trans-human ideals or principles such as obedience to the will of God, but to real human conditions. Second, his description of the life of any one person as being almost completely enmeshed in "association" with all other persons in the world implies that the human conditions to which ethical standards refer must encompass not only (and not primarily) the life of individual persons but rather (and more centrally) the total process of human association. Third, the telicist description of that total process as including the pursuit of "larger aggregates and juster proportions" of the six basic interests implies the standards which must be central in any ethical theory which hopes to gain general assent.

Small states these three conclusions in the following ways. First:

All ethical judgments are virtually estimates of the relation of subordinate parts of conduct to the largest wholes brought *into calculation*. All ethical judgments are not only telic in form; they are not only comparisons of concrete particulars with a generalized standard; that standard is not merely a version of human conditions; but all these facts are parts of the more comprehensive fact that conduct-valuations are always appraisals of the ratio between the particular conduct in question and the largest complex of human conditions that the mind at the moment of judging is able to consider.[88]

Second, applying this observation to "conduct in association," in particular, as distinct from purely individual conduct, *"Our judgment of conduct in association always tends to appraisal of it as good or bad according to its assumed effects upon the largest range of associations that we can take into account.*[89]

Third, providing this observation with more specific content, and simultaneously jumping from descriptions of reality to criteria of moral values, Small "restate[s] the reality in which the sociologist finds the working criterion of moral values":

The life of the individual, according to the view of the individual which we have proposed, is to be considered as a process of achieving the self given in the interests which prompt the health, wealth, sociability, knowledge, beauty and rightness desires, but this process produces and is produced by the social process. Following the same line of analysis, we have as our conception of the social process: *Association is a continuous process of realizing an increased aggregate and juster proportions of the health, wealth, sociability, knowledge, beauty, and rightness satisfactions in the persons associating.* This is the end visible as interpretation and justification of the whole social process. All that goes on among men actually is valued by them with conscious or unconscious reference to its bearings upon some conception of these goods, either severally or collectively. We have no other real measure to apply in a theory of conduct-value.[90]

The purposes of the total social process, which empirical observation supposedly reveals, provide the standards for the ethical evaluation of any single part, or aspect, or conduct within that process. And as empirical observation of the real nature of value judgments supposedly prove, "We have no other real measure to apply...." Assuming the goal of a theory of ethics which will gain general assent, empirical observations of the nature of individual ethical judgments reveal the general characteristics which that theory must have. For example, it must be telic and relativistic. And observations of the nature of human association, including the purposes inherent in the total process of association, in the context of a telicist ontology, reveal what the highest standards of that theory must be.

CONCLUSION

In short, Small was not a preacher's kid who had never been weaned, or a muddlehead who was unable to tell the difference between descriptive and normative statements. He coherently synthesized his scientism, including his empiricism, with his moralism. The peculiar characteristics of his synthesis, and the fact that it is intellectually coherent within its own terms but historically dead, suggest three general lessons about "value-free social science," about the ways in which social scientists do their work, and about attempts to arrive at super-perspectival views of society.

First, the close association, in Small's thought, between sociology and ethics depended, in part, (1) on his conception of scientific objectivity and (2) on the meaning of the notion of a descriptive statement in the context of his telicist ontology. More generally, the meaning of any statement in any discussion of the relationship between science and ethics, as in the recurrent discussions among sociologists about "value-free science," depends in part upon the meanings one gives to the various components of one's notion of "science." The very meaning of the notions of "descriptive" and "nondescriptive" statements is relative. The meaning of "descriptive" and "nondescriptive" varies with the language and with the ontological assumptions within which one is speaking. Hence, those meanings must be clarified before intelligible discussion of the relationship between science and ethics can take place.

Second, Small's conception of the social role of university scholars and of the social mission of universities was the link between his view of American society in his time, on the one hand, and, on the other, his conception of what he should and could do about it, as a sociologist. His conception of the role of university scholars was in a part a carry-over from his experiences in an earlier, very different social position, that of a college teacher, and was in part defined in a language which he took from a nonacademic social affiliation, that of a low Protestant believer.

More generally, the scope and content of a social scientist's social science depend not simply upon what is going on in the society in which the scientist lives, plus the inherited intellectual traditions of a field. The scope and content depend also upon (1) how social scientists perceive what is going on in their society, and (2) the ways in which they define their professional jobs, as determined, (3) by the specific institutional settings in which they work (for example, college, university, free lance, research institute), (4) the ways in which they define the settings, and (5) other social ties and affiliations that they have.

Third, in Small's conception of objectivity, in the way he defined the central ethical problem of American society, and in his proposed solutions to that problem, he attempted to overcome perspectival views of society and of ethics. He wanted both a holistic, super-perspectival science of sociology and paramount standards of moral value to which doctors, lawyers and Indian chiefs, with their limited, perspectival moralities, would defer. He found his social base for super-perspectival social science, and for super-perspectival ethics, in the occupants of a particular social position in a peculiar type of organization, scholars in universities, as he defined universities and university scholars. But his definition of the social role of university scholars, and of the social mission of universities, as distinct both from earlier definitions of college teachers and from later definitions of university scholars, made sense in American society only in the late nineteenth and early twentieth centuries. His thinking about the way to overcome perspectival thought was blatantly perspectival.

More generally, other scholars, too, have looked to the occupants of particular social positions, positions which are supposed to endow their occupants with privileged cognition, as the social source of super-perspectival thought. Mannheim looked to free-lance intellectuals.[91] As Merton has shown, some people, for centuries, have looked to "outsiders" while others have looked to "insiders."[92] But Small's perspectival thinking about perspectival thinking suggests the likelihood that all attempts to locate the social source of super-perspectival thought in the occupants of cognitively privileged positions are doomed.

Suppose, however, that there is such a social position. The occupants of any position whatsoever, including the positions of professor and of sociologist, vary in their definitions of that position. Do all free-lance intellectuals, say, enjoy privileged cognition even though they vary in their definitions of that status? More crucially, they also occupy other, nonprivileged positions. They occupy not a status, but a set of statuses. And those other nonprivileged statuses, such as male or female, married or single, black or white, consumer, American or Uzbek, bring perspectival thinking back in.[93]

Small's perspectival thinking about perspectival thinking casts into doubt all hope of finding social statuses whose occupants enjoy privileged cognition. Briefly and sketchily, and going beyond the central concerns of this book, there are two more promising approaches, each different from the other and from the attempt of Small and of Mannheim to identify the cognitively privileged. First, what are the social sources of the overwhelmingly powerful belief in contemporary American society in heliocentrism as against geocentrism? And what are the social sources of the even more fully consensual belief that there are exactly twenty cigarettes, no more and no fewer, in every unopened pack on every cigarette shelf in every store selling this most peculiarly law-like commodity? Here are genuinely mass-democratic beliefs that exist for social reasons, and there is no element of perspectivalism whatsoever.

Second, following certain leads in Jean Piaget's *The Moral Judgment of the Child*, and in the works of others who have done research on moral development in Piaget's tradition,[94] we might find the source of super-perspectival thought, not in cognitively privileged social positions, but in certain types of continuing, socially constrained relationships between occupants of very different positions. There are relationships in which—because there is no element of power and dependency, or of authority and obedience, or of impersonal market transactions in which each person is oriented to that external, alien force, the prevailing price—each, if socially constrained to continue the relationship, is constrained also to absorb the other's point of view.

Small, of course, did not think along those lines. One of the meanings of the concept of "social process" was that each point in every person's life touches, and is touched by each point in every other person's life. But the common run of humanity, caught up in its daily cares, could not see, much less think consistently in terms of, that fact. It was a peculiar mission of sociology to spell out both the cognitive and the moral implications of this central fact of human life, and to spell them out in a way that synthesized the two. This synthesis reflects the historical setting in which Small worked, and his personal background, and it depended upon the fairly distinctive intellectual methods that this chapter has analyzed. The synthesis depended also, however, on the substance of Small's views of human nature and of the social process, as distinct from his intellectual methods. Briefly, Small could be both scientistic and moralistic if he was scientistic but not mechanistic. In that way he could combine a scientist's faith in causation with a moralist's faith in responsible, volitional selves. The following chapter shows how Small conceived of the relation of human nature to the social process in a way that enabled him coherently and intelligibly to retain both faiths.

6

HUMAN NATURE AND THE SOCIAL

PROCESS

Sociology, for Small, was supposed to be both empirical and theoretical, both ethical and scientific. Turning from the kind of sociology he envisaged to the detailed substance of his thought—as in such concepts as "interests," "association," and "the social process"—this chapter relies primarily on a single source, Small's *General Sociology*, published in 1905.[1]*

General Sociology was Small's treatise.[2] Its goals were, "first, to make visible different elements that must necessarily find their place in ultimate sociological theory; and, second, to serve as an index to relations between the parts and the whole of sociological science" (p. vi). That is, this book is Small's comprehensive summary of his field.

After some 100 pages of introductory discussion of the history, subject matter, and definitions of sociology, Small devotes 300 pages to Spencer, Schäffle and, especially, to Ratzenhofer. He is concerned with showing cumulative development in sociology, with showing that Ratzenhofer went beyond Spencer and Schäffle, and that sociology was building upon Ratzenhofer. Hence, his chapters on Ratzenhofer often fade over into expositions of his own views. And he brings many other social scientists, such as Morgan, Tarde, Simmel, Veblen, Ward, and Ross into these chapters. The result, in Small's judgment, was "a series of generalizations, of concepts, of

---

* All references to page numbers in the text of this chapter are references to this book. In the quotations from Small, all emphases in the original are omitted.

categories" on the frontiers of sociology, which equip sociologists "just as the physicists, chemists and biologists were when they had generalized the elementary phenomena in their fields, and had adopted a working terminology for the notions so generalized" (397–98). The rest of the book, some 300 more pages, consists largely of Small's further spelling out "of the generalizations to which our analysis has led" and of "the precise content of the most important categories" (398). These include such "categories" as "the social process," "association," "social structure," "social function," "group," "interests," and "society." The book concludes with a reprint, with little change, of Small's earlier essay on "The Significance of Sociology for Ethics," and with a brief discussion of "practical sociology."

The central concept in the entire work is "social process."[3] "A process," in Small's definition, "is a collection of occurrences, each of which has a meaning for every other, the whole of which constitutes some sort of becoming." According to Small:

Every portion of human experience has relations which require application of this concept "process". Human association is a process. Every act of every man has a meaning for every act of every other man (513).

What is more, "human association" is a "process" also in the sense that it "constitutes some sort of becoming." The goals, or at least the tendency of the social process are the good life for all people, and a good life which is ever more variegated, colorful and individualized.

More and better life by more and better people, beyond any limit of time or quality that our minds can set, is the indicated content of the social process (523).

If we take the genetic view of the social process, we may describe it in this aspect as a progressive production of more and more dissimilar men. Each change in the social situation affords a new outlet for personal idiosyncrasy, and presents new incitement to variation of conduct and character. The proverb that "it takes all sorts of people to make a world" is only one side of the reality.

It takes a world to make all sorts of people, is equally true of the same reality (590).

As with so many of Small's ideas, however, no single statement, out of context, can convey what was going on in his head, or in his written works. In some contexts, as when Small writes that "the social process is incessant reaction of persons" (205), or that sociologists should transfer their attention from "society" to "the process of human association" (184), the concept of "process" has no temporal component. Or, at least, it has no long-term, evolutionary temporality. "Social process" is virtually synonymous with "interaction." Elsewhere, Small uses the term interchangeably with "growth" (145). Or it becomes almost the equivalent of "evolution" (238–39). In such uses, and when Small defines a process so as to include "a becoming," temporality is inherent.

Many other ideas in *General Sociology* also seem, at the first glance, to be confused or contradictory. Small opposed individualistic views of society and history (44–51). But he asserts that all "social forces" are "lodged in individuals" (532) and that, "In the last analysis, the stimulus of every act is an interest of the individual who acts" (365).

Small writes, "There is neither free will nor free thought nor free feeling in the world of people" because "feeling, thought, and volition are tethered to fixed physical conditions" (412–13). But he also makes "selection of ends," and "attention, valuation and choice" central to "the psychological element in the social process" (636). And he refers to "the spiritual initiative which is superior to mechanical causation" (639). Small writes that human beings are "earth children" who are "not exempt from physical law" and that "All the higher flights of life are anchored to the sordid earth" (407). But, even though we are children of the sordid earth who also have a "spiritual initiative," Small rejects Saint Paul's notion of the war in the members between good and evil, the spirit and the flesh, the human and the animalic (471). If "interests" are located in individuals (281), then what is restraint "in obedience to the general interests of the community"? (239). If the "springs of action" of all people, from the masses building the pyramids to the British royal family "are fundamentally the same" (483), then what is "the individuality which distinguishes man from matter"? (460).

It is not the goal of this chapter to show that Small was full of inconsistencies. Nor is it the goal to show that all apparent contradictions can be resolved into a perfectly coherent theoretical system. All theorists have inconsistencies. None has a perfectly tight system, in which there are no loose ends. But the attempt to make sense of real or apparent contradictions is a useful device for digging into the logical structure and the content of a theorist's work. That attempt forces the reader to read more carefully, to pay close attention to language, and to see content in the light of logical structure and the logic of argument in the light of content. It seems especially important in Small's case to pursue apparent antinomies. Small was a prolific writer. But Henry Elmer Barnes, a friend and colleague, predicted shortly after Small's death "that his permanent influence upon sociology through his writings will ultimately prove slight and ephemeral as compared with the impress of his personality and his personal activities" such as his influence as a teacher, his founding of the Chicago department and of the *American Journal of Sociology*, and his work for the American Sociological Society.[4]

Barnes was right. Who but an intellectual historian reads Small today? Who accepts Small's view of the relation between sociology and ethics? And who practices, or attempts to practice, a synthesizing sociology in Small's tradition? But why did Small's intellectual synthesis die with him? Is there something wrong with it, intellectually, that scholars after Small have noted, leading them to refute and reject him? Or did history, not sociologists, refute Small? Is his synthesis so deeply rooted in his own historical moment, and so much a compromise between conflicting forces at that moment— between moralistic religiosity and scientism; between labor and capital, whose struggles Small observed; between the individualism that he rejected and the socialism that he opposed—that it could not stand the test of time, no matter how lucid the content, and coherent the logic, of his thought?

This chapter, then, will follow up some of the apparent confusions or contradictions in *General Sociology*; will attempt to make sense of them; and will try to assess the balance of intellectually unstable tension as against coherent systematizing in this book. It turns first to what Small meant by "individualism," and what he meant when he claimed to have overcome individualism with his "functional" or "organic" view of society. It concludes that presocial individuals remain the basic units in Small's sociology. Second, it examines Small's view of human nature, of the children of the sordid earth who are superior to mechanical causality. Third, it considers Small's concept of "interests," an integral part of his view of human nature. Fourth, it examines the relation between human nature and the social process. And fifth, it considers the "incidents" or fundamental traits of the social process as additional evidence of the limited extent to which Small overcame the individualist tradition.

THE ORGANIC VIEW AND THE INDIVIDUALIST TRADITION

Small often expressed his opposition to "individualism," and he described the overcoming of individualism as central to his life's work. In 1915, in a letter written in lieu of his attending a class reunion at Newton Theological School he wrote:

> If I should compress into a sentence what seems to me to be the scientific significance of my life, it is that I have been trying to do my part toward shunting the thinking of social scientists from the side track of individualistic and statical interpretation of life onto the main line of functional interpretation.[5]

In place of "individualism," as Small used that term, he put forward concepts such as "the social process," the "organic concept of society," and "association." For example:

> Every man is what he is as a resultant in part of the pressure of the human associations within which his personality has its orbit. The concept "human life," whether we try to construct it for individuals or for the race at large, is a fictitious and unreal picture, unless it includes the notion "association." Association is the universal medium in which the individual completes his existence by merging it into the larger life of all individuals (507).

This view had cognitive, moral, and political implications. First, cognitively, the concept of "social process" means that sociologists are supposed to see in the world not discrete, isolated individuals, or aggregates of individuals, but individuals in interaction (or "association") with one another. Further, sociologists are supposed to look at the full range of ties and affiliations that individual persons have—their entire status-set, as Merton uses that term—in the context of the total societies in which they live. In one example that Small gives, a carpenter is not simply a carpenter, or simply a union delegate, a citizen, or a member of a church. Nor is the carpenter simply a psychological specimen with a nervous system and certain mental traits. Rather:

> He is an intersection of all the groupings which human beings form in the pursuit of all the ends of life, and all the ends of life are epitomised in that single man's character. He is a function of the whole process by which they are working together to organize their physiological, and economic, and personal, and scientific, and aesthetic, and religious interests. Make a cross-section of him, and we find we have in him every fiber of civilization (520–21).

Or, more briefly stated, "the essential thesis of the organic concept of society," in Small's view, was, "Every point in every man's life is related to every point in every other man's life" (567).

Second, this complete interdependence of each with all had certain moral implications. If each affects and is affected by the actions of all, then "Live and let live" is not an adequate moral guide. In the "organic" view of society it is impossible simply to let others live, or for others to let me live. We must "Live and help live" instead. And we must restrain ourselves in the pursuit of our own interests, or the assertion of our own rights.

> There could be no civic society in advance of anarchy, if it did not come into existence, and stay in existence, by virtue of restraint upon interests which would destroy each other, if not restrained. Civic society is practical agreement of many interests not to assert their claim to the full, and it is, beyond this, practical agreement of each of the interests to contribute something toward enforcing the claims of the aggregate interests. Phillips Brooks once said: "No man has a right to all of his rights." The theorem sums up a whole social philosophy (240).

Third, Small was explicit about the political implications of his rejecting "individualism" in favor of an "organic" view of "the social process." An opponent both of socialism and of laissez-faire capitalism, Small charged that:

> ... old-fashioned Jeffersonian democracy was a political philosophy which assumed precisely the individualism rejected above as an optical illusion. All the modern variations of Jeffersonian democracy, in spite of their stalwart and salutary traits, are weak from the implications of this impossible individual, and they are foreordained failures in just the proportion in which they ignore the composite, dependent, social character of the individual (476-77).

Small went on to say, however, that all forms of socialism "imply the opposite misconceptions; viz, that society is the only real existence, and that the personal units have no separate and distinct claims or character sufficient to modify theories devoted solely to the perfection of social organization" (477). In contrast, and in opposition, both to Jeffersonian liberals and to socialists:

> The sort of work the sociologist has to do is needed as a means of reducing the weight of both kinds of prejudice, and of substituting for each a just conception of the intrinsic relation between personal units and the social whole (477).

The similarity between this way of stating the issue—"the ... relation between personal units and the social whole"—and the venerable liberal formula, "individual and society," suggests that Small overcame individualism only to a limited extent. He perceived "association," that is, systems of social interaction. He asserted that there is no "absolute individual," that persons are molded by social interaction, and that selves and individuality emerge out of "association."

> We are in large part what our social set, our church, our political party, our business and professional circles are (496-97).

> The presence of others is necessary in order that I may be myself. The self that is potential in me cannot become aware of itself, and display itself, except by means of reaction with other people[6] (474-75).

But the basic units, the elemental building blocks of "the social process" are individual human beings. In this respect, Small is similar to others in a long line of social philosophers, associated for the most part with the liberal tradition, such as Hobbes, Locke, and Smith. Briefly, social philosophers and social scientists in this tradition have an image of (1) individual human beings, (2) each of whom is endowed with some kind of human nature, or motives, or set of purposes, (3) coming together in some kind of encounter or transaction, (4) out of which bumpings together of motivated individuals, social institutions or societies emerge. Thinkers in this tradition vary in the type of human nature or motives that they attribute to presocial persons. They may have a malign, sceptical view of human nature, as in Hobbes. Or they may see presocial persons as more reasonable—indeed, a bit gentlemanly—as in Smith. They vary in their image of the encounter between presocial persons, from a war of each against all to a rationally calculated exchange of goods and services. And they vary in their definition of the institutional outcome of the encounters—sovereignty in Hobbes; the social contract in Locke; and in Smith, a division of labor between people working and exchanging goods in a system of market transactions. But the general format of their imagery of the origin and operation of social systems is the same throughout.

For example, in Adam Smith's hypothetical tribe, one hunter does not hunt very well. He goes into the woods to hunt deer and comes home without any. It happens, however, that this hunter makes bows and arrows better than the others. For reasons inherent in human nature, including the "natural propensity to truck, barter, and exchange" and a tendency rationally to calculate in one's own self-interest, this hunter trades bows and arrows for the venison that a better hunter has to exchange. Both hunters discover that they have more venison than if each attempted to make his own weapons and to shoot his own deer. The bad hunter who is a good craftsman exchanges with other hunters and becomes a full-time armorer for the tribe. A division of labor, a certain kind of social structure, has emerged out of the bumpings together of presocial individuals who had been pursuing their own individual goals, or manifesting their own individualized human nature.[7]

This individualist imagery is still very much present in American social science today. It informs not simply speculation about the historical origins of human societies, but social-scientific analyses of contemporary phenomena.[8] This imagery is "individualist" because it posits the possibility of an individual person going into the woods to hunt deer and meeting there another individual person. But, of course, such a thing has never happened, never will happen, and could not possibly happen. Only social structures can hunt deer; individual persons cannot. That is, it is possible for an individual who is, let us say, male, and of a given socially defined age, and is someone's son, or brother, or father, or husband (or all four) to go into the woods to hunt deer. And, of course, if that person meets another, then whatever happens between them, whatever new social structures emerge, cannot be the result simply of each person's individualized human nature, or motives, or purposes. For the encounter in the woods between strangers was structured in the first place, with possibilities and constraints that stem from the statuses which the participants occupy in that setting (such as age and sex) and in other settings (such as kinship statuses, or whatever other ones they may occupy).

The individual hunter is a liberal myth that neither Marxism nor classical conservatism ever shared. When liberalism, in the late nineteenth and early twentieth centuries, switched from laissez-faire to statist welfarism, it retained this individualist imagery of what constitutes a society. For example, Hobhouse, whose work marks this transition in England, writes that "the organic view of society ... means that, while the life of society is nothing but the life of individuals as they act upon one another, the life of the individual in turn would be something utterly different if he could be separated from society."[9] Further:

Society consists wholly of persons.... The British nation is a unity with a life of its own. But the unity is constituted by certain ties which bind all British subjects, which ties are in the last resort feelings and ideas, sentiments of patriotism, of kinship, a common pride, and a thousand more subtle sentiments that bind together men who speak a common language, have behind them a common history, and understand one another as they can understand no one else.

Small uses similar imagery. "America is an entity that is made up of people" who illustrate "the wonderful fact of reciprocal influence throughout a society" even though "the persons who compose the society may be at distances from each other varying from residence in the same house to location at opposite sides of the continent" (140–41). And Small, too, shared the myth of the individual hunter. Except that his hunters are lumberjacks.

> The arrangements of individuals into somewhat permanent relationships, or structures, come about, as we have seen, in consequence of utilities which people discover, accidentally or otherwise, in those arrangements. To take one of the simplest cases: Two woodsmen may have no personal interest in each other, but both are trying to earn a living clearing neighboring pieces of forest. The trees are so big that after the trunks have been trimmed neither woodsman alone could move one end of the logs. From sheer economic necessity the personally indifferent individuals combine their efforts. Together they can handle the logs quite easily, and roll them into positions from which they may be floated toward the mill. The skillful combination of efforts between these two men is an instance of social structure, serving as a device to accomplish work. In general, this is the underlying meaning of social structures always (149).

Or more generally:

> In a word, the whole social process is a perpetual reaction between interests that have their lodgment in the individuals who are in contact. More specifically, this reaction is disguised or open struggle between individuals. The conflict of interests between individuals, combined with community of interest in the same individuals, results in the groupings of individuals between whom there is relatively more in common, and then the continuance of struggle between group and group. The members of each group have relatively less in common with the members of a different group than they have with each other (499).

The significance of this formulation depends, of course, upon the meaning of "interests," and on Small's conception of the individual human beings in which they are lodged. It depends on Small's view of human nature. It suffices at this point simply to say, that "interests" are universal, or nearly universal characteristics of human beings. They are, in some of Small's formulations, energies that impel people to do things. Hence, to say that the social process is a perpetual reaction between interests lodged in individuals, is to say that social relationships consist, in part, of the objectifications into interaction of the human nature of individuals. Presocial individuals—not families, hereditary orders, classes, or even dyads —are the building blocks of the social process. In this one crucial respect, Small never overcame the individualist liberal tradition in social philosophy and social science. He insisted on the centrality of "association," as against a purely aggregative view of people in society. But he retained the myth of the hunter.

SMALL'S VIEW OF HUMAN NATURE

Small, in common with many other scholars of his day, wanted to be both scientific and moralistic. His conceptions of science and of ethics, and the fairly distinctive intellectual methods by which he synthesized the two, allowed him to encompass both in a single system of thought, or a single academic discipline. Small also shared with many others in his day a desire to be scientific but not mechanistic. He wanted to have a science of human life, avoiding any "confession of unfaith in the universality of cause and effect in the world ... " (645). But he also believed that there is, in human beings, "a spiritual initiative which is superior to mechanical causation" (639), that human beings have knowledge of situations, make evaluations, choose, and engage in acts of will.

Men do not, as a rule, tread the stage of life in a dream. If they are not socially conscious, they are at least self-conscious. They act for reasons, although not necessarily for good reasons, socially considered, nor with far-reaching vision of the scope of the reasons. In contrast with Tarde's hypothesis, and with the whole genus of single-reaction explanations of which it is a type, we urge that the characteristic factor in the psychological element of the social process, as distinguished from the biological element, is selection of ends. Every effort to locate the dis- tinctively social factor in a state or motion of consciousness less complex and complete than acts of combined attention, valuation, and choice, foolishly tempts fate.

Sentient action is action directed toward ends. Explanation of the social process in terms of stimulus alone, or of reflex action alone, or of subjective change alone, without reference to purpose and volition in view of a purpose, is irresponsible speculation (636).

On its own terms at least, Small's view of human nature allowed him to have it both ways. He could root human beings in the sordid earth, subjecting them to some measure of mechanical causality, and still give a central place in human nature to sentience and choice. There are three different strands, or three vocabularies, in this view. First, although he does not use the metaphor of "levels," he seems to have such a notion in mind when he refers to physical, chemical, biological (or, sometimes, vital), and psychological energies, or components of persons. He can give full deference to "mechanical causation" as regards the more material components in human nature and retain purpose, choice, and volition in the psychological components. For the "vital" components—a way of saying "biological" without sounding materialistic—stand between the psychological and the physico-chemical. They serve to protect, as it were, the psychological realm from too close a contact with the realm where "mechanical causation" holds sway.

Second, "interests"—"the simplest modes of motion which we can trace in the conduct of human beings" (426)—are central to Small's view of human nature. The six basic "interests" are the interests in health, wealth, sociability, knowledge, beauty, and rightness. As seen below, the vocabulary of interests and the vocabulary of physical, chemical, vital, and psychological components in human nature cut across each other. They relate to each other in a way rather analogous to the way in which Freud's vocabularies of id, ego, and superego and of the unconscious, the preconscious, and the conscious cut across each other. Some interests "are generically identical with the factors that compose plants and animals" and "follow the laws of physics, chemistry and biology" (426). Other interests, such as knowledge, are rooted in the psychological components of human nature.

Third, in addition to these two secular vocabularies, Small occasionally uses religious terms. His secular terms replaced the older vocabulary of body, mind, and soul—distinct and separable entities that, like their Freudian parallels, id, ego, and superego, can be at war with each other. Instead, Small had a more unitary view of human nature. He saw no Pauline war among the members but, rather, a combination of energies or motions of diverse types from the physical and chemical, through the vital, to the psychological. But he sometimes also uses a religious vocabulary or religious ideas. He uses phrases such as "spiritual initiative" (639), and "the spiritual environment" (482), and writes of the persistence of each person's influence in the social process that makes death a fiction (611). He has a very weak sense for the demonic in human nature, or for sin. But he does write, "In one fraction of his nature man is an eagerness to be a god" (451), which is precisely the way in which some Protestant theologies define sin. And he attributes the interest in rightness to a sentiment, or "premonition" that is quite similar to the oceanic feelings that Freud associated with belief in religion.

> In brief, men always manifest some species of premonition of a self somehow superior to their realized self, or of a whole outside of themselves with which it is desirable to adjust the self.... This superior self is a more or less vague image of the conscious self, somehow amplified by addition of activities beyond those of the actual self. The whole partly detected around the self is not the commonplace of people and things that the routine of life encounters. It is the mysterious more that broods in and over the familiar surroundings. The real individual is at last, in one fraction of his personality, a wistfulness after that other self, or a deference to that inscrutable whole. In other words, there are distinct sorts of human action which are impelled primarily not by supposed demand for health, or wealth, or sociability, or knowledge, or beauty; but they are to be accounted for as conscious or unconscious efforts either to become the larger self or to be adjusted to the containing whole (466).

Small's simultaneous use of the three vocabularies, or his going back and forth from one to the others, allows him to combine "mechanical causation" with sentience and choice. When Small writes that humans are bound to the sordid earth, and subject to physical laws, he does not make materialist causation cover all of human nature. Rather, "the physical is the necessary vehicle of the spiritual" (457). Hence, "the spiritual" is not absolutely free. But physical laws alone do not determine human action. There is also "sentient action"—"knowing, feeling and willing" (431) in one formulation, or "attention, valuation, and choice" (636) in another. As Small saw the relation between material causation and "sentient action":

> The various materialistic and mechanical philosophies of history, that have attempted to find the secret of human development in the inevitable operations of nature, have not overstated the absolute value of this fundamental and constant factor. They have simply miscalculated its ratio and some of its other relations to all the other factors. There is neither free will nor free thought nor free feeling in the world of people. Feeling, thought, and volition are tethered to fixed physical conditions. This is as true of the rhapsody of the devotee, the exhortation of the zealot, the vision of the poet, the speculation of the metaphysician, as it is of the geographer's search for the North Pole or the miner's delving for gold or coal. All that men do or desire is either a drifting on the tide of physical conditions, or primarily some sort of reaction upon those conditions. The extent to which men can act, and the mode of their action, is not to be deduced from the formulas of an absolutely defined freedom; for that condition exists only in the speculative imagination. On the other hand, the formulas of volition are not to be derived from physical law alone. The scope of sentient action is, however, merely that restricted area to which the individual or the generation is limited by the conditions of physical nature (412-13).

In short, "The physical environment is always present, but it is not all that is present" (424). That environment enters, in some degree and in some way, into every sentiment, emotion, song, or poem or prayer. "But the fact that the same farm produces Websters whom Americans never know and the Webster whom Americans will never forget, proves that the materialistic interpretation of life lacks precision" (424). Processes other than physical causation explain the differences between the different Websters, and make it possible for a child of the sordid earth "to be a self, responsible for his deed and accountable for his fault" (460).

In addition to "physical, chemical and vital energies" (427) there is also "the psychological element in the social process, as distinguished from the biological element, [namely] selection of ends." And, "Every effort to locate the distinctively social factor in a state of motion or consciousness less complex and complete than acts of combined attention, valuation, and choice, foolishly tempts fate" (636). Human beings are subject to material causation. But they also make choices and act for purposes. They act "for the sake" of goals (444).

When we attempt to explain the social process—i.e., to go back one step beyond the statement of human experience in terms of process, to restatement of it in terms of purpose—our problem is, in a word, to generalize the purpose-reactions that occur in typical situations (642).

In focusing on conscious choice or the pursuit of purposes as a central element in human nature, freeing human beings from complete subjection to "mechanical causation," Small is not giving up his scientism. For choices, too, have causes and may be explained. To think otherwise "would be a confession of unfaith in the universality of cause and effect in the world...." But, continuing the same sentence, Small suggests "that every human choice has an explanation, as an effort to adapt means to ends" (645).

Two things seem to be going on at this point in Small's thinking. First, he often associates physical causation with the notion of "environment," with the soil, climate, and topography down on the farm that produced quite different Websters. If choice is central to human nature and to the social process, and choices have to be explained, but are explained as "efforts" of individual persons, then the causes are internal. They do not come from an external, physical environment. Hence, to the extent that physical causation pertains only to the influence of external environments, such causation does not determine human choices. Small can be scientistic without being mechanistic.

Second, note that when Small introduces "selection of ends" as central to "the psychological element of the social process" he distinguishes that element from the biological one. In this context, he does not refer to "physical, chemical and vital energies," but only to the biological. For, in his image, the psychological elements in human nature are "highest" and the physical are "lowest." "All the higher flights of life are anchored to the sordid earth.... We can raise our heads only so far as successful provision for primary material needs grants us partial release from the constant task of life" (407). These metaphors place the realm of the physical and chemical down low, and sentient action up high. Between the two is the biological or the vital. The vitalistic vocabulary that Small sometimes used protects "the psychological element" from too close a contact with anything that has a materialist ring to it. And the energistic vocabulary which he also used in some contexts, as when he writes, "We want to find out what are the deep undercurrents of energy in all association" (234), serves the same purpose. Humans are, in part, material. Small's identification of matter with the material environment is not complete. But we are not dead matter. We have energies of various types, including physical ones. And if even our physical components are energies, then stimulus and response cannot explain our behavior. We are alive, making choices, acting upon the environment. The vitalistic and energistic vocabulary is not very prominent. It is strangely absent from most of the summarizing statements in *General Sociology*. But it, too, served to allow Small to be scientistic while still believing in the centrality, in human life, of sentience, volition, and choice.

THE CONCEPT OF INTERESTS

Cutting across the distinction between the psychological and material elements in human nature is Small's concept of "interests."* Roughly speaking, interests are Small's version of instincts. He defines the concept differently in different contexts. He sometimes uses "interests" as synonymous with "desires" (444). But the term also covers objects of desire. Hence, Small sometimes distinguishes between "'desire' . . . the subjective aspect of choice, and 'want' . . . the objective aspect, i.e., the thing desired" (436). In

*Chapter 31 of *General Sociology*, entitled "Interests," is reprinted in Appendix C.

other contexts, "want" seems to be subjective, to mean the same thing as "desire." "Both something inside men that makes them have wants, and something outside of men that promises to gratify the wants, is implied by the word 'interest' " (196). In this formulation, interests, on the subjective side, are "deeper" than desires or subjective wants. "The activities of men ... all run back to motives that have their roots" in interests (197). This imagery of interests as "deeper," as somehow more basic and primordial, than subjectively experienced motives allows Small to refer, on occasion, to unconscious interests. People may have interests in knowledge, beauty, or rightness even if they are not aware of that fact. The interest in rightness may be "something in the person impelling him, however unconsciously, toward ... moral conduct ..." (435).

Small does not develop, or give sustained atttention, to the notion of the unconscious. He is more concerned with asserting the centrality of sentience in human life, of "attention, valuation and choice" as against "mechanical causation." Nor does he develop all the possible implications of another similarity between his concept of "interests" and Freud's concept of "instincts," the insatiability of their demands. "An interest is a plain demand for something, regardless of everything else. An interest is unequivocal, intolerant, exclusive" (201).

Small goes from this point neither to Saint Paul's nor to Freud's conception of the war among the members. Instead, Small goes on both to observe, and to recommend, balance, restraint, and moderation, with respect both to the interests within an individual and to the confrontation of interests in the social process. An individual is the "resultant of many interests, which have been reduced to a certain working basis of mutual concession" (201-2). In society, people do not have a right to all of their rights. And as seen in the next chapter, balance, moderation, and restraint are central to Small's politics. In his version of "the greatest good for the greatest number," he counts the number of interests instead of the number of people. That policy is most desirable that serves the largest number and greatest variety of interests.

In still another variation of the vocabulary, "an interest is an unsatisfied capacity, corresponding to an unrealized condition, and it is predisposition to such rearrangement as would tend to realize the indicated condition" (433). Whatever the variations in vocabulary, however, "In the beginning there were interests" (196). Small compares them to the concept of the atom in natural science and calls them "the simplest modes of motion which we can trace in the conduct of human beings" (426).

All such notions, of course, risk tautology. Some people sometimes put their fingers into crevices in stone walls because they have an instinct (or interest) to do so; and we know that they have such an instinct because they engage in this behavior. It seems possible, however, to reconstruct Small's concept of "interests," or Freud's concept of instincts, in a nontautological way. Neither Small nor Freud attributes any given type of behavior to a given corresponding instinct. Rather, a given interest or instinct, in different strengths and in varying combinations with other interests or instincts of variable strengths, results in different behaviors. The imagery is of multivariate, contingent relationships and, for that reason, is probably not tautological. But this point is hardly important for present purposes. It is more important to note how Small's concept of interests, however vague and possibly tautological it might be, fits in with his view of human nature, and with his concept of the social process.

First, interests are lodged in individuals. They are the atoms, the elemental modes of motion in individuals, who are, in turn, "The ultimate molecular unit carrying on the [social] process" (428). Now, a very different, more social structural notion of "interests" would begin with the observation that the Latin phrase *inter est* means "is between." Interests stand between people and their goals, as obstacles or as means, whether people are aware of them or not. And to the extent that obstacles, means, and goals are, or involve other people, interests exist between people. They are not motives or desires, but characteristics of social relationships. Given the goal of finding sponsors or advertisers for daytime TV shows geared to adults who are at home during the normal working day, it is in the interest of the TV networks that there be free, compulsory public education for young children, or some other device for getting youngsters out of the house, so that parents can watch TV undisturbed. But Small does not have a sociological concept of interests such as this one. Interests are attributes of persons, not of social relationships.

Second, the six basic interests that Small delineates reinforce

Small's unitary conception of human nature, in which there is no war of the members (even though interests are unsatiable demands), but in which "sentient action" is predominant. Most contemporary social scientists are no longer concerned with the mind-body problem. The division of academic labor has proceeded far enough since Small's day to make them feel that they have no responsibility for thinking about such matters. They can simply distinguish between "action" (mind) and "behavior" (body), or between "action" and "motion" in Kenneth Burke's vocabulary, and leave the study of "motion" to some other department. Or, they can do the opposite, and announce that they are studying only observable behavior. But Small was still concerned with the mind-body problem. For him to have studied only observable behavior would have implied, in his day, a belief in "mechanical causation," in a stimulus-response model of human nature in which "sentient action" and the traditional moral verities could have no place. But to distinguish between "action" and "motion" and then leave "motion" out of social science was no good either. For such a distinction, in Small's day, would have meant mind versus matter, the highest reaches of moral and intellectual insight versus the lower reaches of this sordid earth. Such a view of human nature would have been incompatible with the association between knowledge and virtue; with the conception of social scientists as moral leaders; and with his brand of ameliorist, centrist politics, in which knowledgeable experts have an important place. Hence, Small required a more unitary conception of human nature, in which the material elements are integrated with, but remain in dignified subordination to "attention, valuation, and choice."

Small's bundle of six basic interests—interests in health, wealth, sociability, knowledge, beauty, and rightness—unifies matter in human nature with "spiritual initiative." The health interest consists of "modes of motion which follow the laws of physics, chemistry, and biology" and "exhibit the different forms of vital evergy" (426). It is "the basal interest in every man" and consists of "the impulse of all the physical energy deposited in his organism to work itself out to the limit" (427). It is "the impulsion and propulsion of the frankly material in our composition" (427).

The wealth interest also operates close to the material level. But it represents a distinction between human beings and matter. For it consists of a human drive for lordship over things.[10]

The lordship of man over man occurs wherever force can assert it, and the sense of justice does not estop it. When men cannot or will not lord it over each other, there still remains to them a means of partially completing the circuit of self-realization in the lordship over things. Things subject to personality is the formula of a second stage or phase of the completeness of the real individual. It is part of complete human personality to exercise lordship over things. The savagery of the savage is primarily his inability to lord it over things. In the midst of limitless resources of ores and fibers and forces, he commands nothing, he marshals nothing, he compels nothing to his service. His wealth is raw roots and flesh and pelts, and tools that the monkeys may have used, and used about as well. He begins to be a man in beginning to take completer possession of things, in ordering them about, in molding them to his will, in mastering them at the caprice of his imagination. The truth is, the modern vice is not too much devotion to wealth, but too little. Our materialism is too extensive, but not intensive enough. It puts up with quantitative title instead of qualitative possession (451).

The sociability interest is a drive, which all people have, for human contacts that are not instrumental, that are "of a sort to gratify their pure sense of personality" (458). Comparing the sociability interest with the health interest, Small writes:

Parallel with the desire for bodily integrity is an equally naïve and persistent desire for personal integrity. Each man embodies a claim to be a spiritual integer, an undiminished unit among like whole units. . . . The privilege of standing over against his fellow, with the assured franchise of equal freedom of self-expression, is an implicit demand of every unspoiled man (459).

The knowledge interest, to Small, was obvious. "It is hardly necesssary to insist upon the abstract proposition that the human individual wants to know" (461). Humans want to know both as a means to other goals and as an end in itself. On the beauty interest, Small confesses ignorance. He can write only that "a sociologist who is most painfully aware of his own incompleteness in this section of life may register the bare intellectual perception that life, at its largest, involves feeling of the aesthetic type, and conduct aimed at satisfaction of the feeling" (464). On the rightness interest, Small insists that his assertion of such an interest is not speculative. "Like the substance of our claim, under each of the preceding five heads, it is simply a generalization of facts that appear to be universal in the human individual." Or, if the rightness interest is not universal, then "the variations are to be accounted for by conditions which do not affect the fact that the traits so specified belong to the typical human person" (465). Small rests his belief on this sixth interest on his observation, or claim, that people act not only for the sake of each of the first five interests—health, wealth, sociability, knowledge, and beauty—but also make choices which "are not for the sake of satisfaction of either [i.e., any] sort yet specified" (466). They make choices for the sake of the larger self, or the larger whole beyond the self, of which everybody has a premonition.

These six interests vary from the "frankly material" to the spiritual. The health interest consists of material motions. Wealth is lordship over matter. Sociability entails a drive for the integrity of one's personality, for "the individuality which distinguished men from matter" (460). With the interests in knowledge, and not only instrumental knowledge, and in beauty, humans pursue strictly nonmaterial goals. And with the interest in rightness, the material children of the earth soar above their limited selves to a completed self or to a cosmic whole. As Small sees this hierarchy of interests:

We may repeat that the plot of the whole human drama begins to appear so soon as another interest beside the health interest begins to draw one specimen out of the mass of the human pack, and make an individual of him. The drama starts first in his own person. It begins with the challenge of one interest by another. We may summarize the human animal as a digesting machine. Presently this machine begins to feel impulses that compete with unlimited digestion, and henceforth human history is in the making. It is first and foremost a process of individual-building. One interest after another appears upon the scene and defies the primal interest (470).

But this distinction between the "frankly material" health interest and the other five does not imply a dualistic human nature. The digestive machine is human too, and Saint Paul was wrong to consider the "animal interest . . . not as a factor in man, but as a foe of man" (471). In some contexts, therefore, Small uses the same vocabulary to describe all six interests. They are all energistic, as when Small writes, "One interest is perpetually struggling to express its full energy, and its success would mean the suppression of the energy of other interests" (471). In this energistic conception, all interests are atomic "modes of motion" (426). And each is an impulse or "an unsatisfied capacity" (433). Those that operate closer to matter share characteristics with those that are psychological or spiritual. As a bundle, they cut across the physical, chemical, vital, and psychological levels. As a set of different drives, each insatiable in itself and each, therefore, making concessions to all the others, they convey an image of human nature in which the highest spiritual activity is rooted in matter, but the animalic makes concessions to the spiritual. This unitary view of human nature makes possible Small's optimistic association of knowledge with virtue, and it carries over to his view of "the social process" in general and of politics in particular.

THE RELATION BETWEEN HUMAN NATURE AND THE SOCIAL PROCESS

In the individualist, liberal tradition, as seen for example in Adam Smith's tribe of hunters, social structures result from the bumpings together of persons, each of whom is pursuing some individual motive, or is manifesting some kind of individualized human nature. Small, though he prided himself on having overcome individualism, remained in this tradition.

. . . The social process is a process of realizing the subjective content of the associates. Association is implicit objectification of that which is in the minds of the associates. Association is practical adjustment between the subjective and the objective conditions of the persons associated (545).

There are at least two different ways to conceive of social structures as the "objectification of that which is in the minds of the associates." One way, often expressed in the works of Freud and of Freudians, sees social structures as the collective externalization of the human psyche. The characteristics of the psyche that are externalized into society are socially shared. But the externalization does not come about through any process of interaction between people. For example, Ernest Jones, arguing with Malinowski's claim that there is no Oedipus complex among male Trobrianders, writes:

> There is much reason to think that the ambivalent conflict between love and hate is sharper among savage peoples than among ourselves, hence it is not surprising that they should possess more elaborate institutions subserving the function of guarding them from their repressed impulses: it is as though they had more reasons than we to fear them, or less power of diverting them. As examples of institutions of this kind one may quote totemism and exogamy on the one hand and the innumerable initiation ceremonies on the other.[11]

In this conception, social structures are objectifications of psychic traits which the members of society have in common, in the aggregate. Small's conception was different. The social process is the "objectification of that which is in the minds" of people, not in the aggregate, but in interaction with one another.

> In a word, the whole social process is a perpetual reaction between interests that have their lodgement in the individuals who compose society (242).

> . . . The relation between persons who make up a society is not principally mechanical. One person acts upon other persons, not chiefly by use of physical force, but by communication of thought and feelings and purposes in one way and another (141).

If the process is the objectification of the subjectivities of persons in interaction with one another, and if the essential traits of these subjectivities are the six basic interests of human nature, then it follows, in Small's logic, that "proper" and "essential" social functions are defined in terms of this human nature.

The proper social functions are the activities through which the essential human wants are evolved, gratified, balanced, adjusted between person and person, and then started on their next evolutionary cycle. These functions are by no means identical with operation of the structural machinery which we call institutions. The essential social functions are promotion of the primarily individual functions of securing sustenance, controlling nature, establishing working relations between man and man in the common use of opportunity, acquiring knowledge, developing aesthetic activity, and realizing religion. The forms and combinations of these functions vary infinitely, with variations in the stages of social advancement, and innumerable minor circumstances. They must never be confounded with the routine operation of economic, civic, social, scientific, artistic, or religious structures. These routine performances are functions in the narrow, mechanical sense, but not necessarily in an intelligent human sense (174-75).

In this passage, the concept of "function" is explicitly normative. Given the inherent goals of the social process, the realization of the optimum combination of the six basic interests, then, by the logic seen in the preceding chapter, evaluative distinctions between proper functioning and "the routine operation" of social structures are part of the scientific description of the operation of social structures. Institutions are "devices" for performing functions. But these devices "are likely to be transformed, in the minds of the persons who get their status in society by working with them into ends, to be cherished and defended and perpetuated on their own account" (234). For example:

... the function of a State is to maintain civic order. Russia is maintaining civic order in Finland. Ergo, Russia is discharging the immanent civic functions. The conclusion does not follow. Civic order is merely one of the means to human ends. The enlargement and enrichment of the lives of the people maintaining the order, not order itself, is the criterion of civic functions. Russia is crushing out the life of the Finns. The revolution of the wheels of government according to a despotic system is not discharge of the indicated social function (175).

The molecular units of the social process are individuals. That process is the objectification of the subjectivities of individuals. But as in the example of Finland, social structures can nonetheless be external and constraining. The transformation, by people in power, of means into ends, at the cost of service to the basic human interests, is one way in which this externality and constraint comes about. More generally,

> ... The sociological interest begins with individuals feeling wants. How do those wants bring them into contact with other individuals feeling wants? How do the individuals thus in contact modify each other's wants? How do the wants of the separate individuals become a species of environment, conditioning all the individuals? (21).

In some contexts, in Small, this note of externality and constraint is missing. Formulae such as "All men are functions of each other" (77) sometimes seem to imply that each person in the social process has power equal with all other persons over the content and direction of the process. For example:

> One person acts upon other persons, not chiefly by use of physical force, but by communication of thought and feeling and purposes in one way and another. Through the different agencies that people have at their command, the persons in a society make themselves felt by each other. They are responsive to each other's moods. They accommodate themselves to each other's wishes. They observe nicely calculated bounds of conduct. They balance, and restrain, and instigate, and inspire each other, so that certain common characteristics come to be a sort of ground plan of each individual's personality; certain common impulses move all in like ways and often at the same time; a certain consensus of idea organizes their actions into co-operation and concert; and thus all Americans may be said to share one career, while at the same time each individual has a more special career of his own (141).

This imagery describes an egalitarian world. People do not "react to" or "respond to" each other. They are "responsive to" each other. In other contexts, however, force, inequality, externality, and constraint are clearly present. "For instance, a hundred socialistic German students are mustered into the imperial army and are sworn to defend the Kaiser and the flag. So long as they wear the uniform they are imperialists, not socialists." For "There is something besides the sum of those individualities which is at work in giving them a character." In combination, they are "different from the sum of their characters as isolated individuals" (50).

More generally:

> Our work as students of society begins in earnest when the individual has become equipped with his individuality. This stage of human growth is both cause and effect of the life of human beings side by side in greater or lesser numbers. Under those circumstances individuals are produced; they act as individuals; by their action as individuals they produce a certain type of society; that type reacts on the individuals and helps to transform them into different types of individuals, who in turn produce a modified type of society; and so the rhythm goes on forever (488–89).

Despite externality and constraint, however, and despite the rhythm of individuals creating society creating individuals, Small returns in the end to psychic determinism.

> In short, descriptive knowledge of the social process passes into science of the social process, properly so called, only in the degree in which we become able to restate all that we have found in the way of phenomena of human experience, in terms of the mental influences which are the causal nexus of the whole process (623).

INDIVIDUALISM AND THE SOCIAL PROCESS

There is little room in Small's thought for causal processes in society that operate independently of "mental influences." In Adam Smith, for example, in addition to rationally calculated self-interest, the propensities of human nature, and "sympathy" (in his *Theory of Moral Sentiments*), there is also the "invisible hand" that operates independently of anybody's thoughts, feelings, or intentions. In Marx, in addition to purposive labor as a defining characteristic of human beings,[12] and to the crucial role of class consciousness, there are also external processes such as change in the organic composition of capital and the law of the declining rate of profit which operate independently of purpose or consciousness. In contrast, all or almost all of the characteristics of the social process that Small identifies can be located in the interaction of individuals who are pursuing individual interests.

... The social process is incessant reaction of persons prompted by interests that in part conflict with the interests of their fellows, and in part comport with the interests of others (205).

... The social process is a continual formation of groups around interests, and a continual exertion of reciprocal influence by means of group-action (209).

To be sure, "the pursuit of super-individual ends becomes a part, and an increasingly important part, of the whole social process" (357). But super-individual ends are lodged in individuals who develop loyalties to some larger social whole. And they result from the interdependence of individuals in the social process.

Take, for example, the family, either primitive or modern. From a variety of motives a man and a woman unite to form a family. They thus secure certain reciprocal services. They assure to them-selves certain comforts, conveniences, safeguards, dignities, which unattached persons lack. To each of these persons individually independence is a desired end. These other goods are also desired, and for the sake of them the individuals exchange a certain kind of independence for that kind of interdependence which the family relationship involves. That very interdependence now becomes an end for the persons united in the family. The continued existence of the family is an end in itself. Both man and woman may shortly become aware that this end, which is decisive for them as a family, comes into sharp collision with ends that are dear to them as individuals. Each says in his heart: "I would like to do so and so;" but each is restrained by the thought: "That would break up the family" (538).

Interdependence, as in this quote, is one of the fifteen "incidents of the social process." These "incidents" are "certain traits which we observe in all human associations" that, however, "are often discernible only as tendencies" (599-60). Some of them, such as "attraction" and "repulsion" between individuals are, in effect,

Small's "pattern variables." Others, such as "multiplicity of individuals" are brute facts about the social process in all times and places, as distinct from variables that can take on two or more values. Still others, such as "justice," that is, the balance between the different interests of different persons, read as if they ought to be variables, although Small does not present the polar opposite term. He occasionally used the term "variable," but the language and the logic of variables were not central to his style of thought. Whatever the precise status of each of the various "incidents," however, Small intends them to be a list of universal traits or tendencies in the social process.

Some of these incidents are direct outgrowths of human nature. "To get at the reality of the social process, we must see not only that . . . interdependence is a fact: we must see that this fact is the necessary outgrowth of the fundamental fact of interest" (208). "Attraction" and "repulsion," too, stem out of "interests."

> . . . there are facts about persons which satisfy or antagonize the interests of other persons. People are not therefore like fugitive bits of dust in the air—disconnected with each other. Persons everywhere attract or repel persons (209).

Other incidents, such as "vicariousness" (the incessant interchange of services), "coordination," and "solidarity," (the interdependence of all parts of the social process in relation to external conditions) are variations on the "incident" of interdependence. Others have a somewhat different relation to human nature. "Justice" is the balance of interests. And "individuation," the individuality that distinguishes human beings from matter, works in tandem with "socialization" because the basic springs of action of all people are the same. Hence individuation can come about only through socialization, through a person's distinct combination of positions in the social process. Other "incidents," such as "persistence of the individuals" are less clearly related to Small's conception of human nature, but are attributes of individual participants in the social process. And still others, such as "discreteness or discontinuity of the individuals" (Small's version of the concept of "social distance"), and "continuity of (individual) influence" refer to microsociological interactions between persons. A few of the fifteen incidents, such as "security of status" seem to be neither outgrowths of human nature, nor attributes of individuals, nor traits of microsociological interactions. But most of Small's universal traits or tendencies in the social process suggest, once again, the limited extent to which he had overcome the basically individualist perceptions of society that have always informed the liberal tradition in social thought and social science.

Conclusion

Within Small's own terms at least, his concepts of "interest," "association," and "the social process" were related to one another with a fairly high degree of logical coherence. The social process is the objectification of the interests of persons who are in association with one another. Each interest is insatiable. Hence, the social process at any point in time is in part a struggle between interests and in part a series of mutual concessions that each interest makes to others. Over time, also because interests are insatiable, but depend for their realization upon previously achieved situations, the process consists of the progressively fuller realization of increasingly larger combinations of interests. Small's belief in progress, his view of history, was logically linked to his view of human nature.

Further, given Small's conception of the relationship between sociology and ethics—a conception which is also quite coherent, within its own terms—the evaluative elements of his theorizing, such as his use of "function," fall coherently into place alongside the cognitive components. His dual vocabulary of physical, chemical, vital, and psychological energies, and of the six interests that form a bundle cutting across these four levels, allowed him to be scientific without being mechanic; to assert the centrality of choice in human action without giving up a scientist's faith in the universality of cause and effect; and to have a unitary view of human nature. In this unitary view he could ground human nature in the body without setting the spirit at war with the flesh. He was able, in this way, to play down demonic features in human nature and make the association between knowledge and virtue, upon which the conception of professors as moral leaders rests.

Small, in short, had a reasonable and reasonably coherent view of society, history, and human nature. To be sure, there are loose ends. For example, his different definitions of "interest" do not seem to add up to a single, consistent notion. What is more important, some of the theoretical coherence in Small's work stems from procedures that might strike some readers, half a century after his death, as playing with words. An example might be his use of energistic and vitalistic terms in order to endow children of the sordid earth with spiritual initiative. If he had consistently referred to "biological motions," and never to "vital energies," then his view of human nature could not have been so voluntaristic. But in taking over, without careful scrutiny, a vocabulary current in his day, and in adopting the terms best fitted for arguing the case for his own theory, Small was only doing what most social theorists do most of the time.

Small took the terms "physical," "chemical," and "biological" for granted. Similarly, most sociologists today take over uncritically the vocabularies and sets of metaphors that suit their needs, with little attention to the conclusions inherent in the terms. If they take over the notions of "individual," "motivation," and "personality," then they can easily define "socialization" and "internalized norms." If they start out with "organism" and "operant conditioning," they are less likely to end up with such a concept. If they use the spatial metaphors of statistics—curve, distribution, skewness, "above" and "below" the mean—then they are more likely to see a social world of discrete units existing side by side than they are if they use metaphors of connectedness such as "networks" or "web of group affiliation." Different conclusions are inherent in different terms. We sometimes reach conclusions unwittingly because of our uncritical acceptance of terms; and we sometimes choose terms, unwittingly or not, for the sake of the conclusions inherent within them. In these respects, Small was no different from, and neither more nor less guilty of playing with words than, anybody else in sociology.

If Small is not markedly inferior, intellectually or scientifically, to other and later theorists in sociology, why then, was Barnes correct in predicting that Small's lasting impact in American sociology would not come about through his writings? Why are most of his substantive ideas, as distinct from his scientistic procedural doctrines, virtually dead, while the department and the journal he founded are still alive?

Briefly, and to anticipate some of the conclusions of the final chapter, Small's organizational success brought about his intellectual undoing. In successfully establishing sociology as an academic discipline, he opened the way for specialists and research technicians who no longer had to be concerned with the full range of issues that Small worked on. Sociologists no longer had to have doctrines of human nature, or comprehensive views of history, or theories about the mind-body problem. They could pursue their specialized work. Once established in the universities, it was no longer necessary, or politic, for sociologists to make the grandiose claims for sociology that Small had made. For Small, throughout most of his career as a sociologist, sociology was simultaneously the science of human association and the general, synthesizing science of society, drawing upon and subsuming the more specialized social sciences. This dual definition of the field is summed up in Small's concept of the social process. But once sociology became an established discipline, this ambitious vision was lost. As Small himself noted, late in his life, "In proportion as sociology becomes responsibly objective it will leave behind its early ambition for a hegemony over social sciences" and will become a "technique" for studying the whole of human experience "through investigation of group-aspects of the phenomena."[13]

There seem to be still other reasons why later generations of sociologists have largely ignored Small's ideas. In many respects his thinking was so rooted in his own historical moment that much of it seemed irrelevant after World War I and the Great Depression. His conception of the relationship between sociology and ethics was consonant with the social position of university scholars around the turn of the century. It was inconsistent both with later ideologies of universities as abodes of disinterested learning, and with the later practice of professors working for corporate or government clients who define the problems which professors are supposed to help solve. Similarly, Small's specific political writings, and the general political stance implied by his conception of "the social process," were rooted in turn-of-the-century America. His pre–World War I progressivism and his general sociology were part of a single ideological package.

7

THE SOCIAL PROCESS AND
PROGRESSIVE POLITICS

INTRODUCTION

Small held that his "organic" view of the "social process" implied opposition both to Jeffersonian individualism and to socialism. He was not always explicit about the connections between his general sociology and his politics. But his political writings are full of passages that echo, while making no explicit reference to, his general theories of "interests," "association," and "the social process."[1] Small favored "municipal ownership of natural monopolies," supported unions "both as a means of self-expression by the many and as a curb upon the capitalism of the few," believed that "collective bargaining is among the most constructive of modern inventions," and credited "industrial arbitration and conciliation" with "a margin of accomplishment—as brakes upon the flywheel of capitalism . . ."[2] More generally, he held that "the social movement" of his day "deserves the sympathy and wise cooperation of all who love their kind."[3]

These beliefs have led some commentators to portray Small as something of a radical. Ernest Becker describes Small's politics as "very near to socialism." He calls one of Small's books "a blistering critique . . . of capitalism."[4] And shortly after Small's death, Harry Elmer Barnes described him as a strong critic of capitalism.[5] Small, a Republican who sometimes deserted his party to vote Prohibitionist, saw himself in that light. The subtitle of his novel, *Between Eras*, was *From Capitalism to Democracy*, and late in his life he was still using phrases such as "the radical fault" and "the evils" of capitalism.[6] In contrast, Dusky Lee Smith describes Small, along with most other founders of American sociology, as an apologist for corporate capitalism. Small and most other founders, he argues, opposed only laissez-faire capitalism, and opposed it only to favor corporate capitalism instead. Once corporate capitalism—Big Business and interventionist governmental policies—was established, sociology ceased to be progressive.[7]

More recently, Herman Schwendinger and Julia Schwendinger have interpreted Small in generally similar terms. Following the vocabulary of William A. Williams, they call him a liberal syndicalist.[8] I will argue in this chapter that Smith and Schwendinger and Schwendinger are correct, but are compatible with Barnes. For Small was a critic of capitalism who rejected the socialist alternative. The resulting position was quite consistent with the rest of Small's political thought. It was consistent with his attitudes toward Marx— a mixture of praise, misunderstanding, agreement, and disagreement; with his state-capitalist thinking about "social reconstruction" on "the basis of function"; and with his conception of "objectivity," which assumed the legitimacy of all conflicting interests in society.

ALBION SMALL AND KARL MARX

As with so many half-true descriptions of Small—he was pious and he was secular, he was commited to science, and he was a moralist—it is possible to find considerable support for those who see Small as something of a radical. Small wrote that "socialism has been the most wholesome ferment in modern society" and that "Marx was one of the few really great thinkers in the history of social science."[9] One of Marx's accomplishments was that

> He declared that the world will remain impossibly arbitrary until its theory and its practice center around labor. This was in substance by no means a novel utterance. Adam Smith had said it, but he was appalled by his own irreverence and promptly retracted it. Marx said it with the force, the detail, and the corroborating evidence of a revelation. He is still a voice in the wilderness, but for one I have no more doubt that he was essentially right, and that conventionality was essentially wrong, than I have that

Galileo will hold his place to the end of time as one of the world's great discoverers.[10]

Small also seems to accept the labor theory of value, or something close to it. For example, he writes that a dollar deposited in a savings bank draws interest that has "not been produced by any effort of the depositor" because the bank "forwards the dollar to some point where workers convert it into more than a dollar" (and because the law threatens to punish anyone in the bank who "fails to do what the law requires—in the process which makes that deposit safe and profitable"[11]). Similarly, "there is no conceivable claim to share in the economic output equal in universal validity to the claim based on labor, or, in our more precise technical term 'function.'"[12]

Hence, that portion of profits that represents a return for labor is legitimate. What small traders and artisans call their profits is essentially wages. In contrast:

> The Marshall Field concern, however, has grown to be an organization with such advantages, at both the buying and the selling end of its operations, that its returns are far in excess of the total of labor value of all the managing personnel combined. This is true if we compute those wage values at the prevailing market rate for each kind of service, from door man to general manager. A small number of persons compose the Marshall Field corporation. They are able to assign to themselves in salaries, and to stock as dividends, the whole of the net profits without regard to the proportion which their own labor bears *strictly as labor*, to the labor of the other workers in the business who have no voice in the distribution of this surplus.[13]

Believing in something like the labor theory of value, Small can also accept the concept of surplus value. He calls it a "rudimentary economic fact."[14] "The fact of class struggle," too, "is as axiomatic today as the fact of gravitation" and is "one of the elemental reactions between human beings."[15] But it is not always clear what Small is really saying when he seems to accept certain Marxian ideas. His reading of many points in Marx is questionable. For example, according to Small "the gist" of the economic interpretation of history

... is the homely fact that if there is anything insecure about a man's chances of getting tomorrow's dinner, or anything unjust about the ways in which he is forced to use the chances, there will be nothing quite right about the rest of his mental or emotional or moral life. Or, to express it in the social instead of the individual form, if there are crudities or injustices in our economic system, to that extent those of us who gain by the anomalies will be getting something for nothing, while those who lose by them will be deprived of a square deal.[16]

In the first of these two formulations Small assimilates historical materialism into his image of human nature—of children of the sordid earth, grounded in the physical, who also soar above matter in pursuit of higher goals, but only if their material needs are satisfied. Small also had many explicit and acknowledged differences with Marx. After praising Marx for his economic interpretation of history (as Small misunderstood it), for the concept of surplus value, and for the emphasis on class conflict, Small questions "his assumption that the laboring class and the capitalistic class may be sharply distinguished and precisely divided" and rejects "the keel of his proposed ship of state, viz. the socialization of capital."[17] On both issues Small thought that his social science was more developed, more advanced than that of Marx.

On the belief that proletarians and capitalists "may be sharply distinguished and precisely divided," Small wrote:

For Marx the social campaigner this assumption was convenient and in a large degree correct. For Marx the scientific investigator it was the most fatal mistake. We had no sooner formulated the primary sociological generalization of the universality of social conflict than we made out the equally primary parallel generalization of the universality of co-operation. For certain immediate purposes, human beings may and do form themselves into groups of friends for better or worse, to fight against other groups regarded as absolute enemies. In doing this the other processes of the group life are partially arrested in order that in certain particulars the antagonistic interests of the respective groups may measure strength. These differences having been adjusted, it soon appears that the groups cannot be permanently as exclusive and hostile as they made themselves provisionally. Americans and Spanish, Boers and British, Russians and Japanese, employers and employees, presently discover that in the long run it is the best policy for cooperation to control conflict. Thus it comes about that our last rendering of the social process today expresses it in terms of one stage farther along in its evolution than that which most impresses Marx. We assert the universal fact of class conflict as strongly as he did. We assert the universal fact of co-operation more strongly than he did.[18]

On "the socialization of capital," Small's reading of Marx seems to be erroneous. He writes that all of Marx's "visions of reor-ganized society centered about a state which should be the owner of all productive wealth, while the citizens should be the consumers each of his own shares of the output of production."[19] This description apparently applies to the first stage of socialist society in which the state, commodity production, and commodity exchange continue to exist. Small could not envision, or perhaps could not take seriously, the eventual withering away of the state, the end of commodity production and of commodity exchange, and a society in which "to each according to his needs" holds sway. But this characterization of socialism is inaccurate even for the first post-revolutionary period. For so long as commodity production exists, exchange values continue to exist. And so long as exchange values exist, workers must continue to give up surplus value—for public education and other public services, for support of the aged and infirm, for reinvestment, and for national defense. Hence, it is not possible for individual citizens to be the consumers of their "own share of the output of production." But however accurate or inaccurate Small's reading of the kind of socialist society Marx envisioned, he rejects "the socialization of capital" as a central feature of a new and better society:

From the standpoint of social science it is extremely naïve to suppose that the form in which any constructive principle will be assimilated in a national economic system can be foreseen very far in advance. I must confess that Marx's ideal of economic society has never appealed to me as plausible, probable, desirable, or possible. In essentials Marx was nearer to a correct diagnosis of the evils of our present property system than the wisdom of this world has yet been willing to admit, but his plan for correcting the evils is neither the only conceivable alternative nor the most convincing one. Indeed, from the standpoint of social science any plan at all for correcting the evils of capitalism is premature until the world has probed down much deeper into the evils themselves. Not until we thoroughly understand that our social order now rests on the basis of property, and that it will not be a thoroughly moral order until it is transferred to the basis of function, shall we be in a position intelligently to reflect on social reconstruction.[20]

SOCIAL CONTROL OF CAPITAL

Small was never very clear about the meaning of "social reconstruction" on "the basis of function," either as a general policy or in terms of specific political proposals. But in "The Social Gradations of Capital" he does argue that the degree of control over the use of capital should be proportionate to the extent to which the labor or other contributions of people other than the owner are required to make capital productive. And elsewhere he does make some specific policy proposals. In "Social Gradations," he distinguishes between "tool-capital" that only the owner uses; "management-capital" that "is used by the owner in some sort of dependence upon the acts of others," and "finance-capital" that is used "wholly by others than the owner, and under conditions which he does not and could not maintain by his own individual power."[21] Small's example of tool-capital is a farmer's hoe. His example of management-capital is a grist mill. When a farmer becomes a miller as well, he has a whole new set of relations to others. For with the mill, unlike the hoe, "the cooperation of others beside the owner [is required] in making the capital efficient."[22] His example of a finance-capitalist is the moneylender who "employs his time finding borrowers who will pay for the use of his money while furnishing good security" and who "may by courtesy be said to work."[23] Small writes that "the theory and practice of finance-capital present perhaps the central sociological problem of our time."[24] But in developing his case against laissez-faire capitalism he argues primarily from the characteristics of management-capital.

In an equalitarian society in which all capital were tool-capital, and all citizens lived from their own work, both the free market and unrestricted enjoyment of the fruits of one's labor would be justified.

A society may be near enough for all practical purposes to the truth, if that society depends upon "free competition" to insure economic justice—*provided*, that the members of that society are all alike in depending solely upon their individual labor of hand, or brain, or both, to obtain the results which they will have to exchange with their neighbors. Our present society is assuming the impossible, however, when it dallies with the illusion that there can be "free competition" in a society containing, on the one hand, millions of persons with no assets but their individual powers, and on the other hand thousands of corporations with wealth and credit and legal resources. When the interests of these two types of competitors clash, "free competition" between them is like a boy with a pea-blower besieging the Rock of Gibraltar.[25]

The legal and other "artificial" institutional supports that society provides to management-capital create and sustain these differences in power. A "management-capitalist is not merely . . . exercising his unaided powers . . . but . . . is an individual with powers increased tens, hundreds, or thousands of times by virtue of artificial arrangements, which make him the repository of social powers incomparably greater than his own."[26]

Not only these differences in power, but also the dependence of management-capital and of finance-capital on people other than the owners justify interventionist controls over the use of capital.

The capitalistic ultimatum is that property is property, whether it is a hoe or a house or a railroad, a dollar or a thousand dollars or a thousand million dollars. The dictum belongs in the "important-if-true" class. With only the rudiments of objective social analysis, one may discover that it is not true. On the contrary, it would seem to be axiomatic that in the degree in which the partnership of other men besides the proprietor is necessary to make a type of capital possible and efficient, corresponding partnership of those other men in control of that capital is indicated.[27]

We cannot state too strongly that we are neither asserting nor implying that this phenomenon of management-capital is wrong. We are pointing out in the first place that it is artificial, as compared with tool-capital. The control of the management-capitalist over this large and dispersed wealth is not principally by virtue of his own power. It is principally by virtue of the organized action of society, which gives power not his own to his volitions. This being the case, the terms of this relationship between society and the men whom it empowers to be management-capitalists will always demand closer scrutiny, as to their justice and wisdom, than the simple and obvious resolution of the neighbors to protect the farmer in possession of his hoe.[28]

Our analysis of the social relations of management-capital, therefore, in no way implies doubt about the necessity of management as a distinct economic factor, our discussion takes that for granted, but it aims straight at these two facts: *first, the function of economic management would be relatively impotent without the support of social co-operation; second, this social co-operation morally entitles the co-operating laborers and the co-operating society to a share in controlling the terms under which the management-capitalist shall work, and a larger and more influential share than our present economic system has either realized in practice or admitted in theory.*[29]

Small is not very specific about the nature of these proposed controls over management-capital. In some passages he seems to be supporting limitations on profits and at one point he suggests that no contract involving finance-capital should be legally binding "unless a judicial representative of the community has passed favorably in advance upon the equity of the terms, especially as between either or both of the contracting parties and the now inadequately represented ... civic community."[30] His proposals in other writings were similar, but sometimes more specific. For example, late in his life he proposed the following "comprehensive plan of limiting and distributing corporation profits, and thereby wholesomely restraining both the spirit and the practice of capitalism."

1. Stockholders to receive not more than a maximum rate of

dividends, x, calculated to be enough above the average rate of return upon securities to serve as a premium upon investment in needed industrials.

2. Stockholders to be restrained from evading the prescribed limitations by voting salaries to themselves for services.

3. Premiums, in the form of pro rata dividends on salaries and wages, to be offered as inducements to increase output.

4. Net profits in excess of the rate provided for in 1 to be divided, in some proportion to be determined by experience, between employees of all sorts and the state.

5. The state's share of the profits shall not be available for governmental expenses. They shall go to some holding concern, perhaps an adaptation of the present Federal Reserve banks, to be loaned to the most desirable industrial enterprises— desirable from the standpoint not of private but of public interest.[31]

Small saw this plan as going beyond the "patches," as he labeled the reforms, such as municipal ownership and all the rest, which he had always supported. By the end of his life he came to believe that the effects of such reforms were minimal. But going beyond patchwork reform did not mean socialism. It meant, simply, more political control over profits and over capital investments than earlier reforms had envisaged, including an element of confiscation of capital that the government would reinvest not according to market criteria but in the light of the "public interest." For, in Small's view, writing more than five years after the first socialist revolution in history, "no devices are in sight to which we can pin our faith as feasible and comprehensive substitutes for capitalism, either on its subjective side as the acquisitive spirit, or on the objective side as an economic technique." Instead, "line upon line, precept upon precept, device upon device—must be the formula of practical social philosophy."[32]

In short, Barnes was correct in calling Small a critic of capitalism. He was a critic not only of unrestricted laissez-faire capitalism, but also of patchwork reforms. The radical commentators are also correct, however, in calling him an apologist for "corporate" or interventionist, post–laissez-faire capitalism. In Small's own mind, given his inability to see any "feasible and comprehensive substitutes for capitalism," these two descriptions of him would probably be compatible. They appear incompatible four decades later, after the New Deal, Fair Deal, New Frontier, and Great Society have left American capitalism with grave weaknesses and a critique of laissez-faire capitalism and of patchwork reforms can no longer appear to be a critique of capitalism itself, unless it is coupled with an espousal of the socialist alternative.

POLITICS AND SOCIOLOGICAL THEORY

Small's insistence that the productivity of management-capital and of finance-capital depends upon the cooperation of people other than the owner seems to be a special case of his "organic" view of the social process. "From a very early stage in the social process, if not absolutely from the beginning, men live and move and have their being as members of one another."[33] That dictum applies to the relationship between a management-capitalist and a worker just as it applies to everybody else. But the general notion that each point in every person's life touches each point in every other person's life does not, by itself, have any specific content. Why, in Small's view, is the relation between a management-capitalist and a worker marked not only by class conflict, but also by class cooperation (tending to preclude, therefore, any "feasible and comprehensive substitutes for capitalism")? And why, for Small, should it be? For Small's statements on class cooperation are normative as well as descriptive.

As a mechanism for turning out wealth, the industry of a State demands harmony of the parts co-operating in the industrial process, no less than a battleship needs a maximum of efficiency, and a minimum of friction, in each element of its structure and equipment.[34]

To be sure, Small saw the society in which he lived as ridden with class conflict. For, under current conditions, "There is not and cannot be harmony between people as claimants to the product of industry" and "Each class wants either to retain or to increase its power and to enforce its own estimate of its own economic rights."[35] But class struggle was also leading toward the very institutions that will mitigate conflict. Small sympathized with unions, and supported collective bargaining as parts of the drive toward a "constitutionalism in economic enterprise" that would restrain the power of capital.

> *The unformulated and unconscious struggle today, in all industrial States, is for constitutionalism in economic enterprise, just as the struggle of the late eighteenth and early nineteenth centuries was for constitutionalism in politics.* That is, each economic class wants a fundamental economic order which will contain checks and balances adequate to keep other classes from usurping economic power.[36]

Small's preference for class cooperation, and for political controls over capital short of socialism, seems rooted in his general theory of the "social process," in his conception of objectivity, and in his closely related conception of the proper role of social scientists, and of "the knowledge interest" generally, in the face of social conflicts. Or perhaps his sociology is a generalization of his politics. For, as seen in chapter 3, his political stance was at least partially formed in the 1880s, before he developed his general theories.

The fundamental unity of all human beings is inherent in Small's "organic" view of the "social process." "The social process could not occur at all if a certain measure of the conjunction of interests did not exist among early specimens of the human species." Without a community of interests stronger than that between kin or members of the same clan, such as exists among wolves, human societies would resemble animal societies. "At the same time," however, "the conspicuous element in the history of the race—is universal conflict of interests."[37] Human association is the action and reaction of interests lodged in individuals, of which some conjoin and others conflict. In earliest times, conflicts of interests were more prominent and "conciliation and agreement have been rather resultants of social forces than prime factors in movement." At "the most advanced stages of the social process" however, conjunction of interests becomes more prominent and more important.[38]

One essential step in subduing conflicts was economic growth.

So long and so far as the struggle for existence develops merely material wants, the persons or groups feeling those wants are implacably hostile to all persons or groups whose existence threatens the satisfaction of those wants. As other wants develop, and as means for securing the essential wants increase, the terms on which persons are willing to pursue satisfaction of their wants become less absolute. The social process continues to be largely in the form of struggle, but it is less and less inexorable struggle.[39]

Another step toward the reduction of conflicts was the formation of states. Small does not use the term "state" in the relatively narrow English sense. He uses "state" in the broader German sense of "politically organized society" (as in the phrases *Ständestaat* and *Klassenstaat* that, in English, mean "estate society" and "class society"). The term, in Small's usage "means people so far integrated that a government is one of their bonds of union."[40] States subdue conflict in at least two different ways. First:

The State always brings to bear upon the individuals composing it a certain power of constraint to secure from them, in all their struggles with each other, the observance of minimum established limits of struggle.[41]

States differ in their conceptions of "the proper scope and methods of civic constraint."[42] For example, in Russia and Germany, but not in France, "it accords with the general ideas of decency and order that the government shall require all citizens to attach themselves to some recognized religious body in order to become eligible to certain civic positions." But:

The master-key to the occurrences which take place in all States, throughout their development, is the perception that, whatever the incidents of political struggle in any case, the one constant factor is the civic organization attempting ... to guard the interests of the individuals and groups of which the state is composed, by constraint appropriate to the needs of the situation.[43]

The formation of states, then, represents the stage at which the "social process" went from "absolute hostility" to "relative hostility," or "viewed from the other direction, relative sociability."[44] For some of the interests of all persons are merged into the state, notably their "interest ... in having the struggle of interests within the range of their associations go under the limitation of certain positive rules."[45] This common interest, a shared demand for minimal order, is often weaker than, or contradictory to, individual or group interests. But:

> By virtue of combinations, always stronger than individuals, the modicum of common interest intrenches itself more and more firmly, while the quantum of common interest meanwhile increases. Throughout this process, the State is becoming more and more necessary to the typical individual, but at the same time more and more antipathetic to everything in the individual in proportion as it conflicts with the typical. Here, then, we have the conditions of the irrepressible conflict which the State does not originate, but by means of which the State carries on the social process. *National life is conflict, but it is conflict converging toward minimum conflict, and maximum co-operation and sociability.*[46]

The "social process" in states moderates conflicts in a second way as well. In the "social process" in general, socialization and individuation work in tandem. There is a rhythm of differentiating and integrating mechanisms. The same holds for the social process in states. When minimum material needs—the interests in "health" and "wealth"—are met, people pursue the other basic human "interests" in diverse ways and in varying combinations. They pursue them in diverse associations with others. Hence, the natural movement of the social process is toward greater complexity and flexibility. The state "is constantly differentiating into more and more associations" and in this way "the interests of the individual members, and those of the whole society, are both accommodated to each other and adjusted to the prevailing conditions of life."[47] Historically, this process has meant that middle strata have always emerged between the rulers and the ruled. But, "the classes that have power are always trying to prevent other classes from getting power."

> The world over, those who have power imagine that retention of power by their class is necessary to the stability of society in general. The only decency and order which the despots can

imagine for society is a state of things in which people of their own kind hold sway.[48]

For this reason, "one of the characteristic tendencies of the governing class in States founded by conquest is to set themselves with all possible vigor against social differentiation, and especially against the formation of a middle class."[49] People in power resist the natural tendency of the social process toward differentiation of interests, and therefore toward flexibility and accommodation of interests. The social process generates new, different social groupings that seek a recognized place in society, and their share of power and authority. If allowed their place, the society becomes more complex and differentiated, and the level of conflict goes down. Conflict ensues, instead, because people in power resist. "This program of collision between the powers that be, and the social elements that scarcely have recognized being or power" has continued into modern times:

> In the United States we have the same antagonism of forces rallying about different interests. With approximate abolition of political classes, we have economic strata that use both economic and political means of conflict. The managing class is suspicious of the fitness of the many to share in political and industrial management. Our political campaigns are becoming more and more trials of skill between men, on the one hand, who have the confidence of successful business organizers, and, on the other hand, men who are attempting to organize the fears and the jealousies of those who distrust the political integrity and ability of the economically successful classes.[50]

This, in part at least, is the reasoning behind Small's support for "constitutionalism" in the economy. And, writing some fifteen years later, this seems also to be the reasoning behind this comment on the Bolshevik revolution:

> The irrefutable bad of the Russian revolution, the central reason why every just man who is also clear headed hates it, is that essentially it is *no revolution at all*. It is simply a transfer of that old guilty *dominance* of the Czar to the even more guilty hands of Lenin. There was a certain palliation of the Czar's guilt in the fact that it was not wholly his own. It was thrust

on him. He was born with it bound to him. But Lenin violently usurped it. The tragedy of Russia was and is the absence of a middle class able and willing to create a real revolution by abolishing all dictatorship and introducing a regime of justice to all interests. What needs to be revolutionized in Russia is *dominance* of anybody by anybody. What needs to be substituted more than ever is a start toward a genuine community spirit—everybody trying to accommodate himself to everybody.[51]

The injunction that everybody accommodate to everybody else assumed, of course, that all interests, all classes, all goals are legitimate, if not equally legitimate. Both "the powers that be" and newly emergent "social elements that scarcely have recognized being or power" should compromise. This assumption is built into Small's view of objectivity and into his view of the proper role of a social scientist.

Cognitive Objectivity and Political Compromise

For Small, that social science is most objective that is most holistic. Objective social science embraces the perspectives not simply of warriors, or lawyers, or kings, or priests, but the perspectives of all participants in the social process. A sociologist in the United States in 1900 who studies conflicts between labor and capital, or farmers and railroads, or prohibitionists and anti-prohibitionists, should be able to identify the combinations of interests that each party to the conflict pursues, and should be able to understand them from each party's point of view. That is the spirit in which Small often wrote about the conflicts in his own society. He also took the next step, however, of equating scholarly objectivity with political nonpartisanship. For example, at the conclusion of a section in *General Sociology* on "The Partisanship of Economic Classes," Small noted that by giving to capital "the legal status of a person" through incorporation, capital "becomes a titanic superman, incomparably superior to the natural persons who find their interests challenged by this artificial being" and that the "most significant factor in the modern social struggle . . . is this legally created competition of a fictitious person with each and all natural persons for pre-eminence as a social force." He then went on:

> Of course, such a perception as this leads us to the actual fighting line between capital and labor. We are tempted to turn aside and discuss details and practical issues between these interests. Our present business, however, is not of that sort. The sociologist's duty is to determine the place which all concrete details of life have in the general social process. His work will at last contribute to the adjustment of social conflicts by exhibiting each of them, and each phase of interest involved in them, in its ultimate relations with the whole system of human activities. Meanwhile the sociologist's business is not to agitate, but to investigate. He will do his best work in the end upon concrete questions, by provisionally not working upon them at all. Thus in the present instance there is work enough for many sociologists, in determining typical relations of the leading social interests, without leaving the field of scientific investigation to enlist in the fighting ranks of any particular social class.[52]

In taking this position, associating or almost equating cognitive objectivity with contributions to the "adjustment of social conflicts," Small felt that he was representing "the knowledge interest." People who upheld that interest had a very special role to play in society. In Small's view:

> ... the modern world is tense with strife between stereotyping parties and innovating parties, neither of which is able to subject its contentions to the objective test of adaptation to the essential requirements of the social process. In any joining of issues each interest attacks the others' positions with argument. In the case of two opponents upon any social question, the crudity of the logical process, and the real weakness of both sides, is that each interest is always ready to assault the other's position, but neither will submit to an unprejudiced expert examination of its own.[53]

That is, Small generalizes the specific conflicts and contestants of his day into the "stereotyping" (conservative) and "innovating" sides, and looks at both sides as an objective observer—objective both in the sense of being an outsider and in the sense of understanding both points of view. This stance made Albion Small a representative of "corporate reason" as against the "individualistic feeling" of the contestants.[54] This stance, therefore, made it possible for Small to refer to the difference between him and his kind, on the one hand, and all sides in all conflicts out there in society, on the other, as the most basic conflict of all.

> In other words, the essential conflict today is between the intellectual, the knowledge interest, and all the other interests combined. The primary issue, between groups, within groups, and even between conflicting motives in the individual, is that of *assumption*, on the one hand, and *knowledge*, on the other, as the basis of action. Shall we first of all desire to know, or even consent to know, all the bearings of our conduct, before we choose our course of action; or shall we take refuge in the claim: Whatever is, is right, if it favors us, and whatever is, is wrong, if it balks our wish?[55]

From this position, Small was invariably and inevitably a mediator, and mediation was identified with rationality. For example:

> It is more and more difficult for me to get excited over a quarrel between a labor organization and an employers' organization in which it is evident that the essential capitalistic spirit is as rampant in the one party as in the other. On the other hand, I can easily grow enthusiastic over any program which promises to limit the liberty of either party to beat the other by anything but rational means.[56]

He praised others for being mediators. For example, he praised Abraham Lincoln for his veneration of justice. He defined "justice" in *General Sociology* as "the condition in which there is a balanced proportion between the interests of different persons who are equally entitled to the possession of interests."[57] In a nonscholarly address a few years later he had the same conception. One of Lincoln's greatnesses was that "he has exhibited himself to posterity as a man standing, as it were, between the upper and nether mill stone [sic] of conflicting interests, saying, from his heart of hearts, daily and hourly to Almighty God: 'Show me what justice is and where it is, and by thy grace, so far as it in me is, it shall be done.' "[58] Small urged upon others this stance in favor of the "knowledge interest." For example, in "The Church and Class Conflicts," published in 1919, he warned of the dangers of bolshevism and urged a group of laymen:

(1) to organize and support a permanent commission for investigation into, and report upon, near and remote causes and details of any economic class conflicts which may develop in this country; (2) that the commission be instructed to study such conflicts on the ground, not as attempted arbitrators, but as accredited representatives of associated churches, with the aim of, so far as possible, exhausting all the material facts in the given case, especially those which have any appreciable bearing upon principles of justice; (3) that the associated churches be urged to make provision for the widest circulation of the reports of this committee among the leaders of thought, both ministers and laymen, in their respective bodies; (4) that the commission be charged also with the duty of reporting, from time to time (primarily with reference to their accuracy, their fairness to all the interests concerned, and the competence of their authors to pass the kinds of judgment involved) upon books, pamphlets, and magazine articles which purport to represent Christian principles in economic conflicts; ... [59]

In short, Small's conception of sociology as the study of the total social process, and his conception of objectivity led him to define a sociologist as a person who studies all points of view in social conflicts, and makes no partisan choices. Hence, all conflicting interests are legitimate. Sociologists make two distinct contributions. First, they represent the knowledge interest, and are therefore the tribunal before which all other contestants in social conflicts present their claims. Second, their ability to understand the multiplicity of factors in the social process in general, or in any particular situation, enables them to point out to the contestants, and to society at large, which interests, if given free rein, will be most conducive and least conducive to the realization of other interests. And the maximum realization of the maximum number of interests is the goal inherent in the social process. "The social problem" therefore "is to give freest scope to those interests which actually require for their realization the largest sum of other interests." Or, expressed negatively, "The social problem is to defeat all interests which, in content or possibly even in form, subordinate general interests to special interests."[60] One way to reach such judgments is to consider how "immediate" or "unsocial" an interest is. For example:

... if I am thinking of myself and my immediate interest in physical comfort, I shall want to eat, drink, and be merry, regardless of effects on my larger self or on my neighbors. I shall be a viciously unsocial factor. If a church is interested simply in itself as a church, with care only for its peculiar type of edification now, and forward looking to the triumphs of a judgment day, when it can marshal a certain number of saved individuals as its credentials, that church is a separatist affair, if not antagonizing, at least abandoning, the rest of society, instead of helping to carry on the social process.

On the other hand, *interests are social in proportion as they contemplate themselves as at their highest power when in co-operation with the social process.* As a self-sufficient individual, I am a clog in the social process. As an individual finding my individuality incomplete except as it progressively completes the social process, I am a part of the material and the motive that make society.[61]

Then Small goes on to equate the notion of "co-operation with the social process" with the notion of "common interest."

A State is normal or mature in proportion as the interests operating within it find their adjustment and completion in the progress of the common interest. Each interest is normal in proportion as it lends itself to the completion of the total civic interest.[62]

Small's holistic vision, his demand that sociology study the total social process instead of being a "pseudo-science of fragments" was also a call upon rational people to see a "total civic interest" in virtually every situation of conflict, and a moral injunction to contestants in social conflicts to subordinate their goals to that common interest. Hence, management-capitalists and finance-capitalists should be subject to greater political control, and representatives of the community should have a say in contracts involving finance-capital. Hence also, workers should cooperate with, as well as oppose capital and there should be enough "constitutionalism" in the economic system to make class cooperation possible.

CONCLUSION

There seems to be no way to prove that Small's political beliefs were derived from a coherent theory of sociology with extrapolitical roots. And no way to prove the opposite—that Small's sociology was essentially a generalization of, and elaborate rationalization for his centrist, mediating political reactions to the political and economic conflicts of the late nineteenth century. There is probably truth and error in both contentions. We do know that, in a general way, Small had a reformist, antisocialist position long before he developed his general sociology. That position is clear in his annual reports at Colby in the 1800s, and was one of the factors that led him into empirical sociology. To some extent, therefore, Small's sociology must have been a generalization of his politics. Such a conclusion, however, does not necessarily prove the primacy of politics in Small's thinking. Perhaps both his politics and his sociology were a secularized version of the biblical vision of all human beings as members of one body, and of Small's youthful experiences in a community of believers. Nor would such a conclusion necessarily mean that Small's sociology was merely a doodle on the surface of his politics. For the sociological generalization of the political beliefs, once formed, could presumably color or determine the way Small saw and responded to later political events, much different from the earlier ones out of which his sociology had arisen. Whatever the precise connections, however, and whatever the specific influences back and forth in Small's intellectual and ideological development between politics, religion, and sociology, it is clear that those three strands in his thought and feeling went hand in hand. His sociology was rooted in, or implied, a kind of progressive politics in which increasing harmony was a central goal, and in which professors, experts, and other knowledgeable outsiders who represent the "knowledge interest" played a central role.

By 1930 this brand of progressive politics seemed to make sense to fewer people than it seemed to in, say, 1910. Ten years after Small's death in 1926 it was virtually dead. For example, one tendency of the New Deal, as in the Wagner Act, was to give some legislative advantage to the weaker side in an economic conflict and then turn the two sides loose to see who wins, on any given occasion. Both that practice, and the absence, until the mobilization of World War II, of political controls over capital anywhere near the stringency envisaged by Small, were quite different from his brand of progressivism. To the extent that his sociology was linked to a style of politics that turned out to be unviable, his sociology, too, was bound to remain on library shelves without becoming a living legacy for his successors. The following chapter will review that entire legacy, will suggest some additional reasons why Small's synthesis broke down—historically, not intellectually—and will assess what significance that legacy might have in the future of sociology.

8

CONCLUSION

This book has neglected many aspects of Small's life and thought. For example, I have made no mention of his attitudes toward blacks,[1] toward ethnicity in American society,[2] and toward women;[3] or of the changes in his views of Germany and of German scholarship as World War I was approaching, and of the war itself.[4] I have not gone into his personal life, his family relationships, or his highly traditionalist defense of the family.[5] I have barely mentioned his own civic and political involvements, and have given only passing attention to his intellectual and personal relationships with contemporaries in sociology, such as Ward, Cooley, Giddings, and Simmel, and with scholars in other fields, such as Mead and Dewey, with whom Small has several affinities.[6] But some general conclusions, and some tentative answers to certain questions about Small's work and its significance today, seem possible. First, were there two Smalls, "the indignant ethical man" and "the detached scientist," in Ernest Becker's words?[7] Or did Small synthesize science and ethics? Second, arguing that Small did create such a synthesis, why did that synthesis break down among later generations of sociologists? Third, what are some of the conditions which seem likely to make sociologists today and in the future more or less receptive to Small's vision of a holistic social science, and more or less interested in a synthesis of science and ethics?

As Becker sees Small's work, Small attempted two tasks. First, he tried to create "a socially critical body of knowledge that would attack the ravages of *laissez-faire* capitalism." Second, he "had to do this 'scientifically' and 'objectively'...."[8] The first task required the portrayal of human beings as members of a moral community, of all individuals as participants in the total social process that bound each to all. In pursuit of this task, Small attacked the economists of his day for abstracting economic action out of the total social process, as in *Adam Smith and Modern Sociology*. He wrote *Origins of Sociology* and his other works in the history of social thought as part of this same task.

"The second aspect of Small's work . . ." in Becker's reading of Small, was "the longer-range problem of the science of sociology considered as a discipline."[9] Small tried to make sociology "objective," "scientific," and academically respectable. But respectability in the academy was inconsistent with the claim that sociology was the science of the total social process, as distinct from the more specialized "pseudo-science of fragments." As Becker states the issue, "It was physically and organizationally impossible to be a Wardian, and yet it was cognitively necessary to be a Wardian in order to launch a new type of social inquiry, a broadly relational inquiry with man at the center."[10] Small's first task required that sociology be the science of the total social process. His second task required that Small give up that claim, as he tended to do late in his life. In Becker's reading of Small, he opted in the end for the second task, so that "one gained a new equality with the other social sciences, but one lost social science."

And this is the paradox of Small's career, the two poles of his writings—the tension between the social problem and the objectivity of science. Let there be no doubt that Small himself was personally and at times painfully stretched between these two poles; it shows through all his work. How was the indignant ethical man to be made compatible with the detached scientist? Again and again, in article after article, interspersed with indignant books, the paradox shows forth. On the other hand, confession about how pitifully little was known about social reality: "As to the so-called social sciences . . . they had not passed far out of the homely wisdom stage of development. . . . On the whole, every social scientist . . . has actually, in ninety-five hundredths of his activities been a rationalizer at large, and in only five per cent of his activities has he concentrated upon close investigations of strictly defined problems, by use of an adequate method." Here, decidedly, was the champion of the discipline talking, lamenting that this state of affairs had existed from Herodotus down to 1924, the date of his lament. But on the other hand, listen to his voice—the same man, but a different aspect of his life-problem: "... an inevitable incident of specialization in social science is a drag toward abstraction as a finality; that is, toward dehumanizing of the specialty. Sociologists have no right to assume that they will prove exceptions to this rule. Indeed, I foresee rather the certainty that in proportion as we sociologists become ... efficient in the application of our technique, the tendency to exalt the immediate end at which our technique should arrive, viz., analysis of group phenomena as such, will show itself over-mastering us, as [happened to the older social sciences].... It is not at all difficult for me to imagine a stage in the growth of social science in which there will be sociologists no more concerned about anything beyond certain abstracted group phenomena, regardless of their meaning for human fortunes in general.... " Decidedly, this is the "other" Small, the ethical man conscious of the social problem. The discipline, with its very promise of success as a scientific specialty, now held the forbidding prospect that it would follow the abstractions of the older social sciences, and lose man! But it was precisely in order to put man back into science, that sociology had established itself vis-a-vis the other disciplines.[11]

In contrast to this image of two Smalls, the scientist founding a discipline versus the moralist concerned with reforming laissez-faire capitalism, Jurgen Herbst praises Small for synthesizing science and social reform.

> Small's achievement lay in his demonstration of a logical connection between the empiricism of the historical school [of economics] and the reform activities of the Verein für Sozialpolitik. The German scholars of the historical school, and their American students likewise, had embraced reform activities simply as moral imperatives, naïvely asserting that they were also scientific. Their opponents had not failed to point out the missing link between scientific description and ethical prescription. Small circumvented the problem by introducing the "social process" concept into American sociology.[12]

I, too, have argued at length that Small produced an internally coherent synthesis of science and ethics, in which, starting from premises that are, in principle, empirical, he argues systematically toward the only system of ethics that, in his view, fallible human beings can possibly follow. I have stressed the coherence (along with some loose ends and loose talk) in other aspects of Small's work as well. I have argued that his concept of "objectivity" informed his styles of theorizing, his view of the relation between sociology and ethics, and his political stance as a mediator; that his generalized images of "the social process" and his political views complement each other; that his empiricism was related both to his politics and to his style of theorizing; and that he had a view of human nature which allowed him, logically, to be both scientistic and moralistic.

But the extent to which any two ideas are synthesized instead of juxtaposed, is itself a historically relative matter. The argument—if A, then B, if B, then C; therefore, if A, then C—seems coherent to the point of logical closure to some people, but not to those whose historical experience includes so many contradictions that they would automatically react with a "Yes, but . . ." To the extent that Becker's image of the scientist versus the moralist in Albion Small refers to the internal logic of Small's own thought, that image is, on balance, incorrect. But to the extent that Becker refers to the historical impossibility, after the 1920s, of sustaining Small's syntheses any longer, he seems, on balance, to be right.

Why did the synthesis break down? Not only with Small, but with a whole generation of professors as moral leaders? For example, the intellectual, ideological, and political biography of the economist, Richard T. Ely, is similar to Small's in many respects, including the tension between academic success and reformist zeal.[13] But Ely (born, like Small, in 1854) lived so long that by the time of his death in 1943, little was left of the turn-of-the century professor as moral leader. Only detailed historical research could approach an adequate answer to the question: Why did Small's synthesis break down? To be sure, it is possible to make a purely intellectual critique of Small's sociology. For example, Small does not show, and it is doubtful that, the behavior of human beings in association with one another is reducible to the sum of the individual interests. But other, more political and historical factors seem relevant.

First, as Becker suggests, it was impolitic for sociology to claim to be the science of the total social process if it wanted success and respectability in the academy. And after sociology was securely established, it became unnecessary to make such grandiose claims. In Small's case, at least, sociology's claim to be the holistic social science had been logically linked to the synthesis of science and ethics. When sociology became one special discipline among all the others, one intellectual support for the union of sociology and ethics was lost.

Second, entirely apart from explicit doctrines uniting sociology and ethics, there is some suggestive evidence from Germany in the late nineteenth century that the perception of social relationships— of the central subject matter of sociology—goes along with the making of value judgments among people who are not in power, but that there is no statistical association between moralism and the perception of social relationships among people who are in power.[14] Extrapolating from this study to the history of sociology in the United States, sociology needed moralists to get started. But, once established in the academy, and then (via grants, commissioned research, consultantships and other ties) with centers of power in American society, the moralists were no longer necessary.

Third, Small's image of "the social process," and of sociology as the science of the total process, was linked not only to his union of science and ethics, but also to his politics. It seems to have been, in part, a generalization of political views that he had formed before he became a sociologist. But his politics did not turn out to be viable. Neither during the New Deal, nor during any other period in American politics after Small, has the federal government attempted peace-time controls over the flow of capital to the extent that Small envisaged. Under American conditions, it seems likely that the government that could implement Small's politics could also confiscate capital and initiate a socialist program, while a government that could not or would not confiscate capital could not or would not institute the reforms that Small called for. Left-liberals, therefore, fall short of Small's proposals, and socialist revolutionaries go beyond them. Small is left virtually alone. And to the extent that his sociology is linked to a politics that has gained virtually no assent, an otherwise possible set of heirs is lacking. A political practice that might find social-scientific legitimation in Small's work does not exist.

Fourth, the social position of universities, and the meaning of basic academic values such as free inquiry, have undergone considerable change during the twentieth century. Early in the century, norms of free inquiry were a useful device for resisting localistic pressures—from temperance groups, antievolutionists, religious fundamentalists, or partisans of one or another orthodoxy who tried to give the local campus a hard time. There was little or no notion that free inquiry was incompatible with a university's having its own institutional truth, and proclaiming that truth to society. For example, William Rainey Harper wrote that universities were established "to stand apart from other institutions, and at the same time to mingle closely with the constituent elements of the people" as "the prophet—that is, the spokesman—of democracy." Only much later did free inquiry come to mean that professors had a right to do any research they wanted to do, in collaboration with any outside agency, governmental or otherwise, because a university is a place where all opinions may be heard and, for that very reason, has no institutional truth about, say, Vietnam or the technology of weapons' systems.

Not all the reasons for these changes are clear. Perhaps the Great Depression was a spur to the ideology of universities as seats of disinterested learning in which there should be no institutional truth. Perhaps the greater involvement of universities with the federal government, temporarily during World War I and permanently since World War II, and with business, has created more professional servants of power, for whom it would be incongruous, impolitic, and financially risky to make Victorian moral pronouncements on the destiny of society. Whatever the reasons for these changes, the notions of disinterested learning and of free inquiry as incompatible with institutional truths seem to have made universities more vulnerable to the penetration of outsiders, more available for the purposes, whatever they may be, of whoever has the money to buy professorial time and pay for research equipment. These notions are a virtual reversal of the conception of universities that Small shared with many of his contemporaries. The position of universities in American society can no longer sustain, and the prevailing ideologies of university scholarship are largely incompatible with disciplinary scholars as moral leaders, who standardize measures of value, and create or discover new values, for the rest of the society. Small's synthesis of sociology and ethics no longer has social structural support in universities, and in the position of universities in American society. On paper, it is just as coherent now as it ever was. But the history of American universities in the twentieth century has passed by it. Does that fact mean that this book is of historical interest only? Becker contends that:

> ... Albion Small is contemporary. And the reason is that for the first time since the 1920s there is again deep searching for what sociology is, should be, or might be. The period we are now entering has all the same characteristics as the period for which Albion Small wrote. His career brings out in full relief the whole problem of the meaning of sociology and its failure to be socially relevant in spite of its unprecedented achievement as an objective science. It puts into the sharpest focus the relation of sociology to the crisis of our age.[15]

This characterization of Small's contemporary significance seems somewhat sweeping and overstated. But Becker does remind us that Small's contemporary relevance or lack of relevance to sociology is historically changeable. His call for a holistic science of sociology, as against the kind of research which Mills castigated as "abstract empiricism," probably makes more sense to more sociologists today than it would have made in, say, 1955. For when a society seems static, when people (including sociologists) think that the major framework of a society is not historically and politically problematic, then sociologists are more likely to examine microsociological details within that major framework than they are when the shape of the whole society seems to be in question. When the shape of a whole society seems in question, they will probably be more attuned to Small's vision of holistic social science. Even the nature of research subsidies from governmental and private sources will change from static to eruptive periods. When society seems static, firms and governmental agencies will be more interested in studying small, manipulable details within a society's major framework. When the shape of society seems to be in question, conservative sources of research support will, as with project Camelot, be more interested in studies of entire societies.

Similarly, the apparent relevance, or irrelevance, of Small's union of science and ethics will change from one period to another. Sociologists will vary, over time, in the extent to which they are sensitive to Small's issues in the first place. And they will vary in the ways in which they deal with the relation between science and ethics. Generally speaking, people are more concerned with the ethics of their behavior—whether it be publishing research in sociology, operating on tumors, or driving a cab—when they can see, or see the possibility of, beneficial or dire consequences of their behavior for other people. In periods in which society seems static, power seems well entrenched, and the moral authority of people in power seems unquestioned, sociologists will see little consequences in their work, whether that work seems logically to have conservative, liberal, or radical implications. But when society seems to be in flux but the direction of change seems open-ended, and the moral authority of people in power is eroded, more sociologists are going to think that their work might have beneficial or dire consequences for other people. That reaction would be even more likely if confused citizens, with no clear sense of political direction, turn to them for guidance, and if there is in the sociologists' society no strong, oppositional political movement that many or most sociologists can support. If there were such a movement, sociologists who allied with it could, in effect, delegate their moral and political concerns about the society to the movement and get on with their scholarly research. In the absence of such a movement, they would be more inclined toward activism themselves, and would worry about some doctrinal rationale for synthesizing scholarship, ethics, and political action.

These rationales, too, will vary. Both "value-free social science" and "value-laden social science" can mean many different things. Perhaps those sociologists who are more socialized into, and committed to, traditional scholarly values will develop elaborate rationales, as Small did. One possibility might be a linguistic version of value-laden social science, the counter to the linguistic version of value-free science. This version would argue that some empirical phenomena that sociologists study—"legality" and "justice" might be good candidates—can be studied empirically only by using concepts that have normative or evaluative components that are inextricably fused to their cognitive elements.[16] With respect to such phenomena, and such concepts, this rationale might argue, it is impossible to make empirical statements without simultaneously making value statements as well. Others, perhaps less committed to their roles as sociologists, might have very different rationales, asserting the primacy of ethics, or of politics, and arguing that scholarship is justifiable only as it serves these higher goals. Whatever the variations, however, it seems most unlikely that any American sociologist, in the foreseeable future, could accept Small's version of the union of science and ethics in the precise way in which Small spelled it out. The logic might be persuasive, but the historical moment that made it seem compelling to him is forever gone.

That fact does not mean, however, that we have nothing to learn from Small's logic, or from following the fine details of his argument. It is possible to understand his argument for the ethical significance of sociology only if one follows it from within, on its own terms. It is possible to do that, however, only if one temporarily gives up much of the prevailing wisdom about science and ethics— as in the linguistic version of value-free science, for example. And the experience of giving up that prevailing wisdom so as to think within Small's very different set of assumptions has the permanent impact of teaching Small's readers that the prevailing wisdom on these matters is limited, incomplete, and sociologically naïve. Albion Small knew better.

Appendix A

A letter from Small to William Rainey Harper defending the right of the University of Chicago department of sociology to teach statistics (1894)

MURRAY HILL HOTEL

New York. Dec. 29. 1894

President William R. Harper,
University of Chicago,
Chicago, Ill.

My dear Dr. Harper:—

It is unfortunate for me that I did not have longer time to hear further from you with reference to the matter of statistics. Quite likely I have partially misunderstood your brief statements, but I will reply as intelligibly as I can to the main points as I gathered them.

I have had no thought of disturbing, denying or rivaling the vested rights of the department of political economy in the matter of statistics or anything else. Whatever has been interpreted to the contrary has been misunderstood. I have no wish to change the arrangement by which the general theory of statistics is taught in the department of political economy.

On the other hand, no university department can have a monopoly of the statistical method any more than of the exegetical or of the laboratory method. The statistical method is tributary to the physical, biological and social sciences alike; its relative importance in different cases not being determined by the scope of the department in general, but by the kind of evidence required in the particular problems investigated. In the sessions of the economic association which I am now attending it has been positively stated over and over again by economists, statisticians and sociologists

159

alike that statistics is a primary and essential instrument in some of the most important divisions of sociological inquiry.

Our department of sociology needs statistical instruction, planned with special reference to classes of problems which are of immediate concern to sociologists—vital and moral statistics particularly—which are of secondary interest to the economist. The many divinity students desiring to study sociology increase the demand for this special application of the statistical method.

Without interfering in any way with the prerogatives of the department of political economy, but calculating to use the instruction offered by that department and especially the instruction already provided for in statistical science, I reported to you that the interest of students of sociology made it urgently desirable to introduce instruction in the application of the statistical method to the class of inquiries which they most need to learn how to pursue. In the nature of the case, so long as the instructors in the department of sociology are presumed to be competent, they are the best judges of the subjects which those inquiries should investigate. It is important that an expert statistician should work in co-operation with Dr. Henderson and myself in carrying out plans of investigation directly tributary to our own lines of study.

A chance conversation with Dr. Gould suggested to me that he might be available for both kinds of work—that desired by the department of political economy, and that particularly needed in sociology. Telling him plainly that the suggestion must be regarded as entirely irresponsible, because I had no assurance that my desire for statistical work could be granted, and moreover because I had no right to assume that the suggestion would meet the approval of others concerned, I asked Dr. Gould to outline a double minor in the theory of statistics, and another double minor in the application of the statistical method to sociological inquiry. After I had done this I reported my action to you, and asked if you would get Prof. Laughlin's views of the desirability of an arrangement with Dr. Gould.

If I understood you correctly, Prof. Laughlin thinks that I have committed an offense by not dealing with him in this matter instead of with Dr. Gould and yourself. I most emphatically decline to admit that there is cause of complaint on that ground. There is no more reason why I should consult Prof. Laughlin before finding out what is possible in the line of statistical courses in sociology, than why I should consult Prof. Whitman before endorsing Miss Talbot's request for a sanitary laboratory. Very likely the department of pedagogy, and perhaps psychology and history, and political science, and half a dozen more may want to apply the statistical method, and it would be as absurd to require them to go to political economy for permission, as it would to require the department of political economy to obtain the consent of the department of mathematics if it wanted to use tables of logarithms.

I distinctly recognize the limits of my own freedom in the matter by stating to you that I should be glad, for my part, if a man of Dr. Gould's well earned reputation could take charge of the part of the work preempted by political economy, and at the same time the work which I need. If it is trespass to express such a desire, leaving action upon it entirely to yourself and Prof. Laughlin, I am simply ignorant of the law which created the crime.

If the root of the difficulty in this case is unwillingness to have statistical instruction offered unless the courses are all scheduled with political economy, I would say that I do not care a straw what label is on them. If the sociological rose would smell sweeter under the economic name, by all means let it have the added fragrance! I do not believe, however, that it would be agreeable to Prof. Laughlin any more than to me to have the matter left in such shape that both Dr. Henderson and myself would feel ouselves in the position of interlopers whenever we ventured to consult with the instructor in statistics about his assistance in sociological investigations. It may be wise for the University to place the department of sociology under the supervision of the department of political economy, but I am strongly of the opinion that such is not the case.

Perhaps it was my own invention, but my impression from the talk with you was that Prof. Laughlin regarded my desire to apply statistical methods in a sociological course as a reflection upon his wisdom in conducting the department of political economy. As soon as there is a possibility that the funds of the University will allow it, I propose to ask an appropriation for a sociological museum; and I should say that Prof. Chamberlain would then have precisely the same right to interpret the request as a reflection on his curatorship of Walker. In my innocence I applied for what seems to me necessary: If the interests of the University veto the request, well and good. Whatever be the decision I hope to be absolved from the imputation of desire to encroach upon another department; and at the same time I want to register my protest against allowing one department to handicap another by asserting exclusive control of any method of investigation.

My opinion is positive that the two courses marked out by Dr. Gould could not be improved upon in plan. It is plain to me that they would add greatly to the attractiveness of our offer to students. One or both of these courses would meet wants of a large number of students outside of both departments. It was to me an interesting coincidence that Prof. Richmond Smith, of Columbia, read a paper yesterday describing what would be in his judgment an ideal course in statistics as applied to sociology. It was enthusiastically commended by the whole association. And everybody said that such instruction should be a part of all well equipped departments of sociology. The courses proposed in the paper were almost precisely identical in scope with those which Dr. Gould outlined to you and me. Under such circumstances I do not believe that the University can afford to let any trifling questions about departmental boundaries interfere with the acquisition of such an important element in our instruction. What I am after is the thing itself. I do not care very much about the matter of names and locations on paper. It seems to me that the courses in question ought to be a bond to unite the two departments for practical purposes, not a barrier to separate them. As they cover so much of the ground which is basal to both departments, and which cannot possibly be accurately fenced off, it seems to me scholarly and courteous to recognize the elements which the two departments have in common, in the premises, and not to attempt a too minute limitation of proprietorship.

As I said before I am quite willing to abide by the decision which shall be made from the standpoint of University organization in general, even if that point of view shall necessitate an opinion different from that which I am bound to express.

Sincerely,
Albion W. Small

Appendix B

A letter from Small to Harper urging that the University of Chicago
support a journal of sociology (1895)

THE UNIVERSITY OF CHICAGO
Founded by John D. Rockefeller

Chicago, April 25, 1895

President William R. Harper, D.D., L.L.D.,

My dear President Harper:—

By your permission, I present herewith a statement of some of
the reasons why a journal of Sociology is demanded of the University
of Chicago. Hoping that the Board of Trustees will see fit to
authorize the establishment of such a journal, I am preparing a more
specific statement in form of prospectus which will be ready for your
consideration in a few days.

1. A recent English critic made the following remark:—"Outside a small group of workers, who, however, stand more or less
aloof from the main body of professional thought, we have really in
England at the present day no school of thought producing men
fitted to deal with the science of human society as a whole" (Mr.
Benjamin Kidd, in *Nineteenth Century*, Feb. 1895). The observation
notoriously fits every other country. The foundations of the science
of Sociology have been and are being laid by men who realize this
failure and who appreciate the necessity of combining social abstractions with "a science of human society as a whole."

2. The University of Chicago has made more liberal provision
than any other institution in the world for development of and
instruction in the science of Sociology. Nowhere else in the world are
so many courses of instruction offered. This fact, together with the
fact that equally liberal provision has been made for related

163

departments of social knowledge, has given the University a prominence in these departments, which makes it our duty to use every means of leadership in the formation of opinion about what is desirable right and possible in social action.

3. Sociology is the most recent, the most difficult, the most complex and the most misunderstood of all the sciences pertaining to society. Every silly and mischievous doctrine which agitators advertise, claims Sociology as its sponsor. A scientific journal of Sociology could be of practical social service in every issue, in discrediting pseudo-sociology and in forcing social doctrinaires back to accredited facts and principles.

4. Although everything written under the title or ostensibly written in the domain of Sociology, is eagerly read by increasing numbers of people in all ranks, there is no English or American magazine devoted exclusively or I may say even intelligently to a comprehensive treatment of the subjects properly belonging to Sociology or "the science of human society as a whole."

5. I have been urged by some of the leaders of Sociological investigation in this country, Lester F. Ward the Nestor of American Sociologists among the number, to take the editorship of such a journal, of which every Sociologist feels the need.

6. By issuing such a journal now, we shall have the advantage of being first in the field. We shall not invade preoccupied territory. We shall enlist the good will of men and institutions not committed to the support of a possible competitor and their cooperation will for a long time secure to our journal undisputed possession of ground which it will be greatly to the credit of the University to improve.

7. A journal controlled by the University, while offering freedom of publication for all responsible conclusions and opinions, whether approved by the editors or not, will furnish a needed medium for the exposition of the system of Sociology which the department in the University of Chicago peculiarly represents. I may be permitted to say that if I am right in my views of the scope and method of Sociology, not only the department, but fairly adequate conceptions of the province of the department and of the contributions which it should make to knowledge of right social relations, had been lacking in America until the University of Chicago gave work in Sociology room to develop. The impression which our work has already made upon representative men, the incredulity and opposition as well as the approval which we have met confirms my belief that we have

adopted a scientific platform broader and more secure than the leaders of other tendencies have constructed, or in the present generation can construct. It is the courage of this conviction which spurs me to undertake what I see to be the most formidable task that I have ever encountered.

8. A journal of Sociology would be of direct value to each University department which deals with groups of facts and relations occurring in Society. Sociology, being a synthetic science, cannot gain any authority, except as it builds upon the results of the special social sciences. Sociology constantly emphasizes the necessity of reckoning with the data of Ethnology, History, Comparative Administrative Science and Political Economy. Sociology consequently reinforces the demand of practical men that study of these sciences shall not be pursued as though they were ends in themselves, but in order that the results may be combined for useful purposes in the guidance of social effort. Sociology, therefore, furnishes the setting in which the importance of each special social science is seen in the perspective.

9. The following considerations need not be elaborated:

(a) A journal is needed to work against the growing popular impression that short cuts may be found to universal prosperity.

(b) It is needed to serve as a clearing house for the best that is appearing in the press of the world on sociological subjects.

(c) It is needed both to exert restraint upon utopian social effort and to encourage and direct well advised attempts at social cooperation.

(d) It would advertise the University, and give it additional repute as a moulder of thought.

(e) It would strengthen the department of Sociology and related Departments by attracting students.

(f) It would improve the quality of work done by students in the department by offering a place of publication for meritorious productions.

(g) It would be an additional incentive to the instructors in the department to investigate and publish.

(h) The expense of starting the journal need not be large.

(i) The greatest interest in the subject justifies the hope that it would soon be self-supporting.

10. The following will indicate my opinion, in general of the proper scope of the journal of Sociology:—

(a) It should be primarily technical. By this I do not mean that it should be devoted exclusively to discussions of the methodology of Sociological enquiry, but that it should aim to extend, classify and clarify knowledge of societary relations.

(b) It should be incidentally and secondarily popular. By this I do not mean that it should attempt to attract immature or ignorant readers; but that it should be as free as possible from technicalities which are of professional interest to sociologists alone, and should try to put the results of research in a form which would be interesting to all people capable of forming respectable judgements upon difficult social questions.

(c) It should attempt to present sociological conclusions or problems in such a way that they will be seen to have a double bearing: (1) upon the general or special doctrine of social philosophy held by the theorists: (2) upon the practical decisions of men of affairs. I do not anticipate that such a journal can cater to the latter class of readers in great numbers, but I would endeavor to make its contents available as a resource for middlemen, who could recast them for popular consumption.

(d) It should therefore become indispensable to all thinkers whatever their professional position or special social interest, who need to know the best that has been learned or thought about possibilities of rearranging social effort in the interest of larger usefulness:—Thus (1) Sociologists, scientific writers, leaders, sociological students. (2) Publicists of all kinds except the machine politicians. (3) Journalists, except those who are working for pay regardless of principle. (4) Ministers and others, engaged in promoting humane endeavor. (5) Men connected with state, county, municipal or private charities. (6) Officers of all grades in public school systems. (7) Specialists in particular social sciences who need to relate their part of a subject to the whole from which it is an abstraction.

The primary practical service of Sociology is to show all classes in society the functional significance of the part which each other element in society is performing. The exhibition of these primary facts will go far toward solving many puzzling social questions.

(e) In order to reach each class included under the above suggestions, the journal should contain articles:—(1) Dealing directly with systematic and technical Sociology. The aim of these articles should be to improve methodology, to define lines of distinction and principles of classification among the phenomena and to reach constructive scientific conclusions. These articles should contain the maturest thought about society which our scientific attainments make possible.

2. Designed to show the rational basis or lack of basis beneath proposed plans of state action. These articles should contain diagnoses not merely of isolated symptoms but of social evils in their causes, and they should discuss the possibility of immediate remedies, or of palliatives according to the nature of the conditions in question.

3. Designed to show the relation of the educational factor in civilization to possible social progress. These articles should not deal with the technique of pedagogy, but rather with the subject matter of instruction considered as a societary function—a qualification for effective performance of work by each member of society. These articles should help to qualify teachers to perform their work from the larger outlook of the sociological view point.

4. Designed to interpret the social functions belonging to the church as an organ of society, to instruct clergy and laity and to aid in directing them to intelligent social service.

5. Showing the sociological significance of work done in other sciences.

6. Embodying results of special investigation of phases of contemporary society.

7. Containing records of social movements and experiments. Correspondents in the chief centres of America and other countries should be utilized.

8. Containing theoretical and practical suggestions for administrators of penal and charitable institutions, and for the public who ought to be interested in same.

9. Containing critical bibliographies—exclusive and inclusive—brought down to date and classified.

10. Containing the results of the club work of the department, especially in sifting the new book and magazine literature, thus constituting a means of calculating all the currents of contemporary sociological thought. This department should be extremely valuable because such thought is now so scattered.

11. Containing editorial comments upon current events interpreted by sociological criterians, sociological miscellanies, biographical notes of social workers, news from the Sociological department of the University etc. etc.

Awaiting the decision of the Board upon this general preliminary statement, before entering upon more specific particulars, I remain

Very respectfully
Albion W. Small

Appendix C

Chapter 31 of *General Sociology* (1905)

INTERESTS

Nature—i.e., the physical surroundings in which men come into existence and develop their endowment—is analyzed for us by the physical sciences. We do not know all its secrets, but in studying the social process we have to start with such knowledge of nature as the physical sciences have gained, and we have to search for similar knowledge of the human factor. Men have been analyzed much less successfully than nature. During the past generation, the conception of "the atom" has been of enormous use in physical discovery. Although no one has ever seen an atom, the supposition that there are ultimate particles of matter in which the "promise and potency" of all physical properties and actions reside, has served as a means of investigation during the most intensive period of research in the history of thought. Without the hypothesis of the atom, physics and chemistry, and in a secondary sense biology, would have lacked chart and compass upon their voyages of exploration. Although the notion of the atom is rapidly changing, and the tendency of physical science is to construe physical facts in terms of motion rather than of the traditional atom, it is probably as needless as it is useless for us to concern ourselves as laymen with this refinement. Although we cannot avoid speaking of the smallest parts into which matter can be divided, and although we cannot imagine, on the other hand, how any portions of matter can exist and not be divisible into parts, we are probably quite as incapable of saving ourselves from paradox by resort to the vortex hypothesis in any form. That is, these subtleties are too wonderful for most minds. Without pushing analysis too far, and without resting any theory upon analogy with the atom of

169

physical theory, it is necessary to find some starting-place from which to trace up the composition of sentient beings, just as the physicists assumed that they found their starting-place in the atom. The notion of interests is accordingly serving the same purpose in sociology which the notion of atoms has served in physical science. Interests are the stuff that men are made of. More accurately expressed, the last elements to which we can reduce the actions of human beings are units which we may conveniently name "interests." It is merely inverting the form of expression to say: *Interests are the simplest modes of motion which we can trace in the conduct of human beings.*

Now, it is evident that human beings contain one group of interests which are generically identical with the factors that compose plants and animals. They are those modes of motion which follow the laws of physics and chemistry and biology. The sociologist is not accountable for a metaphysics of those motions. They exist in trees and fishes and birds and quadrupeds and men alike. They are movements that exhibit the different forms of vital energy. These forces that work together in building living organisms are no other in men than in the lower organisms. These forces are incessantly displaying themselves in movements that arrive at certain similar types of results. Viz.: There is the building of living tissue. There is the growth and development of this tissue till it detaches itself from the parent stock and leads an independent life. There is, in turn, the parental action of this organism in giving life to other organisms like itself. All that goes forward in living organisms may be conceived as the working of a complex group of energies which we may call the health interest. In the form of a definition, we may generalize as follows: *The health interest is that group of motions which normally build and work the bodily organism.* That interest has one specific content in a clover plant, another in an oak tree, another in an insect, another in a man. In each case, however, it is an energetic pushing forward toward expression of power which proves to have different limits in the different types; but these puttings forth of power, so far as they go, consist of motions which all belong in one and the same group. Physical, chemical, and vital energies, variously mixed, attain to the life of the plant in one instance, of the insect in another, of the man in another. In short, the basal interest in every man is the impulse of all the physical energy deposited in his organism to work itself out to the limit. This is what we mean by the health interest. It is the impulsion and the propulsion of the frankly material in our composition. Before referring to other interests, we may illustrate in this connection what was said a little earlier about all men being variations of the same elemental factors.

Here is a black man committing a fiendish crime, and here are white men dragging him to a fiendish expiation, and here is a saintly man throwing the whole force of his life into horror-stricken protest against the inhumanity of both. Now, the point is that, in the first instance, the criminal, the avenger, and the saint are storage batteries of one and the same kind of physical energy. The vital processes of the one are precisely similar to those of the other. The same elementary physical motions occur in the life of each. It might even happen that precisely the same quantity of physical energy resided in each of the three. The criminal does not do something to the like of which nothing in the avenger or in the saint urges. On the contrary, the rudimentary energies in the average man move in the same direction as those that betray themselves in the criminal. The health interest is a term in the personal equation of each; but something in the avenger and in the saint inhibits the health interest from monopoly of the man in the two latter cases, while without such inhibition it rages to madness in the former. The saint is not a unit that contains no factor in common with the fiend. On the contrary, saint and fiend are terms which alike cover a certain quantity and quality of the brute. That the fiend is not a saint, and the saint is not a fiend, is not because the make-up of either utterly lacks components of the other character. It is because that which goes to make the fiend is, in the one case, not organized into other interests which modify its workings; in the other case other interests have so asserted themselves that the health interest has been reduced to a completely subordinate role.

In the lowest condition in which we find human beings, they present little to attract the attention of any scientific observer except the zoölogist. They are merely specimens of a higher order of animal. The differences which the comparative anatomist makes out are merely more complex details in the same series which he traces from the lowest orders in the animal kingdom. The horde of savage men is simply a mass of practically identical specimens of a species, just like a shoal of fish or a herd of buffaloes. That is, so long as the health interest alone is in working force, there is no such fact present as a human individual. The specimens in the aggregation are not individualized. Each presents the same dead level of characteristics that appear in all the rest. So far nothing but the animal kingdom is in sight. The properly human stage in world-evolution begins when the differentiation of other interests in some of the specimens of the *genus homo* produces human individuals. In other words, the individual who builds human society, as distinguished from packs of animals, is the human animal varied by the appearance and incessant modification of other than the health interest. [To have] an adequate theory of the human process, therefore, there is need of intimate acquaintance with the human individual, the ultimate molecular unit carrying on the process. This is to be insisted upon for its own sake, but also incidentally for the reason that certain critics of present tendencies in sociology insist that the sociologists are entirely on the wrong track, since they start by leaving individuals out of the account. These critics assert that the sociologist cares only about societies, but that the things which he thinks he knows about societies are necessarily wrong, because we cannot know societies without understanding the persons who compose the societies.

The criticism seriously misinterprets the sociologists. Instead of ignoring the individual, nobody has seen more clearly than the sociologists that we must stop taking a fictitious individual for granted, or still worse, assuming that it is unnecessary to take a real individual into the account at all. Nobody has more strenuously insisted that we must analyze human personality to the utmost limit in order to posit the real actor in association. The sociologists have therefore quite as often erred in the direction opposite to that alleged by these critics. They have invaded psychological and pedagogical territory, and usually without equipment to do respectable work. They have been tempted to this sort of foray by encountering in their own proper work the need of more knowledge of the individual than is available. It is true the sociologists think that, when division of labor is fully organized, study of the individual, as such, will fall to others. But the social fact and the social process will never be understood till we have better knowledge of the individual element in the fact and the process. Professor Baldwin spoke for sociology as truly as for psychology when he said:

> It is the first requirement of a theory of society that it shall
> have adequate views of the progress of the social whole, which
> shall be consistent with the psychology of the individual's personal

growth. It is this requirement, I think, which has kept the science of society so long in its infancy; or, at least, this in part. Psychologists have not had sufficient genetic theory to use on their side; and what theory they had seemed to forbid any attempt to interpret social progress in its categories. As soon as we come to see, however, that the growth of the individual does not forbid this individual's taking part in the larger social movement as well, and, moreover, reach the view that in his growth he is at once also growing into the social whole, and in so far aiding its further evolution—then we seem to have found a bridge on which it is safe to travel, and from which we can get vistas of the country on both sides.*

In this connection we may adopt another remark of Professor Baldwin:

... one of the historical conceptions of man is, in its social aspects, mistaken. Man is not a person who stands up in his isolated majesty, meanness, passion, or humility, and sees, hits, worships, fights, or overcomes another man, who does the opposite things to him, each preserving his isolated majesty, meanness, passion, humility, all the while, so that he can be considered a "unit" for the compounding processes of social speculation. On the contrary, *a man is a social outcome rather than a social unit.* He is always, in his greatest part, also someone else. Social acts of his—that is, acts which may not prove anti-social—are his *because they are society's first;* otherwise he would not have learned them nor have had any tendency to do them. Everything that he learns is copied, reproduced, assimilated from his fellows; and what all of them, including him—all the fellows, the *socii*—do and think, they do and think because they have each been through the same course of copying, reproducing, assimilating that he has. When he acts quite privately, it is always with a boomerang in his hand; and every use he makes of his weapon leaves its indelible impression both upon the other and upon him.

It is on such truths as these, which recent writers have been bringing to light, that the philosophy of society must be gradually built up. Only the neglect of such facts can account for the present state of social discussion. Once let it be our philosophical conviction,

* Social and Ethical Interpretations, p. 81.

drawn from the more general results of psychology and anthropology, that man is not two, an *ego* and an *alter*, each in active and chronic protest against a third great thing, society; once dispel this hideous un-fact, and with it the remedies found by the egoists, back all the way from the Spencers to the Hobbeses and the Comtes—and I submit the main barrier to the successful understanding of society is removed.*

At the same time, there should be no difficulty in getting it understood that, while biology and psychology have to do with the individual when he is in the making, sociology wants to start with him as the finished product. There is a certain impossible antinomy about this, to be sure; for our fundamental conception is that the individual and his associations are constantly in the reciprocal making by each other. Nevertheless, there are certain constant aspects of the individual which furnish known terms for sociology. They are aspects which present their own problems to physiology and psychology, on the one hand, and to sociology, on the other; but in themselves they must be assumed at the beginning of sociological inquiry.

To the psychologist the individual is interesting primarily as a center of knowing, feeling, and willing. To the sociologist the individual begins to be interesting when he is thought as knowing, feeling and willing *something*. In so far as a mere trick of emphasis may serve to distinguish problems, this ictus indicates the sociological starting-point. The individual given in experience is thought to the point at which he is available for sociological assumption, when he is recognized as a center of activities which make for something outside of the psychical series in which volition is a term. These activities must be referred primarily to desires, but the desires themselves may be further referred to certain universal interests. In this character the individual becomes one of the known or assumed terms of sociology. The individual as a center of active interests may be thought both as the lowest term in the social equation and as a composite term whose factors must be understood. These factors are either the more evident desires, or the more remote interests which the individual's desires in some way represent. At the same time, we must repeat the admission that these assumed interests are like the atom of physics. They are the metaphysical recourse of our minds in

* Baldwin, p. 87.

accounting for concrete facts. We have never seen or touched them. They are the hypothetical substratum of those regularities of conduct which the activities of individuals display.

In this connection the term "interest" is to be understood, not in the psychological, but in a teleological sense.* The sense in which we use the term is antecedent to that which seems to be predominantly in Professor Baldwin's mind in the following passages:

> The very concept of interests, when one considers it with reference to himself, necessarily involves others, therefore, on very much the same footing as oneself. One's interests, the things he wants in life, are the things which, by the very same thought, he allows others also the right to want; and if he insists upon the gratification of his own wants at the expense of the legitimate wants of the "other," then he in so far does violence to his sympathies and to his sense of justice. And this in turn must impair his satisfaction. For the very gratification of himself thus secured must, if it be accompanied with any reflection at all, involve the sense of the "other's" gratification also; and since this conflicts with the fact, a degree of discomfort must normally arise in the mind, varying with the development which the self has attained in the dialectical process described above. . . .

> On the one hand, we can get no doctrine of society but by getting the psychology of the *socius* with all his natural history; and, on the other hand, we can get no true view of the *socius* without describing the social conditions under which he normally lives, with the history of their action and reaction upon him. Or, to put the outcome in terms of the restriction which we have imposed upon ourselves—the only way to get a solid basis for social theory based upon human want or desire, is to work out first a descriptive and genetic psychology of desire in its social aspects; and, on the other hand, the only way to get an adequate psychological view of the rise and development of desire in its social aspects is by a patient tracing of the conditions of social environment in which

---

* Here again we have a term which has insensibly grown into force in sociology, and it would require long search to trace its history. It may be found almost indiscriminately among the sociologists. Its use sometimes leaves the impression that the author attaches to it very little importance. In other cases it seems to be cardinal. No writer has made more of it than Ratzenhofer, *Sociologische Erkenntniss*, chap. 2, *et passim*.

the child and the race have lived and which they have grown up to reflect.*

The somewhat different concept of this element "interest" which we posit may be indicated at first with the least possible technicality. We may start with the familiar popular expressions, "the farming interest," "the railroad interest," "the packing interest," "the milling interest," etc., etc. Everyone knows what the expressions mean. Our use of the term "interest" is not co-ordinate with these, but it may be approached by means of them. All the "interests" that are struggling for recognition in business and in politics are highly composite. The owner of a flourmill, for example, is a man before he is a miller. He becomes a miller at last because he is a man; i.e., because he has interests—in a deeper sense than that of the popular expressions—which impel him to act in order to gain satisfactions. The clue to all social activity is in this fact of individual interests. Every act that every man performs is to be traced back to an interest. We eat because there is a desire for food; but the desire is set in motion by a bodily interest in replacing exhausted force. We sleep because we are tired; but the weariness is a function of the bodily interest in rebuilding used-up tissue. We play because there is a bodily interest in use of the muscles. We study because there is a mental interest in satisfying curiosity. We mingle with our fellow-men because there is a mental interest in matching our personality against that of others. We go to market to supply an economic interest, and to war because of some social interest of whatever mixed or simple form.

With this introduction, we may venture an extremely abstract definition of our concept "interest." In general, *an interest is an unsatisfied capacity, corresponding to an unrealized condition, and it is predisposition to such rearrangement as would tend to realize the indicated condition.*† Human needs and human wants are

---

* *Social and Ethical Interpretations*, pp. 15, 16, 21, 22.

†Professor Dewey's formula is: *"Interest is impulse functioning with reference to self-realization."* Our formula attempts to express a conception of something back of consciousness, and operating more generally than in facts of consciousness. Whether this philosophical conceit is defensible or not, is unessential for the remainder of our analysis. All that is strictly necessary for sociology proper is the later analysis, which might be performed in terms of "interest," either in our own or in the psychological sense, or of "desires" in a more empirical sense. Indeed, the latter is the method to be applied in the following discussion.

incidents in the series of events between the latent existence of human interests and the achievement of partial satisfaction. Human interests, then, are the ultimate terms of calculation in sociology. *The whole life-process, so far as we know it, whether viewed in its individual or in its social phase, is at last the process of developing, adjusting, and satisfying interests.* *

No single term is of more constant use in recent sociology than this term "interests." We use it in the plural partly for the sake of distinguishing it from the same term in the sense which has become so familiar in modern pedagogy. The two uses of the term are closely related, but they are not precisely identical. The pedagogical emphasis is rather on the voluntary attitude toward a possible object of attention. The sociological emphasis is on attributes of persons which may be compared to the chemical affinities of different elements.†

To distinguish the pedagogical from the sociological use of the term "interest," we may say pedagogically of a supposed case: "The boy has no *interest* in physical culture, or in shop-work, or in companionship with other boys, or in learning, or in art, or in morality." That is, attention and choice are essential elements of interest in the pedagogical sense. On the other hand, we may say of the same boy, in the sociological sense: "He has not discovered his health, wealth, sociability, knowledge, beauty, and rightness *interests.*" We thus imply that interests, in the sociological sense, are not necessarily matters of attention and choice. They are affinities, latent in persons, pressing for satisfaction, whether the persons are conscious of them either generally or specifically, or not; they are indicated spheres of activity which persons enter into and occupy in the course of realizing their personality.

Accordingly, we have virtually said that interests are merely specifications in the make-up of the personal units. We have several times named the most general classes of interests which we find serviceable in sociology, viz.: *health, wealth, sociability, knowledge, beauty,* and *rightness.* We shall speak more in detail of the content of these interests in the next chapter.

* Quite in harmony with this formula is the conclusion of Professor Ludwig Stein, *Die sociale Frage,* 2d ed., p. 519. Closely connected with this conception of the social process is Stein's formula of the ultimate social imperative: p. 522.

† Probably it is needless to say that the term "interest" in this connection, whether used in the singular or the plural, has nothing to do with the economic term "interest."

We need to emphasize, in addition, several considerations about these interests which are the motors of all individual and social action: First, there is a subjective and an objective aspect of them all. It would be easy to use terms of these interests in speculative arguments in such a way as to shift the sense fallaciously from the one aspect to the other; e.g., moral conduct, as an actual adjustment of the person in question with other persons, is that person's "interest," in the objective sense. On the other hand, we are obliged to think of something in the person himself impelling him, however unconsciously, toward that moral conduct, i.e., interest as "unsatisfied capacity," in the subjective sense. So with each of the other interests. The fact that these two senses of the term are always concerned must never be ignored; but, until we reach refinements of analysis which demand use for these discriminations, they may be left out of sight. Second, human interests pass more and more from the latent, subjective, unconscious state to the active, objective, conscious form. That is, before the baby is self-conscious, the baby's essential interest in bodily well-being is operating in performance of the organic functions. A little later the baby is old enough to understand that certain regulation of his diet, certain kinds of work or play, will help to make and keep him well and strong. Henceforth, there is in him a co-operation of interest in the fundamental sense, and interest in the derived, secondary sense, involving attention and choice. If we could agree upon the use of terms, we might employ the word "desire" for this development of interest; i.e., physiological performance of function is, strictly speaking, the health interest; the desires which men actually pursue within the realm of bodily function may be normal, or perverted, in an infinite scale of variety. So with each of the other interests. Third, with these qualifications provided for, resolution of human activities into pursuit of differentiated interests becomes the first clue to the combination that unlocks the mysteries of society. For our purposes in this argument we need not trouble ourselves very much about nice metaphysical distinctions between the aspects of interest, because we have mainly to do with interests in the same sense in which the man of affairs uses the term.* The practical politician looks over the lobby at

---

* We might reserve the term "interest" strictly for the use defined above, applying the term "desire" to the subjective aspect of choice, and "want" to the objective aspect, i.e., the thing desired. Precisely because the term "interest" is in current use for all these aspects of the case, we prefer to retain it.

Washington, and he classifies the elements that compose it. He says: "Here is the railroad interest, the sugar interest, the labor interest, the army interest, the canal interest, the Cuban interest, etc." He uses the term "interest" essentially in the sociological sense, but in a relatively concrete form, and he has in mind little more than variations of the wealth interest. He would explain the legislation of a given session as the final balance between these conflicting pecuniary interests. He is right, in the main; and every social action is, in the same way, an accommodation of the various interests which are represented in the society concerned.

It ought to be plain, then, that our analysis of society, first into the operative interests within the units, and then into personal units, is not the construction of an esoteric mystery, to be the special preserve of sociology. It is a frank, literal, matter-of-fact expression of the reality which society presents for our inspection; and it is the most direct step toward insight into the realities of society. Social problems are entanglements of persons with persons, and each of these persons is a combination of interests developed in certain unique proportions and directions. All study of social situations must consequently be primarily a qualitative and quantitative analysis of actually observed mixtures of interests. Whether it is a problem of getting the pupils in a school to do good work, or of making the religious force in a church effective, or of defending a town against illegal liquor traffic, or of organizing laborers for proper competition with employers, or of securing an enlightened national policy toward foreign peoples—whether the particular social situation or problem which we have in hand fills only the four walls of our house or reaches to the ends of the earth, in every case the primary terms of the problem are the particular interests of the particular persons who compose that particular situation.

The phrase "properties of numbers" survives in many minds from their earliest encounters with arithmetic. Whether or not it was good pedagogy to use the phrase we will not inquire, but the idea and the program behind the phrase may furnish an analogy for our present use. The boy who simply makes change for the papers he sells on the street corner has this at least in common with Newton, and Laplace, and the bookkeepers, and the actuaries, and the engineers, who carry on the most complicated mathematical calculations, viz., they are concerned with the "properties of numbers." So far as the problems of each go, they must learn, somehow or other, to know the properties of numbers under all circumstances where they occur. In like manner, people who seek social intelligence, whether they are street gamins hustling for a living with help from nobody, or social philosophers attempting to report the past and to foretell the future of the human family, all are dealing with the properties of persons. Just as the chemist must very early get familiar with certain primary facts about his "elements," their specific gravity, their atomicity, their relation to oxygen, etc., etc.; so the sociologist, whether amateur or professional, must early get a working knowledge of the essential peculiarities of persons. Sociology accordingly involves first of all a technique for detecting, classifying, criticizing, measuring, and correlating human interests, first with reference to their past and present manifestations, and second with reference to their indications for the future. The sociological study that is provided for in university courses is not like the instruction in law, which is calculated to make men the most effective practitioners under the code that now exists. All our programs of sociological study are more like the courses in pure and applied mathematics which a West Point student is obliged to take. They are not expected to give him specific knowledge of the situations which he may encounter in a campaign. They are supposed to make him familiar with the elements out of which all possible military situations are composed, with the means of calculating all relationships that may occur between these elements, and with the necessary processes of controlling theoretical and practical dealings with these elements under any circumstances whatsoever.

Every real social problem throws upon the sociologist who undertakes to deal with it the task of calculating a unique equation of interests. General sociology is a preparation for judging a concrete combination of interests very much as general training in physiology and pathology and clinical observation prepares the physician for diagnosis of the new cases which will occur in his practice. He may never meet precisely the same combinations of conditions and symptoms which he has considered in the course of his preparatory training, but he is supposed to have become familiar at least with all the general types of conditions and symptoms which can occur, and to have acquired ability to form reliable judgments on the specific nature of any new combinations of them which he may encounter.

Suppose, for instance, we are dealing with the practical problems of law-enforcement in a particular town in a state which has a prohibition law. There are certain very familiar types of persons who persist in treating the situation as though it were an affair of two and only two simple factors, viz., the law on the one side, and its violation on the other. The fact is that both the law and the violation are expressions of highly complex mixtures of interests, and neither the law nor the violation precisely represents the actual balance of interests in the community. On the one hand, the law was derived from a co-operation of at least these six factors, viz.: first, a high, pure, moral interest that was uppermost in certain people; second, an interest in good social repute, spurred by a state of conscience that condemns the liquor traffic, but without enough moral sympathy with the condemnation to act accordingly, unless lashed to action by the zeal of the first interest; third, a political interest in making capital out of a policy which would win certain voters; fourth, a business interest, in getting the trade of certain people by opposing a traffic that they oppose, or in creating difficulties for a traffic which is indirectly a competitor; fifth, a personal or family interest, in preventing or punishing a traffic which has inflicted, or threatens to inflict, injury upon self or relatives; sixth, an interest in the liquor traffic itself, which calculates that opposition may be fought more adroitly when it is in the shape of positive law, than when it is vague and general. In every particular case these six sorts of interest that create the law will be subdivided according to circumstances, and the relative influence of each will vary indefinitely. We no sooner realize these facts than we are aware that in its substance, its force, its spirit, the law is not the absolute, categorical, unequivocal factor that it is in its form. While it has no uncertain sound as a statutory mandate, expressed in impersonal words, it has a most decidedly quavering quality when traced back to the human wills whose choices give it all its power.

On the other hand, if we analyze violation of the law, we find that it arises, first, from thoroughly immoral interests—greed of gain, contempt for social rights, willingness to profit by the physical and moral ruin of others; second, the interest in satisfying the drink appetite. This ranges from the strong and constant demand of the habitual drunkard to the weak and intermittent demand of the man who uses liquor somewhat as he uses olives or citron or malted milk. Third, the interest in personal freedom. There are always people in considerable numbers who want to do whatever others presume to say they ought not to do. This faction includes elements varying from hopeless moral perversity to highly developed moral refinement. Fourth, business interests not directly connected with the liquor traffic: belief that trade follows the bartender; desire to keep solid with the interests directly dependent upon the liquor traffic; competition with other towns that are said to draw away trade by favoring liquor sellers; etc. Fifth, political interests: desire to use the liquor interest for personal or party ends. Sixth, social interests. Friends are directly or indirectly interested in the liquor traffic, and influence must go in their favor, from the negative kind that allows hands to be tied and mouths closed, to the positive kind that manipulates influence of every sort to obstruct the operation of the law. Seventh, legitimate business interests.

This rough analysis of the situation shows that, instead of two simple factors, viz., law and lawlessness, we are really dealing with a strangely assorted collection of interests, awkwardly struggling to express themselves in theory and in practice. We are not arguing the question how to deal with the liquor traffic, and we are not implying an opinion one way or the other about prohibitory laws. We are simply showing that, whether we are dealing with one kind of a law or another, we may be very uncritical about the ultimate factors involved. The two facts in question, viz., the law and the violation, prove to be in reality the selfsame persons expressing different elements of their own interests. The father of the prohibitory policy has been known to plead with a judge not to pass sentence on a liquor-seller in accordance with his own law. The same persons who sustain the law also violate the law in some of the different degrees of violating and sustaining referred to above. The law on the one hand, and the violation on the other, are nothing but shadows, or apparitions, or accidents, except as they reflect the actual balance of interests present in the members of the community. The real problems involved are, first, to discover whether the law or the violation most nearly corresponds with the actual desires lodged in the persons; and, second, to devise ways and means of changing the balance of desires in the persons, in case immorality proves to be the community choice.

It is both a social and a sociological blunder to proceed as though the law were something precise, invariable, and absolute. The law is an approximate verbal expression of social choices which are mixed, variable, and accommodating in a very high degree. The law has no existence, as a real power outside of the continued choices of the community that gives it effect. In a very real and literal sense it is necessary to get the algebraic sum both of the law-abiding and of the law-violating interests, in order to know just what the psychological choice of the community, as distinguished from the formal law, really is.

This illustration has been carried out at such length because it is a kind of problem with which all of us are more or less in contact, and our ways of dealing with it frequently show practical disregard of the elementary significance of the operative interests concerned. The main point is that, for theoretical or practical dealing with concrete social problems, we need to be expert in detecting and in measuring the precise species of interests that combine to form the situation. To carry the illustration a little farther, some of the states in the American union agree to prohibit both intemperance and ignorance. In general, all of us, both communities and individuals, condemn both vices. We put our condemnation in the shape of laws regulating the liquor traffic, on the one hand, and laws establishing free and perhaps compulsory education, on the other hand. When we attempt to define intemperance and ignorance, however, we find that we have infinitely varied points of view, and that our desires are correspondingly varied. We consequently lend very different elements of meaning and force to the formal laws. Some of us think that intemperance begins only when a man gets physically violent, or fails to pay for the liquor he consumes; and that ignorance means inability to read and write. Others of us think that intemperance exists whenever fermented or alcoholic liquors are swallowed in any form or quantity, and that ignorance is lack of college education. Accordingly, the phenomena of the continued consumption of liquors, in spite of laws against intemperance, and of persistent non-consumption of school privileges, in spite of laws against ignorance, are equally and alike inevitable manifestations of the actual assortment of desires out of which the community life is composed. We repeat, then: The problem of changing the facts is the problem of transforming the interests (desires) that make the facts. Social efficiency, on the part of persons zealous to alter the facts, involves skill in discovering the actual character of the desires present, knowledge of the psychology of desires, and tact in the social pedagogy and politics and diplomacy which convert less into more social desires.

These statements imply all the reasons for the study of fundamental sociology. From first to last, our life is a web woven by our interests. *Sociology might be said to be the science of human interests and their workings under all conditions,* just as chemistry is sometimes defined as "the science of atoms and their behavior under all conditions." Man at his least is merely a grubbing and mating animal. He has developed no interests beyond those of grubbing and mating, or those tributary to grubbing and mating. Every civilization in the world today carries along a certain percentage of survivals of this order of interests, and societies still exist wholly on the level of these interests. On the other hand, some men develop such attenuated spiritual interests that they pay only perfunctory and grudging tribute to the body at all, and live in an atmosphere of unworldly contemplation. Between these extremes are the activities of infinitely composite society, moved by infinite diversities of interests. These interests, however, as we have seen, are variations and permutations of a few rudimentary interests. *Our knowledge of sociology, i.e., our systematized knowledge of the human process, will be measured by the extent of our ability to interpret all human society in terms of its effective interests.*

Appendix D

The Annual Phi Beta Kappa Address: The Social Value of the Academic Career (1906)*

If the world were governed by its wisdom instead of its selfishness would universities be promoted?

If public policy in every nation were settled by a Council of Elder Statesmen; if these men were placed in conditions which excluded gain or loss of wealth or position, and at the same time permitted gain of prestige by loyal devotion to public service; if the Elder Statesmen presided over a system of investigating commissions, charged and empowered to gather all accessible facts bearing upon questions of public policy; if they were the men best qualified by education and experience to pass competent judgments upon the findings; would they decide that a quota of men devoting their lives to academic careers is demanded by the interests of the nation?

An attempt to answer this question may seem to imply a claim to the Elder Statesmen's qualifications. To avoid the appearance of such presumption, let our answer not be dogmatic. Let us try to peer as far as we may into the sort of evidence which the Elder Statesmen might fairly be expected to consider. Let us bring into focus as much as we can of the horizon which their vision would survey.

Let us also at the outset be agreed about the words to be used. For our present purposes, let the word *university* stand for the activities whose aim is primarily to transmit any portion of the permanent knowledge which men have acquired, and also to increase the sum of permanent knowledge. The university is there-

* Delivered before the Beta of Illinois Chapter of Phi Beta Kappa in the Leon Mandel Assembly Hall on 11 June 1906. Printed in the *University of Chicago Record* 11 (1906).

fore present, in whole or in part, not only in the capacious institution which cherishes all the knowledges, from agriculture to metaphysics, but in its degree also in the detached school of mines, or physiological institute, devoted to a strictly limited range of investigation. For our purposes the university which is on trial must be distinguished from the not-university which we may call the *school*. In order to make the basis of distinction plain, we may contrast knowledge, the image that reality forms in our minds, with the sum of devices which the mind invents to make those images clear and available as mental equipment. Spoken language, written alphabets, multiplication tables, the rudiments of drawing, the elements of mechanics, the uses of simple tools, are knowledges to be sure; but when measured by the whole range of the knowable they are less knowledge than vehicles of knowledge, and keys to knowledge, and modes of applying knowledge. On the other hand, every manner of truth, independent of our attempts to represent it or reflect upon it, has a rank of its own, quite distinct from the mind's apparatus for learning or using the truth. As an absolute problem, the question whether the mind first gets knowledge or the apparatus of knowledge is of course very much like the scholastic problem of the priority of the chick or the egg. Practically, if we mean by "knowledge" any substantial part of mature mental acquirement, there is no choice, either for children or their teachers, whether we shall first acquire knowledge or the apparatus of knowledge. With the qualifications to be mentioned in a moment, it is virtually a decree of fate that we must first serve an apprenticeship acquiring the apparatus of knowledge before we can advance very far in the acquirement of knowledge itself. The *school* is that division of our educational machinery which is charged with superintending this novitiate. The *university*, for our present purposes, means that portion of our educational machinery which takes for granted the apparatus of knowledge and concentrates attention upon the substance of knowledge.

Let us not proceed without providing against misconceptions of these distinctions. We know, and we must presume that the Elder Statesmen would know much better, that these antitheses are not absolute but relative. In the last analysis, what goes on in the kindergarten differs only in degree from what goes on in the seminar, and the laboratory, and the academy of science. We cannot acquire the apparatus of knowledge without incidental acquisition of knowledge; and probably no gain of knowledge is entirely without effect upon our apparatus of knowledge. Measured, however, by the maturest knowledge in our possession, not to say by the range of knowledge which scholars are already trying to control, it is usually late, if ever, in the school career, that we cease to deal chiefly with the symbols and the forms of knowledge, and pass to principal dealing with the substance of knowledge.

The story of "The Boston Tea Party," for instance, may entertain a child in the nursery, before he has an inkling of those larger connections of the episode that led a maturer mind to say of a related incident: "The fate of a nation was riding that night." Some version of "The Boston Tea Party," with previous subsequent events, might be a part of that child's school curriculum for years. By means of this thought-material the child might gradually acquire elementary concepts of chronology, of geography, of government, of legal rights, of national rivalries, of military achievements, of political democracy; and at the same time he might advance many steps toward logical correlation of his ideas. Yet this boy might never arrive within sight of those precise problems of economic, legal, and moral relations implied by "The Boston Tea Party," which occupy the exploring frontier of the serious social sciences. That is, the boy might never grasp much more than the form and the symbol of the last knowledge that the incident suggests to the maturest minds. He might never suspect the essential relations that the event involved.

On the other hand, the knowledge that a Newton or a Darwin gains may presently alter the whole symbolism, or even the technique, of knowledge which schoolboys have to learn. While there is a sense, therefore, in which the child and the sage necessarily apply their minds to one and the same thing, I resort to this convenient distinction between relative limitation to symbols of knowledge, and relative dedication to the substance of knowledge; and I would apply the terms "school" and "university" so as to connote a contrast in the degree in which the program inclines in the one direction or the other. Furthermore, I use the phrase "academic career" as synonymous with partnership in university work as thus defined, and contrasted with school work.

Of course, we are thus dealing with shifting boundaries, and it is no part of my purpose to discuss the points where they should be drawn, or whether they should be drawn at all. Neither do I ask whether the school and the university should be parts of one organization, or independent organizations, or what *modus vivendi* should exist between them in either case. I raise none of the familiar pedagogical questions of methodology, either of school or university, or about transitions from one program to another. I do not even stop to inquire whether our Elder Statesmen would think there is any problem left, after it had been admitted that the truth which we begin to learn in the kindergarten has no ending till the maturest minds have exhausted their utmost powers of search. On this ground alone they might be willing, as I would, to rest the case for social promotion of the academic career. They might declare that the logic of the matter is conclusive. They might call attention to the fact that, long before the regime of the Elder Statesmen had arrived, one of the most crucial phenomena in history was an almost unstinted dedication of treasure by naïve democracies to the support of the people's schools. The Elder Statesmen might point out that by this policy those democracies logically committed themselves to promotion of the academic career. True, but it is a far cry from logic to appreciation, and thence to appropriate action. Our question then is virtually this: What perceptions of the worth of the university must pass current in the general mind in order that democracies may place fair appraisal on the academic career?

Unquestionably, the case would present itself to the Elder Statesmen from at least three points of view. They would ask: What role has the university played in civilization? Has it seen clearly when others' eyes were dim? Has it invariably had constructive convictions, and the courage of them?

Again, they would ask: How looks the university of our own time? Is it a parasite or a producer? Is it a pensioner on social privilege, or a purveyor to social needs? Is it living unto itself, or is it enriching the general life? Does it on the whole make the life-problem of the people at large harder or easier? Whatever its function, is it worth what it costs?

Then they would inquire about its promises and its prospects. Has the university reached the limit of its usefulness? Has it undeveloped resources? Can it do anything for society which cannot be done otherwise just as well?

Whether or not the case will be different when the Elder Statesmen actually come to ask the questions, no one may venture to predict. At present, we are bound to confess that a perfectly conclusive argument could not be made in favor of the university in answer to either question. Its record is not wholly without spot or blemish. Its character has not been uniformly consistent and creditable. Neither the Platonic Academy, nor the cloisters of the schoolmen, nor the lecture halls of modern Germany have served their day and generation without margin for reproach. The university of today is impeachable on more than one count. It is not even so well founded that it is certain to survive competition with other institutions already appropriating some of its functions. Yet these concessions are platitudes. They merely say that the university is a human institution, that it has shared the fortunes and fallibilities and uncertainties of all human institutions. The same confessions must be made for family, and school, and church, and state, with every minor human association. There is no absolute impeccable institution with which to compare the university. Our appraisal of it is necessarily a comparison of relative merit. Our question then is: As human institutions go, how must we rate the university in the scale of social values?

To answer such a question in favor of any institution, we must find that it has a distinctive function, that this function makes for the appreciation of life-values in general, and that no other institution offers equally credible promises of performing the function. With this understanding we may not hesitate to submit the case of the university, as it is made up of accomplished past, of active present, and of prospective future.

I shall not attempt to present any novel claims, but shall merely voice the judgments about which there is the least difference of opinion among university men. I shall argue the worth of the university for two main reasons. I do not mean that the whole merit of the university is expressed in these two details. I mean that these are real merits, and that they alone amply entitle the university to a first-rate place in social appraisal.

My formula of the first claim for the university will not be accepted off-hand. It has a decidedly strange appearance. The strangeness, however, is in the form rather than the content. I submit then, first, that *the university has the function of standardizing social measures of value.*

It will probably be a long time before the claim ceases to be urged that the primary function and the chief justification of the university is "mental discipline." There is doubtless a sense in which the conception is valid. It is quite as certain, however, that the meaning ordinarily carried in the conception has very precarious psychological sanction. So far as mere intellectual feats are concerned, whether of strength or of precision, it is by no means certain that the university ever has been foremost, or ever will be. There are a thousand occupations which cannot be pursued without developing a degree of mental alertness and responsibility that the typical college student does not attain. If we mean by mental discipline the habit of taking in all the significant facts of a situation, and of carrying on the action most appropriate to the situation, it is rank superstition to suppose that the university can monopolize such discipline. The university is presumably the best place in which to develop the habit of mind peculiarly appropriate to the academic career, but it is rather humorous pedantry to assume that this mental habit, considered strictly as an intellectual regimen, is of a higher order than the mental habit developed and exercised in the management of a factory or a railroad or a newspaper or a department store. Real mental discipline involves the complete series of mental processes from stimulus to volition, and not merely single volitions, but organized and correlated volitions. It is a part of the naïve provincialism of our educational tradition to assume that vicarious mental discipline is possible. No man ever became a convincing speaker or writer merely by studying language, or merely by practicing composition. One becomes expert in using language by confronting occasions that call for thought and by learning first to do the appropriate thinking, then to control the words that adequately express the thinking. No one ever became a competent navigator merely by studying navigation, nor a lawyer by studying law, nor a financier by studying political economy, nor a chemist by studying chemistry, nor a physician by studying medicine. I mean in each case that the merely academic discipline in the subject is after all only a fraction of the experience necessary in order that abstract thinking may take its place as a competent factor in complete mental habit. The decisive mental discipline in either case comes in the course of practicing the subject, not in the mere preliminary of thinking about it. We can, consequently, maintain that the university stands in a class by itself as a promoter of mental discipline, only by putting an utterly arbitrary valuation upon certain factors of mental habit.

Not thought alone, but thought in its whole functioning with life, is the proper measure of mental discipline. As merely approximate illustrative statements, it is quite possible that one might acquire more real linguistic discipline by a month as a newspaper reporter or proof reader than by a year studying language; more practical judgment of financial relations by a month as a bank clerk than by a year as a student of economics; more steadiness of social perspective, and reliability of sociological judgment, by a month in a charity organization society than by a year studying sociology. If it is merely a matter of mental discipline, in a defensible sense of that term, the activity in which the mental habit is exercised is a drill-master immeasurably more efficient than any indirect stimulus of mental action.

What then becomes of the traditional claim for college education on the ground of mental discipline?

My answer is that the claim is a mistaken rendering of the facts. The university is only one among many centers in which mental action is developed to high degrees of precision and power. There is no way to prove that the mental habit formed in the university is superior, either in precision or in power, to the intellectual processes exercised in many other pursuits. I would even go so far as to say that, up to the time of assuming the responsibilities of instruction, the typical mental habit in the academic career suffers, in point of accuracy and reliability, when compared with that of coordinate mental types in business careers. The value of the academic career, so far, is not because of superiority in mental discipline, but in spite of certain inferiorities in that respect.

We may return, then, to our proposition that the primary service of the university is its contribution to the standardizing of social values. I mean that the university systematically directs the mind away from vulgar centers of attention. It thereby enlarges the range of interests with reference to which judgments of value are formed. By so doing, the university discredits provincial standards of value, and proposes standards which do justice to all the interests of life.

The typical situations of "practical" life are suggested by the questions: How can I accomplish the day's task? How can I turn out my tale of work? How may I solve my problem? How may I win my case? How may I cure my patient? How may I make my profits? How may I promote my special scheme? How may I reach my particular kind of results? Since the bulk of life necessarily consists of asking and answering these questions, is there any use in trying to turn attention in other directions? These questions tend to make us all believe that our particular purposes are the supremely important purposes; that the means tributary to the purposes share the value of the purposes themselves; that, therefore, the means are virtually as important as the ends; and, consequently, that beyond these means and ends life contains nothing of first-rate value. All this tends to make life mechanical, and in proportion as our tasks are bound to the primary needs we tend to become virtually not only mechanical but materialistic.

But life is not alone a mechanical grinding out of tasks. Life is only rudimentary until it begins to be a mental possession and control of mechanical achievement, and a moral appraisal and assortment of purposes according to some valid standard of value. Life consists not merely of doing our work, but of thinking our work, of thinking about it, and through it, and around it, and over to other men's work, in comparing and contrasting kinds of work, in finding what work is most worth doing and why it is worthier than other work, and in aiming to reduce the ratio of less worthy work for the sake of enlarging scope for worthier work.

Life cannot pass into this phase, or even remain in it if the transition has once been accomplished, unless all men for a part of their time, or some men for all of their time, adjourn the kind of work that brings visible results and give themselves to thinking, which at first produces no visible results. We must get some sense of the perspective of life. We must get some inklings of the goings forward in nature and in society that have made the setting for our part of the life-drama. We must in some measure locate ourselves in the stream of time, in the cosmic process, and in the human process. We must think about what other men have done, whether well or ill. We must learn to understand it. We must discover its meanings. We must place it in a scale of comparative values. We must learn from other men's work that the purposes among which it is possible to choose are of many sorts; that they are not of equal worth; that some results are not worth getting because they exclude the getting of better results; that other results are supremely worth striving for, because even the endeavor insures the enlargement of life.

Now the university, like all other human institutions, is not fully here. It is a becoming. It has not realized itself. It is finding itself in feeling its way along toward its competent function. Yet, in its groping, experimental, unconscious fashion, the university has always been, first, a place for survey and analysis and appraisal of past human achievements, for judgment of their quality, and for reflection upon the conclusions they enforce about the direction of future purposes.

This is the real meaning of the Delphic phrase "liberal culture." In contrast with mere technical training—and I do not raise the question whether liberal culture and technical training are mutually exclusive terms; I am now contrasting the merely technical with the evaluating phrases of a mental process which may contain both elements in varying degrees—in antithesis, then, with the technical aspect of mental experience liberal culture is that gift of the university which releases men from the gearing of routine, and admits them to the freedom of sentiment, of preference, and of judgment. It transforms life from an autocracy of will into a constitutional empire of will enthroned upon reason.

The vast majority of men never analyze back of the question: How may I do the thing I am resolved to do? How shall I till my soil, or make my bargain, or please my friend, or hurt my enemy? The first task of the university is to create the habit of asking: How shall I go about to decide what is worth resolving to do? In a world of physical cause and effect how fully may I become acquainted with the laws of cause and effect? In a world of human motive, how far may I look into the sources and tendencies of human motive? In a world of undeveloped material resource, and of unfulfilled moral destiny, how far may I see ahead into the rational direction of human effort? In the large perspective of past, present, and future, what modulation of my own individual thought and will must I adopt, in view of the whole system of thoughts and wills in which my moral processes have a part?

The university is of value to society, first, because it is the peculiar home of these questions. In its program the prime consideration is not the processes of life, but the meanings and proportions of the purposes which the processes serve. The university is a sort of board of arbitration sitting in judgment upon the claims of conflicting human interests. The university is only secondarily concerned with the question: How may we do the things that we want to do? The primary inquiry of the university is: How may we decide what we should want to do? Whether we have in mind the mediaeval trivium or quadrivium, or the array of electives offered by a modern university, the motive that distinguishes the university is the purpose to use each and all of these knowledges to form habits of distinguishing the true from the false, reality from illusion, essentials from accidents, the permanent from the transient, the more important from the less important, the end from the means.

In pursuance of this primary aim the university is perforce a corrective of all excesses on the side of individual interests. The university always tends to measure values in terms of all things rather than of some things, of all men rather than of some men. The multiple standard of value which the university adopts is never in principle arbitrary. It is never presumed to be complete so long as a factor of human conditions is omitted which might help in appraising other factors or the whole human situation.

Now, it is not necessary to prove that the university has always had a correct view of life, nor even that the university has always been nearer to an adequate view of life than other leaders of thought and action. The main point is that the university has always stood for the attempt to reach ultimate appraisals of life-values, while the majority of men have pursued their several ways, assuming that their special interests were sufficient sponsors unto themselves. The university has always tried to bring all these eccentric interests under judgment by some common standard. When the nations have been entangled in wars, the universities have thought not merely of war, but of rights and justice and peace. When the majority have been absorbed by material concerns, the universities have cultivated the goods of the mind. When spiritual interests have been controlled by superstition, the universities have fought the battles of enlightenment. Even when the universities have been wrong in detail, they have been salutary in principle, they have stood for the value of the unseen, as against the obsession of the apparent. Even though the rendering of life for which they contended was mistaken, it always contained something which proved to be not the least useful reagent among the forces of the time. Among all the centrifugal policies that confused society the university has been the one institution which has stood for the contrasted program of so investigating all reality that it would reveal and sanction a centered and concentering version of life.

We may accordingly submit this side of our case to the Council of Elder Statesmen. Since the individual and the technical standard of value always has the preference with naïve men, social adjustments are much more difficult than they need be, until full scope is assured to the academic career. The university brings to consciousness the implicit demand of society for a common standard of value. The university establishes a tradition of surveying life from a standpoint outside the immediate interests of the individual. The university takes the lead in adopting a meridian line indicated not by special interests but by the purposes and destinies of all men.

I have no misgivings about the judgment of the Elder Statesmen upon this claim. To test our faith, however, they might raise this objection: "Does not the brief which you submit for the university prove too much? If the claim is admitted, does it not make the university supersede the church? Is not all this business of correcting standards of value the essential function of the church? Are not church and university natural competitors? That one may increase must not the other decrease?

Instead of feeling a temptation to take up the gauntlet thrown down for the church in defiance of the university, it would be much more in accord with my sympathies if I should turn aside from the course of my argument to plead the cause of the church as earnestly as I contend for the university. Happily it is not necessary in this case to magnify one social institution at the expense of another. If we were to discuss the supposed objection in detail, the key to the rejoinder would be that the apparently common function of church and university is easily resolved into variety of functions. When church and university function at their best, neither will displace the other, but each will reinforce the other. In a word, while the prime function of the university is discovery and justification of ultimate standards of value, the prime function of the church is maintenance of influences that impress the importance and authority of ultimate standards, and that exert constant moral pressure toward practical application of the standards. Neither university nor church can perform its utmost social service without complementary services of the other. The Elder Statesmen would not need to be convinced, for instance, that the political iconoclasts of France, whose correction of the church has tended toward destruction of the church, have thereby embarrassed the progress of the state. While abating much unnecessary evil, they have arrested much necessary good. Some day saner Frenchmen must repair the damage at heavy cost.

Let us suggest the whole scope of our reply by a somewhat obvious analogy. I confess to such ignorance of music that an orchestra concert is to me hardly more intelligible than a drama in an unknown tongue. My attention always wanders far afield. Often, for instance, during the program I have occupied myself with the problem: Why does an orchestra need a conductor? If he is not himself a player, is he not superfluous? Each member of the orchestra is an artist in his own right. Each is supplied with the part of the score which indicates the contribution required of his instrument. Each is presumably competent to render his own part precisely as it is written. All these parts fit as accurately into one another as the interchangeable wheels of a standard watch. Why could not these artists simply "follow copy" and produce the same results without the intervention of a conductor?

The answer to the query is found in very elementary sections of psychology and sociology. Like the rest of mankind, musicians are not machines. They are nervous organisms. They are temperaments. They are sensitive and varying moods. They are personal equations. They are functions of factors which do not affect all equally at a given time. If they should rely upon their own initiative, their attempts to adjust themselves to each other would certainly degenerate into bathos if not chaos. There is need of a common emotional stimulus, a reduction of the individual tone and rate of reaction to terms of a single denominator, in order that the music, which is a unified expression of the composer, may have a unified rendering by the orchestra. This, then, is the factor furnished by the conductor.

Though religion and education are alike in having their location primarily in the individual, yet there must always remain a ranking social function for religion which relates it to education somewhat as the conductor of an orchestra is related to the training that makes artists with the separate instruments.

I have left myself little time to speak of the second count in favor of the university. I have done so, not because it is less important, but because among us it is more familiar. I now remark that *the cardinal function of the university is more than the standardizing of values; it is the discovery of new values.*

The world's working presumptions are overwhelmingly static, not dynamic. Everything that we call knowledge, or belief, or custom, or rule, or law, or institution, is not merely an accomplished achievement; to a certain extent it is prohibition of further achievement in the same line. It is not merely an assertion of what is; it is a dogma of what must continue to be. Every vested interest, whether material or spiritual, is a claimant to finality in its premises. Its word goes out to the rest of the world: "Change how you will. As for me, I am here to stay. As I am, so I should be and so I will be." The burden of proof rests hard upon the dynamic innovator. He must fight for his interests or his convictions, and he must fight against the strong entrenchments of established order.

No human institution, therefore, can reconstruct itself wholly from within. This is one reason why the church alone cannot save the world. The church is a purveyor of spiritual values, but it is a factor both of the strength and the weakness of the church that it must needs presume its own values to be final. The logic of life, on the contrary, proves that there is no value known to men so pure that it may not turn out to contain alloy. No truth is absolutely safe from admixture of error. No institution is assured that, whether in its original ideas or in outliving its adaptations, it is not perpetuating mistaken judgments.

While, therefore, the naïve presumption of most men is frankly and obstinately static, the verdict of life as a whole, the ultimate arbiter of all presumptions, is that the decisive principle of life is dynamic. The essence of the human lot is not instability, still less confusion; but it certainly is a function of movement, reconsideration, revision, readjustment, readaptation. While it is the typical impulse of each distinct interest to insist upon its own finality, life as a whole demands persistent search for new knowledge that may cause reappraisal of old values. Society cannot afford to leave a function as important as this to accident or unorganized impulse. The university is the one human institution pledged in principle to serve the world by continually testing the possibility that conventional presumptions may be wrong. The university is the organization of the world's constructive doubt. The university is criticism perpetually mobilized in the service of faith. The university is the sworn detector of untenable beliefs in the interest of ultimate belief.

When the Phi Beta Kappa society was founded, there was no such sharp distinction as I have drawn between these two leading functions of the university. Scholarship still meant, very largely, thinking the things that others had thought, because they had thought them. Scholarship means today, very largely, thinking things that others have not thought, although they have not thought them.

Moreover, the university cannot yet appeal its case to such a

Council of Elder Statesmen as I have imagined. The university is making its record before a world that is unconvinced and unconvincible by any arts of verbal persuasion. The world's appraisal of the university will depend at last upon the success with which scholars of the modern type commend higher values in place of lower values, and substitute larger truth for lesser truth.

I have not asked the question: *Can the individual afford to pursue the academic career?* If the question were to be raised, I for one would phrase it in this form: *Can a man free to choose afford not to pursue the academic career?* But this confession of pride in a glorious vocation might seem inconsistent with the argument I have urged. I have not contended, however, for appraisal of the university upon any exceptional grounds. I have not argued that it is the one social institution of importance. I have not asked for it a place of higher honor than the farm, or the shop, or the market, or the court, or the church. Such comparisons are not in question, and scholars should of all men be content to let such appraisals take care of themselves. I have asked: "Does the university serve a real human need? Is there a social function for the scholar? Does society have a use for the academic career?" If so, irrespective of the relative esteem in which other institutions should be held, the university must constantly gain recognition as socially indispensable. Popular judgment must tend to correspond with the presumed opinion of the Elder Statesmen.

Meanwhile, in the degree in which wisdom instead of impulse controls social policy, the attitude of society will be represented more and more, not by the question, How may we confine the demands of the university within the narrowest limits? but, How may we make the university the most effective instrument of social service? The importance of the academic career to society, not the personal wishes of persons pursuing the academic career, will and should determine the scale upon which universities shall be promoted.

In proportion as we actually believe that abundance of life means progressive appropriation of spiritual values; in the ratio of our working faith that truth makes free; it will become a cardinal point of social policy to mobilize the university to the limit of its possible effectiveness. I merely mention three necessary items in this program.

In the first place, social interest demands that the academic career be made attractive to men whose intellectual initiative is of the highest order. When our views of life are so rectified that we rate the work of the university, not as a luxury, but as a social necessity; when we realize that the work of the university determines the depth and breadth of the spiritual foundations of society; we shall be convinced that no men are of so large mental caliber that their powers would be wasted in the academic career.

In the second place, in order to command the services of the best type of men for the university, a minimum condition is that their positions shall be made absolutely secure. I am not referring to the popular myth that university professors are liable to martyrdom for their opinions. So far as my knowledge goes, universities in modern times have to their charge many more sins of tolerance than of intolerance. I am not acquainted with any responsible calling in which questionable mental or even moral fitness gets the benefit of more generous doubt than that which hedges university professors. I mean that in order to command the services of enough men of the type needed for the best quality of university work, a standard of life must be assured which will permit university men to appropriate their share of the spiritual values which they are making known to others. The university career is inconsistent with material luxury. The man who dedicates himself to spiritual aims should reconsider his sincerity of purpose if he finds himself envying the rich. He is not supposed to want his wages chiefly in material goods. Nevertheless he knows that the laborer is worthy of his hire. He knows that his work is of more real benefit to society than many of the occupations by which men get great wealth. He has no quarrel with unequal distribution of material goods, but he does resent the injustice if his kind of work cannot command sufficient recognition to provide for himself and his family a secure basis for those spiritual goods which he values more than wealth. Society cannot in the long run secure enough of the type of men who might serve it best in the university, unless the material rewards of the academic career are sufficient to insure the modest comfort of the family, the education of children according to the highest academic standards, and adequate provision for declining years.

It is betrayal of a professional secret, but it must be confessed that the condition just mentioned, though logically and ethically fundamental, is in practice secondary to the last condition that I shall name. The university man would in the end do his work for society more thoroughly if he were more insistent upon his personal rights. In actual practice the consideration that is more effective than all others in attracting the right men into the university career, and in holding them there when they are tempted toward other occupations, is *adequate facilities for investigation.* The typical university man is aware of unsolved problems. He is conscious of power to increase knowledge. He asks nothing better than use of the necessary tools of his profession. If his hands may be free, if his time may be sacred to his task, if the material may be supplied for his research, nine times out of ten he will persistently sacrifice himself and his family for the sake of his specialist's part in the world's work. The Council of Elder Statesmen will doubtless calculate social programs in terms of human welfare instead of material wealth. They, if not their predecessors, will stop some of the waste in the present apportionment of capital between production of commodities and promotion of knowledge.

In closing, may I venture to speak a word in the name of the university, not merely to younger scholars, but to all scholars? Let it be this:

Carry your scholarship, not as your defense against the world, but as your investment in the world. Pursue your scholarship, not as seclusion from life, but as dedication to life. Value your scholarship, not chiefly for its enrichment of yourself, but for its contribution to human service.

Appendix E

An autobiographical letter by Small (1915)*

THE UNIVERSITY OF CHICAGO

THE GRADUATE SCHOOL OF ARTS AND LITERATURE

May 26, 1915

Rev. M. F. Johnson,
   Rock, Mass.
My dear Classmate:
   Your note of the 18th arrived while I was on a rapid trip to Baltimore and New York.

   I am very sorry that it will be impossible for me to be with the Class on June 8th. I should certainly be of the number if it were within my power.

   As you request, I sketch my antecedents and history as follows:

   My father, Albion Keith Parris Small, was born in Limington, Maine, Aug. 26, 1821. His father died when the boy was only four years old and the latter was apprenticed as a farmer's boy to an uncle until he was twenty-one years of age. He learned the occupations of farmer, tanner, shoemaker, etc. on a typical Maine farm of the period. When he came of age my father immediately declared his independence and started to earn his way through preparatory school and college. He succeeded in graduating at Waterville College in 1849 and became principal of Hebron Academy for a short period. He entered Newton Theological Institution probably in the fall of 1851. After remaining one year only he was made to believe by the man who was at the time bishop [sic] of the Maine Baptist churches, Rev. Adam Wilson, that he was a Jonah running away from his duty if he wasted any more time on the frivolities of book

   * Reprinted with the permission of Andover-Newton Theological Seminary and with thanks to the cooperation of Ellis O'Neal, Andover-Newton librarian.

learning, and he accepted the pastorate of a vacancy in Buckfield, Maine, where the denominational leaders of the state desired to create a church. The young man was at first pastor, sexton, choir leader, deacon, Sunday school superintendent, and with the exception of his wife, the total church membership. After half a dozen years, however, in which in addition to the performing of the above functions, he had secured subsistence for himself and wife, and presently for the first child, by cultivating a piece of land, he was called to the First Baptist Church in Bangor, Maine. Meanwhile he had succeeded, largely by the labors of his own hands, in completing and paying for a respectable house of worship, and a church which has since proved self-sustaining had been organized. He had gained good repute, not merely in the town but in Oxford County, as has been testified to the writer by a large number of persons who have since given a good account of themselves in the world, and have attributed to his influence some portion of the stimulus which spurred them to the attempt to make something of themselves.

He was pastor of the First Baptist Church in Bangor from 1858–1868, and was credited with being one of the most useful men in the city in creating the spirit which furnished more than its quota of recruits for the Civil War. He was elected chaplain of several Maine regiments, but was requested by the mayor of the city to continue his work at home for the reason that it was thought on all sides that he could be of more service there than at the front. He was for a short time a representative of the Christian Commission in the army of the Potomac. For the six years following 1868 he was pastor of the Free Street Baptist Church in Portland, Me. From '74 to '84 he was pastor of the First Baptist Church in Fall River, Massachusetts. From '84 to '94 he was pastor of the First Baptist Church, Portland Me. Then for a short period he served the church in Fairfield, Maine, and for another short period the Biddeford Church. He died in Portland, Maine, just before completing his eighty-eighth year.

My mother was Thankful Lincoln Woodbury of Cornish, Maine. Her ancestors on one side were a branch of the Hingham Lincolns, her grandfather having been a sailor and a soldier in the Revolutionary War. She is still living in Newton Center, Massachusetts in her ninety-third year.

My early schooling was in the public schools of Bangor, Maine, until I was fourteen; in the high school of Portland, Maine, from fourteen to eighteen. In Waterville College, then Colby University, received my bachelor's degree in 1876; graduated at Newton 1879. Studied in the University of Berlin '79-'80, and in Leipzig and the British Museum '80-'81; was elected Professor of History and Political Economy at Colby University during this study period and began work September, 1881. Was allowed leave of absence during the year 1888-89 and spent the time at Johns Hopkins University where I was at the same time giving one course in American Constitutional History, and received the degree of Ph.D. in 1889. At that time the unique honor of an invitation to make an address at the ceremony of the conferring of the degrees came to me. So far as I know, this distinction has never before, or since, been conferred upon a candidate for the doctor's degree at Johns Hopkins. During the summer of 1889 I was elected the successor of Dr. Pepper on his recommendation, as President of Colby. In the winter of 1891-1892 I was invited by Dr. Harper to become one of the original heads of departments in the projected University of Chicago, and resigned the following June to accept the position. Since October 1892 have been head of the department of Sociology. Since 1895, editor of the American Journal of Sociology, and since 1905, dean of the Graduate School of Arts and Literature. In 1881, married in Berlin, Valeria Von Massow, whose paternal ancestors were members of the Prussian landed gentry and for several generations officers in the Prussian army. We have only one child, a daughter, born May 16, 1882. She married Hayden B. Harris of Chicago in 1906 and has three boys, 6, 3, and 1 year of age respectively. In May 1872 joined the Free Street Baptist Church of Portland, Maine.

"The notable features of my life and work" are of the quiet sort which are recorded in the bibliography that stands against my name. The chief titles are in *Who's Who*. If I should compress into a sentence what seems to me to be the scientific significance of my life, it is that I have been trying to do my part toward shunting the thinking of social scientists from the side track of individualistic and statical interpretation of life onto the main line of functional interpretation. This, I assume, is rather cryptic, but I take the risk of being counted in the future among those who helped to bring about the transition in thought which will be traced back in its beginnings, at any rate, to our generation.

As to my "ideals and purposes for life," I do not know that there is any way of expressing them by which I would rather be judged than in the sermon delivered in a Sunday evening series, July, 1914, a copy of which I send herewith.

All of the above except the introductory paragraph has of course been dictated for you in your official secretarial and historical capacity. I wish more than I was conscious of wishing when I started out, that I might have the opportunity to be in personal exchange of reminiscences and purposes which the narrowing circle of our class will stimulate at the meeting. I might add that I was last Sunday at Union Church in Pelham Manor, N.Y., near my daughter's residence, and had the pleasure of seeing my oldest grandson, aged six, receive a Bible as a prize for having been present at every session of the Sunday school for the school year closing that day. He has promised to have his younger brother with him during the sessions of the coming year.

I want to greet through you every member of the class who will be present.

Sincerely,
Albion W. Small

Appendix F

"Some Researches into Research" (1924)*

In plain English, research, at its lowest terms is merely trying to find out things. Whatever I may say more will be an expansion of the commonplace that there are innumerable varieties of research. From the most simple to the most subtle they have this one common trait, that they are attempts to find out things.

Without affecting precise classification, but using the handiest labels, I will cite a few samples.

There is first *Naïve Research*. All research at its best is only glorified childish curiosity, whether of the race or of the individual. How do things look, feel, smell, taste; how are things put together; how are things seen; what are things good for; who are people? who can lick who? etc., etc. Such as these are the takeoffs in the Marathon of science. They are of the same initial kind with the researches that lead to globe-circling through the air, to weighing the heavenly bodies, to discovering a new star or new dimensions of an old one. They are all alike attempts to pass from not-knowing to knowing: Franklin with his kite and key; "Theodore Roosevelt . . .[illegible]"; the early anthropologist collecting curios, etc., etc.

There is second, at a solemnified extreme, *Socratic or Dialectical*

* This was an informal address to the Research Society—connected with the Department of Sociology in the University of Chicago. A long introduction has been omitted. In view of his approaching retirement, the speaker was strongly affected by the prospect that he would not again have a conference with an equal number of graduate students. His remarks were accordingly addressed to them, not to his colleagues in the Faculty, and were in the nature of paternal suggestions rather than didactic formulas. With the consent of the editors, the colloquial form has been retained. A. W. S. [Albion W. Small papers, Box 2, Folder 12, in the Department of Special Collections, University of Chicago Library. Reprinted with permission.]

Research. In this class belong all attempts to find out things outside the mind by deriving them from relations traced between previously formed conceptions of things inside the mind. Whether we analyze the world in terms of our preconceived conception of "virtue," or whether we appraise manners and customs according to their treatment of our codes about claret or ice water, or sex, the process is essentially one—an attempt to establish eternal absolutes by the test of home-made absolutes. Orientals and Occidentals, Germans, Frenchmen, Englishmen, Americans, each size up the other by the measure of previously adopted notions, each of himself and of the other. A friend of mine has recently been interviewing the high financiers of Paris and Berlin. He writes that in Berlin he hears from the bankers precisely the same charges against the French which he had just heard in Paris against the Germans. In each case, too, those charges will stand as finalities until Providence provides a different research method. Meanwhile, each nation will fail to understand the other. I have a delicious acquaintance, who affords me unfailing diversion, largely because he tells people behind my back that I have *no religion*. That is his inference from my telling him to his face that I have no use for his theology! He reminds me of returned missionaries whom in my childhood I used to hear reporting their adventures among people whom they described as having no religion!* We know now that such reports were merely recitations of preconceptions which inhibited conversion of observed facts into knowledge. Yet for a long time [illegible] dated social science was comprised out of such pseudo-evidence.

There is, third, *Pedantic Research*, the expenditure of enviable ingenuity upon things that don't matter. Among the men whom I heard four or five times a week each, during my first semester in Berlin, was Professor Zeller, reputed at that time to be the foremost historian of philosophy in Europe. His subject was *The Pre-Platonic Systems*. After I had learned enough of the language to know what the lecturer was talking about, I found one Monday morning, that he had introduced the problem, When was Plato born? Hour after hour he [illegible] all the gear of archaeology, chronology, astron-

---

* At about this point in the typed manuscript there is the following handwritten addendum, with no clear indication of where it is supposed to be inserted: "In each case the things alleged are declared to be distinctions [distinctive?] and exceptional characteristics of the other nation."

omy, history, philology, folk lore and heaven knows what not, to make a case for the date 429, or 428, or 430. After he had consumed the lecture hours of an entire week, he arrived at the conclusion— nobody knows, and it wouldn't make any difference if they did! This was research after its sort, but it was a sort that falls short of infamy only by affording an awful example of the abuses that are possible under a dignified name.

I mention, third [sic], *Partisan Research*, a variety of the second species [illegible handwritten insertion]. Indeed there are only two families of research, the subjective and the objective: but the family likeness is not always the most ready finding mark.

Partisan research assumes some supposedly indisputable standard for measuring the conduct of the people concerned, and justifies or condemns them by that test alone.

The instance of partisan research that comes most frequently to my mind and serves to illustrate all the rest, is that of my former colleague Von Holst in writing his *Constitutional History of the United States*. Von Holst assumed the role of interpretor of Americans to themselves. He came from Germany into a political atmosphere which he did not understand, and he made the capital mistake, for a scholar, of adopting a partisan doctrine as key to the interpretation, instead of suspending judgment until he had made a demonstrative canvas of the facts.

In 1830 the issue which had been slurred over in 1789, in order to make any constitution at all possible for the former British colonies, was forcing its way toward a decision. It was the question whether the American states were many or one, or if both many and one, whether finally and decisively many or one. Opinions upon this matter at the outset were not divided along the lines of parallels of latitude, but events were tending to align the northern states in support of the union idea, and the southern states in assertion of state sovereignty. The textbook on *American Constitutional Law* that I studied in college elaborated the proposition that the Declaration of Independence *created a sovereignty* over the thirteen colonies previously subject to the sovereignty of England. The first piece of research that I ever undertook was the task of investigating the records of the colonial and continental congresses in 1775 and 1776, together with the records of the constitutional conventions from 1787 to 1789, to see whether that version of American sovereignty had historical support. My problem was, Did anybody ever claim or exercise any intercolonial sovereign rights in America between July 4, '76 and the adoption of your [our?] present constitution in 1789? (except [illegible] single contemporary document amend earlier than the violent partisan arguments [illegible] began in 1830). Incidentally I discovered that there was not a trace in Von Holst's volumes of any such appeal to the records [illegible]. In the preliminary skirmish in that year, 1830, Senator Hayne of South Carolina maintained the states-rights view, and Daniel Webster of Massachusetts in a speech which became famous, crystallized the doctrine of national sovereignty. Although I had been taught the Websterian doctrine along with the Lord's Prayer and the Ten Commandments [illegible insert], my studies into the documents proved that neither Hayne nor Webster had given a completely objective account of the facts; but that as a statement of occurrences Hayne's version was much nearer the reality than Webster's. The latter formulated the north's partisanship for effective mobilization in the Civil War, but it was a historical fiction. The point of the illustration is that, instead of conducting the necessary process of research, Von Holst waived all that; treated the pertinent historical evidence as negligible; swallowed the Websterian doctrine without testing its credentials; and made a series of volumes which purported to be history, but which merely peddled the Websterian partisanship; which branded every attitude and act of the south in accordance with its view as treason; and which glorified every act of the north in accordance with its view as patriotism [illegible handwritten insertion].

In reality, from 1775 to the close of the Civil War we were slowly evolving a nationality which had been meanwhile merely an unlegitimized vision of a portion of our people. From 1830 to the reconstruction period our political reasoning, particularly in the north, if it could be called research at all, was mostly snap-judgment research, which got its force not from facts but from reiteration. Such facts as it did assemble were marked in advance for a death sentence or a halo. This pseudo-research not merely beclouded and distorted the past, but it added insult to injury by reciprocal misrepresentation.

A fifth type of attempt to find out things, I will call *Pickwickean* or *Curio-hunting Research*. From the beginning, it has occupied the time of more so-called historians than any other. It is the sort of historical puttering that is like nothing so much as the proverbial hen clucking over her one chicken. It is historical rag picking, fussing around after finds that mean nothing. Local histories are mostly composed of nothing else than this flotsam and jetsam— whether Washington took command of the Continental Army under this particular elm in Cambridge or that particular elm, or some other kind of tree, or no tree at all; whether Lafayette was entertained in this house, or that, or none now standing; whether Benedict Arnold camped on the right or the left bank of the Kennebec at a particular halt in his Quebec expedition; whether the president of the southern Confederacy died on a plantation or in New Orleans, etc., etc. Most researches into genealogy are of this type. Possibly they may show that such and such a person is eligible for membership in the Daughters of the American Revolution, or the Colonial Dames, or the Society of the Cincinnati: but beyond such catering to private and petty sentiment they are worthless.

I should not have expanded these illustrations at such length, if it were not for the fact that I have reviewed very few pieces of research in my life which were not vitiated *in some degree* by the worm-eatings of one or more of these spurious types of research. A part of the necessary equipment of a scholar is ability to detect these perversions in others and to check them in himself.

I shorten the possible list and pass, sixth, to the first genuine type of research that I will mention, namely the kind of *Practice Research* that leads to a respectable Doctor's Dissertation.

The essentials of genuine practice research are, first, *a problem*, something not known, to be found out; second, *a method, a technique*, a means adequate to the end, a procedure which appears to be a feasible way of arriving at the something not previously known.

Probably no type of research has provoked more ridicule than the practice type, since Johns Hopkins imported it as an academic institution from Germany in 1876. Nobody competent to understand the meaning and the value of the institution has ever ridiculed it, except in his lighter moments, when he has allowed himself to toy with things sacred.

The graduate students' practice research as a condition of promotion to the Doctor's degree, need not necessarily propose the most exigent problem within that part of the field of knowledge to which he is devoted. It need not necessarily ask and try to answer a question of the first importance. The main thing is that the researcher shall apply means adapted to the end and adequate to the end. The experience of gripping the appropriate tools, and of turning out a workmanlike job, is both an evidence of good faith and a promise of more important work after the apprentice period is closed.

I have thus referred to five types of research which should be left as soon as possible among cast-off childish things and a single type of real research which still necessarily exhibits more academic limitations than may be allowed to cling around research of the highest rank. I will not try to indicate the countless types of research that recur between this first grade in the scale of genuine scientific research and the highest grade that may be reached. What I have been elaborating in all that I have said is the commonplace that there are innumerable varieties of research. Research differs from research as one star differs from another star in glory. While I am in the paraphrasing mood, I may as well add another adaptation of apostolic idiom, viz:—one genuine type of research may not say to a less esteemed but also genuine research, I have no need of thee. Those kinds of research which seem to be more feeble are necessary. Wherefore look to it that they receive their due share of honor.

I simply remind you that the ideal of science is the kind of research which aims to shed light upon permanent or recurrent aspects of reality; or within the social field, research which tries to find out things that are to have long leases of influence upon human relations.

If I may trust my own impressions—in the absence of precise statistics—the largest number of genuine research sociologists today are at work upon problems of the *survey* type. Next in number come the *social psychologists*. Then, among the also-ran, are the few, among whom I belong, the methodologists or general sociologists.

Although the general sociologists at present affect the majority as archaeological specimens, in comparison with the up-to-date social surveyors and social psychologists, yet the general theorists will be necessary, and I have no doubt will continue to be necessary, although in relatively small numbers. I will not put up a defense or apology for them, nor try to make it appear that they are the kind of shock troops most needed in the present state of the campaign. I know they are not, but I believe they still have an indispensable function.

I will remind you, further, that at its best research is an abortion, even if it actually finds out things, unless it links itself up with a technique and a philosophy which put the discovered things together so that they will yield the most meaning.

I do not know who first made the familiar remark that "there is nothing so misleading as a fact." This truism has given Professor Park one of his favorite subjects for discourse and analysis, viz:— What is a fact? Every person who takes upon himself the responsibility of a researcher should endeavor to assure himself about the answer to that question.

As a single illustration of the ambiguity of an occurrence supposed to be a fact, I take a pending instance, or pending when this paper was first read. When Hiram Johnson's candidacy for the presidential nomination was announced, it was stated that former Postmaster General Frank Hitchcock, one of the most stalwart of the stalwarts in the national Republican organization, was to manage the Johnson campaign. Nothing could be much more definite, precise, positive and concrete—Hitchcock is the Johnson campaign manager. That is supposed to be a fact, but is it, or is it only a protruding angle of a fact, the whole of which does not appear? Apparently some more of the fact is that there is a break in the Republican ranks. One of the leaders is backing a man who is running contrary to most of the leaders' wishes.

I have no inside information about the case, but from the first announcement I have had a very confident theory or guess, to this effect:—The fact is that there is no break in the Republican organization—at least not along the supposed line. Hitchcock is not a rebel. He is not backing Johnson to win. Johnson is not even running. Whether he knew it himself before the delegates were chosen, my theory does not attempt to decide. My guess is that Hitchcock is using Johnson as a decoy to lead somebody else out of the running, and Hitchcock is serving his party instead of fighting it.

Whether my guess is correct or not is non-essential to my argument. Even if the illustration were wholly fictitious it would picture reality. The matter in hand is that, even in the case of what seems to be a most unequivocal social fact, there is always plenty of room to apply a technique of interpretation which may connect the particular item with all its hidden relations, and give it a significance precisely contrary to its ostensible meaning.

The lawyers have a saying, apropos of the Ranke type of historical credulity, that "there is nothing so misleading as a document." A document is apparently a *fact* with which there can be no [contention?]. I fancy, however, for example, that until the German war is forgotten, Wilson's [documentation in?] the "fourteen points" will rank as an outstanding confirmation of that saying. So long as historians discuss twentieth-century events, they will rack their brains, and arrive at divided opinions, over the apparently obvious, viz:—what in the devil did the "fourteen points" mean anyway in relation to the entire diplomatic game behind the scenes?

These two types of situations connect up with my reminder a moment ago that my type of sociologist—which I frankly and resignedly admit is now in the reserve, not on the main front of the fighting line—must always have a certain function, and therefore a certain value, whatever may be the type of research which is foremost in a given period.

I might expand this remark in terms of analogy with architecture.

The first thing an architect needs to know, when consulted about plans for a building, is the general purpose of the building—whether a home, a warehouse, a factory, a railroad terminal, or what. Then a second thing for the architect to know is the lay of the land in the proposed location, its contour, its surroundings, its relation to the neighboring buildings already erected or in contemplation. I have just heard of a departmental group in a certain university that became enthusiastic over plans for a building which they thought would be ideal for their use. The architect promptly discovered that the building as proposed would completely shut off the sunlight from an adjoining university building and make the latter useless for its particular laboratory purposes. [Illegible insert.]

Correlation is a necessary part of construction. There is a close parallel between this phase of the architect's function and that of the methodologist. Moreover, it seems probable to me that, the deeper men in the future get into the literal realities of human relations, the more they will realize the necessity of employing the methodologist's type of research as a means of coordinating each special research with all the others.

Going back to my main thread of discourse, and summarizing further analysis that there is no time for in detail, I repeat that there are many kinds of social research after we eliminate all those that are merely amateurish if not fraudulent. There are many varieties appropriate each in its way, to as many different varieties of problems; just as one and the same condition of human tissue may present distinct problems to the physicist, the chemist, the physiologist, the pathologist, the neurologist, the psychologist, etc. There is no stationary, and absolute, and constant hierarchy of rank among legitimate types of research, any more than there are orders of nobility among the words in human vocabularies. The word that conveys the timely meaning is the ranking word at the moment. So of the kind of research which finds out the thing most sought for at the moment. Like all other things human, researchers have their relativities. These relativities are terms of relationships both between phenomena and between human attitudes toward the phenomena and between [illegible]. There is no more certain mark of provincialism among scholars than a tendency to set up a caste status that assigns conventional prestige to one type of objective research over other types. Research is bound to give place to research as ocean waves to one another.

Time would fail me to analyze the differences between types of positive research of which authentic specimens are within our knowledge. I reduce all that to the brief formula:—

Research that can establish its legitimacy before the bar of science differs from other research of equal legitimacy; a) in the kind of subject matter which it selects, b) in the kind of procedure which it adopts.

For an example under the first head we may cite the *Chicago Tribune's* "Enquiring Reporter." Each morning he or she asks the opinion of half a dozen people picked at random about some subject of casual interest. This is "research" after its kind, but it is research as near as possible to zero in scientific value. First because its subjects are of such ephemeral interest, second because we can only guess at the degree of representative character with a handfull of individual opinions. At the other extreme would be an attempt to discover the contexts of composite opinions in the U.S. as to a national attitude towards other nations. I am not construing comparative feasibility of solutions now, but merely contrast between trivial and scientific problems.

As an example of differences in *method* which distinguish subjectivistic from positive procedure, certain inquirers would attempt to solve the second problem by digesting the contents of American fiction for the last decades in so far as it pictures reactions to its [?] subject. And on the other hand there is such a procedure as the *Literary Digest* is developing in sending return postal cards by way of questionnaire to millions of voters.

Neither of these two methods is conclusive, but one is several degrees nearer to objectivity than the other.

I cannot take time to enlarge upon these alternatives, but will merely hint at further details. For example, suppose all the social scientists in the United States should agree to concentrate their research resources upon one of my special interests: the Sociology of Property. It would be a wholly appropriate division of labor for one group of men to devote themselves to the purely historical aspects of property phenomena, from the earliest times and among as many peoples as could be investigated, down to comparative constitutional and legal aspects of property in our own time, especially in our own country. It would be a second wholly appropriate division of labor for these sub-groups to investigate separately the workings of (a) economic, (b) political, (c) religious, (d) other cultural factors in the shaping of property institutions from time to time, and in constituting both strengths and weaknesses in contemporary property institutions, our own first of all. It would be a third wholly appropriate division of labor if another combination should devote itself to the present workings of our property institutions, measured by our present conceptions of tendencies which promote and hinder the general welfare. It would not only be an appropriate, but we shall someday see that, for intelligent people, it will someday be an indispensable division of labor for a fourth group to supplement the work of all the others by carrying on the methodological researches in demand for correlating the findings of such investigations as those just specified, so as to discover ways and degrees in which they may supplement one another, ways and degrees in which they challenge one another, locations of gaps which criticism will detect between the results arrived at by the several groups, and so as to project the next kinds of research needed to complete objective interpretation, both as a social culmination and as a point of departure for the next developments in the human process in this connection.

Obviously each of these subdivisions of scientists would need to use a technique and a procedure more or less different from those of the others. My emphasis here is on the point that it would be not scientific but snobbish for the people in any one of these groups to betray the feeling that their type of procedure is research *par excellence*, while the other people's procedure is something of lower rank. No human wisdom could correctly assign proportionate values to the different divisions of complex research. This kind of snobbishness was under the spotlight when Menger and Schmoller were contending respectively that the *psychological* or the *historical* method was the one thing needed in economics.

Moreover—and this has been in principle the central contention of the sociologists from the beginning, both against other social scientists and among themselves—each one of these special divisions of research might be objective to the limit of its means and still be abortive in the degree in which its procedure and its findings remain insulated from the procedures and finding of other investigators. It is essential to the acquisition of knowledge that, in the end, all research shall become *cooperative* research. Knowledge is limited in the degree in which cooperative research falls short of covering the entire range of the knowable.

There is neither bitterness nor even regret in my unhesitating admission that the kind of research to which my generation of sociologists were forced to restrict themselves rather narrowly, even if it is [illegible] with having begun research at all, is now very much out of vogue. That is the way of the world, and from the standpoint of the world, not of the individual nor of the single generation, it is turning out to be a good way. I certainly would not change it if I could, except to accelerate it. I wish we could speed up the process so that each generation might shoot its bolt as early as possible, and then retire to the veterans' home to make way for fresher troops in the fighting line. That process is going on irrepressibly, however, albeit a little retardedly. But it is quite possible that thirty years from now that variant of survey technique which we are beginning to call *social ecology* may have arrived at developments which will make today's surveys look archaic.

Another quite credible alternative is that the critique of group values, values already realized, values demanded in order to fulfill current movements in the human process, techniques of realizing values—such problems as these may in thirty years have assumed primary importance [?] to social science in America.

In short we are infants at large in the field of research.

What I am interested in saying now may be taken as a warning to you of the student generation not to imagine, as each generation probably always will in its earlier years, that you have come to change all that, under mandate to do a job that will set things permanently to rights. In brief, don't fool yourselves with the idea that your kind of research is the final pattern of research. Don't imagine that your type of research problem is to become the capstone of the arch of knowledge. Don't imagine that your sort of findings will turn out to furnish the missing clue to complete explanation of human affairs.

On the contrary, if we may infer anything from the recorded phenomena of human thought, the precise opposite will be the fact. So far as my observation goes, research that has amounted to anything has usually opened up more questions than it settled. In the contrary instances, "arrest"* has been a danger signal that the research has somehow run off on a wrong track and [illegible] banality and [illegible]. Unless the precedents in past experience are freaks, your generation will live to see the types of problems that you are most concerned with now not solved, and the results put in cold storage for future consumption, but treated like squeezed lemons. More juice will be sought from expected harvests of other varieties of fruit: while your kinds of research will look to your successors as archaic and obsolete as the researches that seemed so luscious to my generation appear to you now.

Let me immunize myself still further against suspicioning jealousy when I allow myself to be a little more specific for the sake of illustration. I wish I could do a skilled laborer's part of the work that the social surveyors are doing. I can't. I'm not equipped for it. I'm painfully aware of it. I am sorely tempted to envy them, but I succeed in applauding them without a lingering twinge of jealousy. I simply say that I'm not a kill-joy in my animus when I warn them that their time will come; because the indication of the past is that following them a generation will appear whose work in its time and place will be as much better than theirs as theirs is an advance upon ours.

The characteristic work of the present generation of social surveyors reminds me of three outstanding movements in social science a generation ago, not a likeness in themselves but a likeness in their relativities. The first was pursuit of the clue that all subsequent developments in the western world were evolutions from

---

* In the typewritten manuscript the word "arrest" is crossed out and is replaced with the handwritten insertion "apparent finality."

the Teutonic village community. The idea came over to us from Germany, but in England E. A. Freeman set it forth with picturesqueness that captivated my contemporaries. Its influence was at its peak while I was spending my first sabbatical year at the Johns Hopkins, 1888-89. Under the stimulus of Herbert B. Adams, a generation of eager young men enlisted to evangelize historical science with the gospel of Germanistic communist evolution. I mean all these three cases as illustrating the crudity of assuming that something was a finality which presently proves to be mostly a passing fashion.

The second movement with which I compare modern surveys is the cult of *sources, archives.* This is the variant of historical program associated most prominently with the names of Pertz and Waitz and Ranke. It impelled many people to seek and find pearls of great price. It left a permanent impression of inestimable value upon the best trained students of history. In its turn, however, it led to confusion of values, to disproportionate emphasis, to dilettanticism, and even superstition. In many cases, the cult of sources degenerated into magnification of the ancient, regardless of the question whether the particular specimen had anything to commend it except its ancientness. People excavated so busily for "sources" that they forgot to ask—Sources of what? For a while they stopped asking the question, What is it worth while to get evidence about? Enough for them that they brought to light a scrap out of the past, even if it told no more about important relations in the past than historians a few thousand years hence will be able to learn about the civilization of our year of grace from the average contents of the boxes deposited in the cornerstones of our post offices.

The third movement of which I am reminded—and I am speaking of these instances as having fallen within my own experience—is that eruption of historical and economic monographs which burst forth in Germany in the seventies, and a little later in this country. They were the first fruits from the planting of the so-called Historical School, in the fields of both history and economics. This movement too was a vital manifestation. It justified itself in the long run, but during the period of its exhuberance it was overdone. It ran into minutiae that were not only trivial but beclouding. It left on deposit formidable quantities of unorganized abracadabra, large portions of which have never proved worth assorting.

L.

I must confess that much of this accumulation, in each of the three cases, was in the course of that *Practice Research* which has its place in technical training, even if its results may not be of first-rate value. My chief reference here is to the fact that it is necessary now to go back to books and monographs written nearly thirty years ago to find very dogmatic expressions of either of these three movements in the tone of their extremest confidence. Yet in each case the protagonists of the movement had more or less of the feeling that it was a conclusive gospel.

It would be easy to draw similar parallels with present movements in *social psychology*. Again I protest that I would give all my old boots, and I would buy new ones for a lot of barefoot youngsters if I could thereby fit myself to make a contribution to social psychology. I know I can't, and as such I enthusiastically applaud those who can. It is beyond my powers of imagination to picture a time when social psychology will ever cease to be a necessary factor in social research. On the other hand, if the fortunes of other divisions and eras of science furnish any guides, there will come longer or shorter periods when social psychology will become relatively sterile, when it must lie fallow while other fields are producing their quota; when its methods will have reached the point of diminishing returns for their system of cultivation, just as a series of types of social psychology have already had their day, but now seem to be closed incidents.

All of this makes for the perception which I want to lodge [?] with you, that research runs in cycles. Nor are these cycles altogether unlike that aspect of the wind of which scripture reminds us. We cannot always tell whence they come nor whither they go. They are not logical. They move in accordance with laws to which we have only vague clues. For various reasons, both subjective and objective, the research that is timely today is untimely tomorrow. Its technique at a given period, however faulty when tested by the most nearly universal logic which a later period may control, may have genuinely served its purpose at its time; but its subject matter and its methods may have been left behind by shifting of the main strategy of research, and they may have lost their relative importance for the whole operation of scientific conquest.

I do not venture my next remark as a prophecy in detail, but merely as an illustration of what is possible. It seems to me quite likely that, before men of the present graduate student generation have reached the retiring age, the center of attention in social science in general and particularly in sociology, may have changed from its present objectives to precisely opposite types of problems. Thirty years from now sociological attention may conceivably be trained upon problems like these:—(1) The Sociology of Nationalism and Internationalism, (2) The comparative influence of tradition and of contemporaneous culture upon scales of value in national groups, (3) The objectives of a scientific civilization, e.g., How may we decide whether occidental or oriental preconceptions of life values are nearest to a rational [illegible]?, etc.

Problems of each order that I have named are directly in the line of march of human knowledge and nobody is wise enough to foretell when either of them may come into precedence in the order of the day.

Now if you have been able to see any plot in these rambling remarks, you will have realized, as I do at this point, that without any intention to that effect, I have drifted into partial conjugation of the irregular verb *to be*. I have noticed a few of the forms of its past and present tenses when predicating the noun *research*. The line of least resistance now runs in the direction of its future tense.

The first impulse of one in my position—poised to discover who is to be his successor—is to utter himself not in the subjunctive, nor yet in the indicative mood, but to express himself in the most pontifical of imperatives—"Do my way and be saved! Do any other way and be damned!"

I confess that for several years past I have had my seasons of depression over the prospect that your generation will not go my way, but will go its own way. I have felt keen sorrow over indications that your generation will not build directly upon the work of my generation, any more than my generation built directly upon the work of Lester F. Ward. I have even committed to paper several schemes of research which in my judgment would best economize the resources of the sociologists in the next one or two or three generations. After allowing a certain temporary indulgence, however, to that very human weakness, I have come back to the saner conclusion that I would not handicap future generations with my prescriptions if I could. In the long economy of the ages, it turns out that, on the whole, each generation knows its own business better than any previous generation could have defined it.

One of the most philanthropic men I ever knew, a constant and liberal giver to a wide range of patriotic, charitable, educational, religious and individual purposes, left a will disposing of a large estate in ways which he intended to be to the greatest advantage to his children and grandchildren. It was a will that represented years of study, with the advice of other men of wide experience. He is not yet a decade dead, but already changes of circumstances have occurred, which neither he nor anybody else could have foreseen, which have made his will operate in a direction precisely contrary to his purpose toward his descendants.

This is such a mysteriously moving world that the most capable people may count themselves happy if they have had wit enough for their own day's work, without presuming to foreordain the work of other people for tomorrow.

You will make mistakes, as your predecessors did, but they will be less calamitous mistakes than if you should allow your predecessors to do your planning for you. There is more wisdom than any of us have assimilated in the vagrant aphorism—*Sufficient unto the day is the job thereof.* From time to time you will arrive at your own evaluations of the sort of thing it is then most worth while to try to find out. You will have the nose for news that will scent out the particular clews most needed in your type and stage of research. You will have at least as much ingenuity as your predecessors have had in adapting procedure and inventing apparatus of investigation suited to your particular sort of problems. You will have your own tests of the validity and the invalidity of the methods proposed for solving your species of problems. You will probably have as much to show for your work as any generation in the past. I hope it will be relatively more. Anyway, it must, and should, and will be better work than it could have been if any one with the outlook of any previous generation had been able to come to life and direct it.

My attitude toward the entire retrospect and prospect may be expressed in the fervent hope that, when your generation reaches the retiring age, it will have to its credit as great a distance as the passing generation's record shows between point of departure and point of arrival, and that you will be as confident as we are now that the best is still in the future.

Notes

INTRODUCTION: THE COHERENCE OF SMALL'S THOUGHT

1. Edward Cary Hayes, "Albion Woodbury Small," in Howard W. Odum, ed. *American Masters of Social Science: An Approach to the Study of the Social Sciences Through a Neglected Field of Biography* (New York: Henry Holt and Co., 1927). Reissued in 1965 by Kennikat Press, Port Washington, N.Y., pp. 149–87. The quotation is from pp. 149–50. According to the unpublished "Listing of Ph.D. Degrees: Department of Sociology, 1895 to Present," University of Chicago, compiled by Morris Janowitz and dated 1 July 1968, Edward Cary Hayes received a Ph.D. in sociology from Chicago in 1902.

2. On this general point see Gladys Bryson, "Sociology Considered as Moral Philosophy," *Sociological Review* 23 (1931): 26–36; Bryson, "The Emergence of the Social Sciences from Moral Philosophy," *International Journal of Ethics* 42 (1931–32): 304–23; and Bryson, "The Comparable Interests of the Old Moral Philosophy and the Modern Social Sciences," *Social Forces* 11 (1932–33): 19–27. On Small in particular, see Jurgen Herbst, "From Moral Philosophy to Sociology: Albion Woodbury Small," *Harvard Educational Review* 29 (1959): 227–44.

3. See Carlo Antoni, *From History to Sociology: The Transition in German Historical Thinking*, translated by Hayden V. White (Detroit: Wayne State University Press, 1959).

4. Throughout his life, Small made numerous references in his published work to Schmoller and other economists of the German historical school, or to that school in general. These references often reiterated the association of social science and ethics in the thinking of these economists. For example, "Thirty years ago Schmoller uttered the defiant economic heresy: 'The entire economic demand is nothing but a fragment of the concrete moral history of a given time and a given people.'" Small, *The Meaning of Social Science* (Chicago: University of Chicago Press, 1910), p. 45. Emphasis in original omitted. Another example, out of many possible examples is: " . . . as the German economists have been declaring since 1870, *there are no economic questions which are not at last moral questions.*" Small, "The Social Gradations of Capital," *American Journal of Sociology* 19:6 (May 1914): 724. Emphasis in original.

5. The biographical information in the paragraphs that follow is from the autobiographical letter by Small that is reprinted below as Appendix E and from other sources. I am grateful to Mr. Ellis O'Neal, Jr., librarian of the Andover-

Newton Theological School, Newton Centre, Massachusetts, for making this letter, and other archival sources, available. The other sources include Thomas Jack Morrione, "The Early Life and Works of Albion Woodbury Small," unpublished M.A. thesis, Department of Sociology, University of New Hampshire, 1967, which includes references to, quotations from, and reprints of a number of primary sources on Small's early life and schooling that I have not examined directly; the chapter by Hayes cited above in n. 1; Ernest Cummings Marriner, *The History of Colby College* (Waterville, Maine: Colby College Press, 1963); Small's obituary by Thomas W. Goodspeed, *AJS* 32 (July 1926); and various other sources.

6. Small's printed "President's Report to the Board of Trustees of Colby University," 10 June 1890, pp. 16-17. Colby College Archives.

7. Small thought that his course was the first sociology course ever given in the United States. But he was mistaken. He apparently tied for second. For details on this point, see chap. 3, n. 18.

8. On this point, see Richard J. Storr, *Harper's University: The Beginnings* (Chicago: University of Chicago Press, 1966), pp. 7-34. Briefly, in 1888 the American Baptist Educational Society was founded as a spin-off from the Baptist Home Mission Society. Officials of the education society approached Rockefeller for support of the institution they proposed to found, before the Chicago site was eventually chosen. Rockefeller sought out the advice of various Baptist professors. One of them, the president of Rochester Seminary, who favored an exclusively graduate institution in New York, became his son-in-law in 1889. During that same year, Rockefeller told the pro-Chicago, pro-undergraduate group that if he contributed to a college in Chicago, he would want to do so through the denominational education society. And a few months later, he made a pledge, conditional upon the society's raising additional funds. And by certain other features of his dealings with the society, Rockefeller, in Storr's judgment (p. 32), "made certain that the paternity of the new institution was clearly established. The college in Chicago was to belong to the Baptist denomination and not to a single Baptist who happened to be very rich."

9. For some examples of the extent to which Small anticipated the work of the later "Chicago School," see chap. 3, below.

10. Among the nine papers by Simmel in *AJS* are "The Number of Members as Determining the Sociological Form of the Group" (8:1-46, 158-96), "The Sociology of Secrecy and Secret Societies" (11:441-98), and "Superiority and Subordination as Subject Matter of Sociology" (2:167-89, 392-415). Other German authors published under Small's editorship include Thon, "The Present Status of Sociology in Germany" (2:567 et seq.), Schmoller, "On Class Conflicts in General" (20:504-31), Toennies, "The Present Problems of Social Structure (10:569-85), and a number of others. Small also published articles on sociology in France, in Italy, and in Czechoslovakia. But the number of articles on sociology or the history of social thought in Germany listed under "Sociology, General and Historical" in the *Index to Volumes I-LII, 1895-1947* of the *AJS* (Chicago: University of Chicago Press, n.d.) published while Small was editor is far greater than the number of articles on any other country, largely because of Small's numerous papers that were later printed as *Origins of Sociology*, cited in n. 12 below. Later in his life, Small seems to have regretted the extent to which this German orientation had led to a relative neglect of Durkheim and of French sociology in general. (There was only one contribution by Durkheim to the *AJS*, in vol. 3, as against Simmel's nine articles.) In a review of a French book in *AJS* 19:6 (May 1924): 752-53, Small writes that the book's "inadequacies are too

evident to the naked eye" and then goes on as follows: "The same may not be said with equal confidence of our attitude toward Durkheim. On the contrary, I suspect that most American sociologists would be willing to confess that they have not given him the attention which he probably deseves," and that the same was true of the relation of American sociologists to French sociology in general. He had already made some similar remarks in the previous issue of *AJS* (March 1924), 608–9, in a review of Durkheim's *Education Et Sociologie*.

11. Small, *The Cameralists: The Pioneers of German Social Polity* (Chicago: University of Chicago Press, 1909).

12. Small, *Origins of Sociology* (Chicago: University of Chicago Press, 1924).

13. Small, *General Sociology: An Exposition of the Main Development in Sociological Theory from Spencer to Ratzenhofer* (Chicago: University of Chicago Press, 1905), pp. 242–304.

14. Jurgen Herbst, *The German Historical School in American Scholarship: A Study in the Transfer of Culture* (Ithaca: Cornell University Press, 1965). Herbst estimates (pp. 1–2) that between 1820 and 1920 almost 9,000 American students studied in Germany and reports (pp. 130–31) that of 116 American economists and sociologists responding to a survey that was published in 1908, 59 had studied in Germany between 1873 and 1905. Of this number, 20 had received German doctorates. Herbst gives considerable attention throughout the book (e.g., pp. 154–59) to German influences on Small's thought.

15. Many observers have noted the predominance of former clergymen and of sons of clergymen among the founders of American sociology. For example, Roscoe C. Hinkle and Gisela J. Hinkle, *The Development of Modern Sociology: Its Nature and Growth in the United States* (Garden City: Doubleday, 1954), p. 3 (although they fail to note that some of those whom they list as having been ministers were also sons of clergymen, including Small and George Vincent). It is by no means clear what conclusions we can draw from the predominance of clergymen and the sons of clergymen among the founders of American sociology. This predominance does not necessarily mean that sociology was an especially clerical discipline or was especially imbued with religiousness, as compared with other academic disciplines. Stephen S. Visher in "A Study of the Type of the Place of Birth and of the Occupations of Fathers of Subjects of Sketches in Who's Who in America," *AJS* 30:5 (March 1925): 551–57, reports results of a mail questionnaire survey to all persons in the 1922–23 edition of *Who's Who in America*. The A. N. Marquis Co., publisher of *Who's Who in America*, sent out the questionnaire at the author's request. Replies were received from 18,356 people, about 80 percent of those still alive when the mailing went out. Using the occupational data from the census of 1870 as the base, Visher reports (pp. 553–54), "In proportion to their numbers in the general population, the professional men have contributed more than twice as many notables born about 1870 as the business men, nearly twenty times as many as the farmers, about forty-five times as many as the skilled laborer class, and 1,340 times as many as the unskilled laborer. Moreover, according to these data . . . twice as large a percentage of clergymen's sons became such conspicuously valuable members of society as to win a place in *Who's Who* as was the case with the sons of other professional men combined." If sons of clergymen were overrepresented in *Who's Who*, why should they not be over-represented among the prominent founders of American sociology? I have attempted to compare the fathers' occupations of the presidents of the economic, historical, political science, and sociological associations between 1890 and 1930. Somewhat

surprisingly, these data were difficult to find in the standard biographical sources and many former presidents of the disciplinary associations were not even favored with obituaries in the disciplinary journals. As of this writing, the data are too incomplete to be conclusive. They do suggest, however, that sons of clergymen were much more frequent among the presidents of the American Sociological Society than they were among the presidents of the other three associations.

16. Small, *General Sociology: An Exposition of the Main Development in Sociological Theory from Spencer to Ratzenhofer* (Chicago: University of Chicago Press, 1905), pp. 245 and 247. Emphasis in original omitted.

17. Small, *The Meaning of Social Science* (Chicago: University of Chicago Press, 1910), p. 277.

18. This paper was published in *Publications of the American Sociological Society* 1 (1907): 55–71, and in *AJS* 12:633–55.

19. *Origins of Sociology*, p. v.

20. See, for example, many of the articles in journals such as *Transaction* (now called *Society*), *Catalyst*, *The Insurgent Sociologist*, and the *Berkeley Journal of Sociology*; the controversies over disguised observation in social research, with contributions by Lloyd Humphreys, Nicholas von Hoffman, Irving Louis Horowitz and Lee Rainwater, and Kai Erikson in the section entitled "Sociological Methods: Should Sociologists Snoop?" in George Ritzer, ed., *Issues, Debates and Controversies: An Introduction to Sociology* (Boston: Allyn and Bacon, 1972), pp. 45–91; the papers in Tom Bottomore et al., *Varieties of Political Expression in Sociology* (Chicago: University of Chicago Press, 1972: first published as vol. 78, no. 1, of the *American Journal of Sociology*); the debates over the participation of social scientists in Project Camelot, as in Irving Louis Horowitz, "The Life and Death of Project Camelot," *Transaction* 3 (1965): 3–7, 44–47; occasional articles in *The American Sociologist* such as Alvin Gouldner, "The Sociologist as Partisan: Sociology and the Welfare State" 3:2 (May 1968): 103–16, and numerous others; and some of the recent publications of Duncan MacCrae, such as his review of Rawls's *Theory of Justice* in *Contemporary Sociology* (1973) and his paper on "Utilitarian Ethics and Social Change" in *Ethics* 78 (1967–68): 188–98. Note also that the American Sociological Association took the first steps since its founding in 1905 toward a code of ethics for sociologists only in 1961, and that the first draft of such a code, intended to stimulate discussion and to provide an opportunity for ASA members to record their "reactions, criticisms and suggestions" was published in 1968. See *American Sociologist* 3:4 (November 1968): 316–18.

2. THE COMING SCIENCE OF SOCIOLOGY

1. Small, "Outline of Course in Sociology," (printed but unpublished, Colby College, n.d.), pp. 3–4. Although this "outline" is undated, the subtitle is "Privately Printed for the use of the Class of '93 in Colby University." As noted below in chap. 3, Small's course in sociology was a modification of the course in moral philosophy that, in the nineteenth century, college presidents traditionally taught to seniors. Hence, it seems likely that Small wrote this "outline" sometime during the academic year 1891–92, perhaps before the possibility of going to Chicago had arisen, for use during the following academic year. Whether or not this "outline" is Small's first writing in sociology is a matter of somewhat arbitrary definition. In 1889 Small presented *The Dynamics of Social Progress: An Address* (Concord, New Hampshire: Republican

Press Association, 1889) to the Sixtieth Annual Meeting of the American Institute of Instruction. In this address, which is quoted below in chap. 3 in another context, Small praises Lester Ward's *Dynamic Sociology*, "In spite of glaring faults, among which is gratuitous and illogical deprecation of Christianity ..." (pp. 14-15). Quoted in Thomas Jack Morrione, "The Early Life and Works of Albion Woodbury Small" (unpublished M.A. thesis, Department of Sociology, University of New Hampshire, 1967, p. 71).

2. Albion W. Small and George E. Vincent, *An Introduction to the Study of Society* (New York, Cincinnatti, Chicago: American Book Company, 1894), p. 31. This book is often cited as the first textbook in sociology. The authors' preface states that "this book is the first of its kind" (p. 5) and that since the founding of the department of sociology at the University of Chicago in 1892 "applications for information about a suitable college textbook in sociology have been incessant" but that "no such textbook exists ..." (p. 6). But this claim, too, is a matter of definition. Perhaps *Sociology: Popular Lectures and Discussions Before the Brooklyn Ethical Association* (Boston: James H. West, 1890) qualifies as a textbook. This volume, which addresses itself as "collateral" to various works by Spencer, Fiske, Wallace, Huxley, and other secularist, evolutionist thinkers, contains papers by numerous authors on such topics as "The Scope and Principles of the Evolution Philosophy," "Primitive Man," "Growth of the Marriage Relation," "Evolution of the State," evolution of law, of medical science, or mechanical arts, and of the wage system; and "Evolution and Social Reform." Compounding the definitional issue is the fact that a few years after the book was published, in a note on pp. 848-49 of "Some Demands of Sociology upon Pedagogy," *AJS* 2:6 (May 1897): 839-51, Small wrote that *Introduction* "is not a textbook in sociology but a path-maker in methods of observing and arranging societary facts." Then as now, those who would be pathmakers deny that they write texts.

3. Small, "The Scope of Sociology: II," *AJS* 5:5 (March 1900): 617-47. The quotation is from pp. 617-18. A passage in Small's *General Sociology* (see n. 4), p. 48, may explain Small's use of "correlation" in the last sentence of this quotation. Small writes: "Science is knowledge of things in their correlation. If they have no correlation, there is no material for science. If there are no recurrences, no regularities, no uniformities in societary events, there is no possibility of the rudiments of all science. There can be no descriptive classification." In this usage, when sociologists demonstrate "correlations" they are demonstrating (a) some kind of interrelatedness between different social phenomena, which interrelatedness (b) illustrates some general or recurrent pattern.

4. Small, *General Sociology: An Exposition of the Main Development in Sociological Theory from Spencer to Ratzenhofer* (Chicago: University of Chicago Press, 1905), p. 5.

5. Ibid., p. 45.

6. Small, "The 'Social Concept' Bugbear," *AJS* 19:5 (March 1914): 653-56. The quotation is from p. 654. This brief work is an unsigned editorial, but Small is listed as the author in the table of contents to this volume of the *AJS*.

7. Small's review of Herbert Spencer, *The Principles of Sociology: Vol. III*, in *AJS* 2:5 (March 1897): 741-42. The quotation is from p. 742.

8. Small, "The Scope of Sociology: I," *AJS* 5:4 (January 1900): 506-26. The quotation is from p. 526.

9. Small's review of Carroll D. Wright, *Outline of Practical Sociology: With*

Special Reference to American Conditions, in *AJS* 5:1 (July 1899): 116-22. The quotation is from p. 117.

10. Small's review of Schäffle, *Bau und Leben des Socialen Koerpers*, Zweite Auflage, in *AJS* 2:2 (September 1896): 310-15. The quotation is from p. 312. The context of the quotation is: "I believe that candid study of this new edition of *Bau und Leben* will do much to end unedifying contentions about things upon which there is more radical and general agreement than the disputants imagine."

11. *General Sociology*, p. 131. In a very different context, Small was seemingly less charitable in his view of Spencer's value as a sociologist. In correspondence with President Harper about possible members of the Chicago Department of Sociology, written after Small had accepted the job at Chicago but before he had arrived on campus, Small wrote to Harper, "Will you endorse me in offering our 'human fellowship' to Spencer. I think it would catch him. He is a good organist, and might be of some service in that line in *the chapel exercises*." Emphasis in original. Letter from Small to Harper, handwritten on Colby stationery, dated 12 August 1892. (University of Chicago Archives: The President's Papers, "Small, A. W.")

12. *General Sociology*, p. 131. Emphasis in original omitted.

13. Ibid., p. 173. Emphasis in original omitted.

14. Ibid., p. 177.

15. Ibid., pp. 176-77.

16. Ibid., p. ix. Emphasis in original omitted.

17. Small, *Origins of Sociology* (Chicago: University of Chicago Press, 1924), p. v.

18. Small, "Points of Agreement among Sociologists," *Publications of the American Sociological Society* 1 (1907): 55-71. This paper and the accompanying discussion were also printed in *AJS* 12. The pagination in the notes that follow is the pagination in *Publications*.

19. Ibid., p. 59. Emphasis in original omitted.

20. Ibid., p. 67. Emphasis in original omitted.

21. Ibid., p. 69. Emphasis in original omitted.

22. Ibid., p. 63. Emphasis in original omitted.

23. Ibid., pp. 64-65.

24. Ibid., p. 55. Emphasis in original omitted.

25. Ibid., pp. 55-56.

26. Small, "The Scope of Sociology: I," p. 507 of *AJS* 5 (not p. 507 of the continuation in vol. 6).

27. In the 1960s and 1970s the issue of one sociology or many sociologies has most often been posed in these same political terms, as when radicals call for a "New Sociology" or a radical sociology. They are, in effect, the obverse of Small. For a different view, in which a radical favors "one sociology," see Paradepp Bandyopadhyay, "One Sociology or Many: Some Issues in Radical Sociology," *Science and Society* 35:1 (Spring 1971): 26. Herman Schwendinger and Julia R. Schwendinger argue that Small wanted to make both Marxism and Spencerian laissez-faire theory ideologically unacceptable. See Schwendinger and Schwendinger, *The Sociologists of the Chair: A Radical Analysis of the Formative Years of North American Sociology* (New York: Basic Books, 1974), pp. 239-40. There is no evidence, however, that Small regarded his Spencerian colleague at Yale, William Graham Sumner, as beyond the pale, and the Schwendingers themselves note (p. 290) that the differences between Sumner and the other founders of American sociology "can be considered bourgeois 'family' differences."

28. One of the few places in which Small writes explicitly about this topic is the unsigned editorial, "Free Investigation," in *AJS* 1:2 (September 1895): 210-14. Small's authorship may be inferred from (a) his editorship of the *Journal* and the fact the other editorial statements in the early years of *AJS*, not by Small, were initialed by the author; (b) his writing style; and (c) the similarity between the opinions about large corporations expressed in the editorial and the views in Small's signed writings on the same topic. In this editorial Small answers a correspondent who cited the case of Edward W. Bemis, a member of the Chicago Department of Sociology whose contract was not renewed, as showing that "an educational institution founded by the arch robber of America ... exhibits a determination to throttle free investigation of sociological or economic subjects wherever there is any danger of running counter to plutocratic interests." Small wrote that Bemis was a contributor to that issue of *AJS* (he was the author of one book review); that further contributions from him, on any subject in which he was competent, would be welcome; and that "This *Journal* will not be equivocal in exposing the usurpations of capitalism, or in explaining principles to which the people must learn to hold corporations accountable." Small was not inclined toward the vigorous defense of academic freedom. He did not jump to the defense of E. A. Ross at Stanford, or of Veblen. As a former college president, he was inclined to give university administrators the benefit of all possible doubts in cases of controversial firings, and his editorial called on the public to do that, in effect, in the Bemis case. But he took for granted the standard beliefs in free inquiry and free discussion. His stand on Ross in particular, and some of his more general attitudes in these matters, are expressed in a letter from Small to President Harper of the University of Chicago, written on the stationery of the Palace Hotel in San Francisco and dated 31 January 1901. Small wrote: "I am convinced that Ross deserved all that he got though I am still of the opinion that it would have been wiser to have endured him until he could have been dropped more quietly. It was astonishingly like the Bemis case in many particulars, though not in all.... I still think that we are missing a chance to quiet [?] the popular ideas about universities if we omit to engage Ross for the Summer Quarter. Nothing that he could say could hurt us, but on the other hand his engagement would [illegible] the guns of people who are [?] to claim that the 'proprietary institutions' are afraid of the things that such men can say.... I am convinced that Ross and probably Howard are men who are about to make themselves impossible in a University." (University of Chicago Archives: The President's Papers, "Small, A. W.")

On the Bemis case there is, in the same source as the above, an undated document, most probably in Small's handwriting, which appears to be a draft, with crossings-out and rewritings, of a statement that a number of people, other members of the Chicago faculty or perhaps only of the sociology department, were to have signed. The document speaks of Bemis's "campaign of abuse." It asserts that "Instead of erring by teaching offensive views," his offense "was that he did not seem to present any distinct views whatever." " 'Freedom of teaching' has never been involved in this case." For a different view, see Schwendinger and Schwendinger, pp. 491-94.

29. Throughout most of the nineteenth century, Small's own alma mater, Colby College, was a good example of the older conception. It was chartered in 1813 as the Maine Literary and Theological Institution. It was Baptist and Jeffersonian. The only other college in Maine, Bowdoin, was a college of the "standing order" in religion and was Federalist in politics. These religious and political differences, intertwined with campus rivalries, continued to affect the position of the two colleges, usually to

Colby's advantage, for some two decades after Colby was founded. See Ernest Cummings Marriner, *History of Colby College* (Waterville, Maine: Colby College Press, 1963), pp. 11-13, 15, 43 et seq. A petition for aid to the Massachusetts legislature in 1819 (Maine did not become a separate state until 1820) argued that since the state supported one form of institutionalized truth at some colleges, it should support another form at Colby: "Your petitioners, in conclusion, cannot refrain from stating what is believed to be a fact, that neither a professed Baptist nor Methodist is now to be found among the instructors at Harvard, Williams, or Bowdoin. Considering ourselves pointedly excluded from the government of these institutions, and believing that the religious instruction offered is of a kind not the most correct, we humbly petition for aid to our Institution." Quoted in Marriner, p. 21. When Gardner Colby, a prominent Baptist merchant, made his big gifts to the college in the 1860s, one of his terms was "that the President and a majority of the faculty shall be members in good standing in regular Baptist churches." (Records of trustee meeting of 8 August 1865, quoted in Marriner, *History of Colby College*, p. 162.) In the 1880s the only eminent research scholar on the faculty, William A. Rogers, an internationally known physicist and astronomer, and one of only four Americans who was an honorary member of The Royal Microscopical Society, was, in Marriner's words, "One of the few faculty members . . . who was not an avowed Calvinist Baptist." He was, instead, a Seventh Day Baptist. Marriner, p. 226.

30. Small, *Origins of Sociology*, p. 6.

31. Ibid., p. 19.

32. Ibid., p. v.

33. Small, "The Significance of Sociology for Ethics," in the *Decennial Publications of the University of Chicago: Investigations Representing the Departments: Political Economy, Political Science, History, Sociology, and Anthropology* (Chicago: University of Chicago Press, 1903), pp. 111-49. This volume has pagination throughout, plus separate pagination for each paper. The quotation is from p. 119 of the volume, p. 9 of Small's paper. The emphasis here has been changed. We have added the emphasis on "pure science." The emphasis in the original text is on the phrase, "What is worth doing?" In context, Small was emphasizing this question as a question for "pure science" in contrast to "the ultimate practical problem," namely (and with emphasis in the original), "How may the thing worth doing be done?"

34. Small and Vincent, *Introduction to the Study of Society*, p. 70. The insertion of the phrase "investigation of" into the description of "Dynamic Sociology" is based on a sentence in the paragraph preceding the one quoted here which reads, "Dynamic Sociology proceeds to investigate means of employing all the available forces of society in the interest of the largest human welfare."

35. Small, "Points of Agreement," p. 67.

36. Small, *General Sociology*, pp. 94-95. All emphasis in original. In virtually the same passage, as it appears in "The Scope of Sociology: II," *AJS* 5:5 (March 1900), Small refers to "the general *kinetic* question" instead of "the general *dynamic* question." A footnote (p. 645) to the term "kinetic" announces a forthcoming paper giving reasons "for following the physicists in use of the terms 'dynamics,' 'statics,' and 'kinetics.'" The note goes on to explain that, in Small's usage at that time, "dynamics" includes "the theory of the social forces in general, while 'statics' is the theory of correlating, and 'kinetics' of the evolving activities, or of 'order' and 'progress.'"

3. Politics, Pedagogy, and Social Research

1. Small and Vincent, *Introduction to the Study of Society*, p. 15. The quotation that follows is from the same page.

2. Ibid., p. 17.

3. Small indicates on p. 492 of *General Sociology* that Vincent wrote this section of *Introduction*.

4. Small and Vincent, p. 99.

5. Ibid., p. 17. It is conceivable that Small picked up the idea of direct field observations while studying history at Johns Hopkins during the academic year 1888–89. For such work had gone on at Johns Hopkins before Small went there. See John Johnson, Jr., "Rudimentary Society Among Boys," *Johns Hopkins University Studies: History and Political Science* 2, no. 11 (1884): 5–56. The editorial introduction to this paper begins (p. 5): "When the publication of the Johns Hopkins University Studies began, it was not anticipated by the editor that any contributor would descend lower in the scale of institutional subjects than Towns, Parishes, Manors, etc. But Mr. John Johnson, Jr., after contributing to the First Series a valuable paper on "Old Maryland Manors" . . . yielded to the influence of a teacher's environment, upon a farm-school for boys, and began to study the agrarian customs and institutional instincts of rudimentary citizens of our larger republic. At first sight, such a study of juvenile society may appear boyish and somewhat trivial, but a nearer view of the customs and institutions of the McDonogh Boys will convince the reader that they are worthy of scientific observation. So curiously picturesque, however, is the life of this juvenile society that some readers may suspect Mr. Johnson of having written a kind of political romance with a socialistic moral. But his statements are all matters of the strictest fact, recorded with the conscientiousness and painstaking fidelity of a local historian. Modern students are finding historical and sociological materials in such imaginative writings as Plato's Republic, More's Utopia and Bacon's Nova Atlantis, but there are few scholars who have thought it worth while to utilize the wealth of fact and illustration for institutional history which lies at our very doors."

6. Arthur W. Dunn, *An Analysis of the Social Structure of a Western Town: After the Method of Small and Vincent* (Chicago: University of Chicago Press, 1895).

7. Small, "Scholarship and Social Agitation," *AJS* 1:5 (March 1896): 564–82. The quotation is from p. 581.

8. Letter from Small to Harper, typed on departmental stationery, 24 November 1894. (University of Chicago Archives: The President's Papers, "Small, A. W.") The man whom Small recommended for the post was Dr. E. R. L. Gould.

9. Letter from Small to Harper, typed, dated New York, 29 December 1894, ibid. Henderson is, of course, the Chicago sociologist, Charles R. Henderson, author of numerous works on criminology, "dependent, defective, and delinquent classes," settlement houses, other charities, and other topics.

10. Letter from Small to Harper, handwritten in ink on departmental stationery, 12 August 1899, ibid. There were, of course, many other factors in the failure of the early seeds to germinate until Park and Burgess joined the department. One factor, among others, was the relative absence of research training of individual graduate students before Park and Burgess arrived. According to interviews with Ernest W. Burgess (April and May 1962), when a student wrote a dissertation under Small he was assigned a topic, wrote it up, and submitted the manuscript to Small to be accepted or rejected. Park and Burgess, according to the latter, were the first

members of the department to guide students' dissertations. The full story on these matters would take us far beyond the confines of a book devoted to Small himself. For example, Henderson, one of the very first social scientists to have the idea of university-affiliated research institutes, would figure prominently in that story.

11. Small and Vincent, p. 16.

12. Marriner, *History of Colby College*, p. 225.

13. Small and Vincent, p. 17.

14. The following information on Robins and on Colby under his presidency is from Marriner, pp. 196-218.

15. Small, "The Presidency of President Robins," *Colby Alumnus* (1919-20), 146-54. See pp. 148-49.

16. Small, "The Class of 1876," *Colby Alumnus* (1925-26), pp. 42-44. Small writes (p. 43) that under Robin's predecessor Colby "was not a college" but "a forlorn attempt to prove that it was the repository of a germ capable of becoming a college." But during his four years there Colby became "in essentials a college" and each of his classmates "was the beneficiary of the quickening influences which began to be felt the moment Dr. Robins took up the thankless task of leadership."

17. Small, handwritten report headed "Department of History, 1883-84" and addressed "To the President and Trustees of Colby University," Colby College Archives. Although political economy was new and disreputable at Colby when Small first taught it there, it was, unlike sociology, not new and disreputable in the United States as a whole. The Reverend John McVicker began teaching political economy at Columbia in 1818; Thomas Cooper first taught that subject at the University of South Carolina in 1820; and the subject was introduced to Yale in 1825. At that time, however, political economy was barely separable from moral philosophy, and the two subjects were often taught by the same man. On these points, see pp. 310-13 of Gladys Bryson, "The Emergence of the Social Sciences from Moral Philosophy," *International Journal of Ethics* 42 (1931-32): 304-23.

18. A passage (pp. 16-17) in Small's printed *President's Report* to the Colby trustees, dated 10 June 1890, reads as follows: "By making the study of Moral Science follow, in the winter term, immediately upon the study of Psychology, I have been able to give, in the Summer term of the Senior year, a more favorable position to the History of Philosophy. I have also changed the subject matter of this course, and instead of attempting to trace the development of metaphysical philosophy in any portion of history, I have introduced the class to modern sociological phil-osophy. To the best of my knowledge this is a line of study which has never been opened to undergraduates in American colleges. The field to be surveyed is but partially explored, and it is impossible to present as exact data as in the older sciences; but I am sure that the plan of study which I have outlined is a profitable one with which to complete the college curriculum." Morrione ("Early Life and Works of Albion Woodbury Small," pp. 63-64) points out that Small was wrong in thinking this was the first sociology course in an American college. William Graham Sumner, who went to the newly founded chair in economics and social science at Yale in 1872, had taught sociology there before Small taught it at Colby. Small's course apparently ties for second with that of Frank W. Blackmar who had been at Johns Hopkins with Small and began teaching sociology at the University of Kansas in 1890. (See Hayes, "Albion Woodbury Small," p. 156.) Small, Blackmar, and E. A. Ross, who went to Johns Hopkins a year after Small left, are three sociologists who had studied at Johns Hopkins. Two of them, Blackmar and Ross, were first exposed to, and impressed by,

Lester Ward's *Dynamic Sociology* while students there. Herbert Baxter Adams taught *Dynamic Sociology* at Johns Hopkins and invited Ward to speak to his "seminary" during the academic year 1888-89, when Blackmar and Small were there. (See p. 74 of Frank Blackmar, "Lester Frank Ward," *AJS* 19:1 [July 1913]: 73-75.) On Ross, see pp. 99-101 of R. Jackson Wilson, *In Quest of Community: Social Philosophy in the United States, 1860-1920* (New York: John Wiley and Sons, 1968). Small does not mention meeting Ward at Johns Hopkins, and he had apparently read Ward before going there. At the time of Ward's death he recalled that when he went to Johns Hopkins he found only one member of the faculty who was familiar with *Dynamic Sociology*. (See p. 77 of Small, "Lester Frank Ward," *AJS* 19:1 [July 1913]: 75-78.)

19. Marriner, pp. 246 et seq.

20. Small to Harper, handwritten on departmental *AJS* stationery, undated. (University of Chicago Archives: The President's Papers, "Small, A. W.") The date is, of course, 1895 or later, the year of the founding of *AJS*.

21. Small's review of J. H. W. Stuckenberg, *Introduction to the Study of Sociology*, in *AJS* 3:6 (May 1898): 855-59. Small cites (p. 856) his "ten years' experimentation with sociology as a subject for graduates and undergraduates" and goes on as follows: "The only sociological instruction which can be made useful enough to justify displacement of time-tested subjects is drill upon definite sections of sociological problems by teachers sufficiently sure of themselves to keep most of this methodology out of sight." He reasserts (p. 858) his opinion that "the way to begin to study society is to begin," and cites Small and Vincent and other "methods of studying a local community" as examples of what he means.

22. Small, "Some Demands of Sociology upon Pedagogy," *AJS* 2:6 (May 1897): 839-51. A note on p. 851 indicates that this paper was presented to the Buffalo meeting of the NEA on 10 June 1896. The phrase quoted here is from p. 840.

23. John Dewey, *My Pedagogical Creed* (Chicago: University of Chicago Press, 1897). This is a book by Dewey, not an anthology that Dewey edited. Small's paper was the only one in the book by another author.

24. Among these papers are the following. "The Next Steps in College Development," an address at the Decennial Celebration of the University of Chicago, *The University Record* 6 (1901): 35. "The Social Mission of College Women," *The Independent* 54 (1901): 261-66. "Co-education at the University of Chicago," *Proceedings of the National Education Association* (1903): 288-97. "The Social Value of the Academic Career," *The University of Chicago Record* 11 (1906): 21-31. "The Doctor's Dissertation," *Proceedings of the Ninth Annual Conference of the Association of American Universities* (1908): 41-73.

25. George Edgar Vincent, *The Social Mind and Education* (New York: Macmillan, 1897). Reviewed by Arnold Tompkins in *AJS* 4:1 (July 1898): 99-102. This review is not included in the "Book-Review Index" of the *Index to Volumes I-LII, 1895-1947* of the *AJS*.

26. See Vincent's obituary, by Ernest W. Burgess, in *AJS* 46:6, 887.

27. Small, handwritten report addressed "To the President and Trustees of Colby University," dated 29 June 1885, p. 6. Colby College Archives.

28. Small, printed report of the department of history, addressed "To the President and Trustees of Colby University," dated 20 June 1888 and included in the *President's Report* of that year, pp. 21-23. The quotations are from p. 21.

29. Unsigned editorial, "The Russian Experiment," *AJS* 27:2 (September 1921):

232-33. The "Subject Index" of the *Index to Volume I-LII, 1895-1947* of the *AJS* (p. 93) attributes this editorial to the *New York Evening Post*. This error was presumably occasioned by the fact that the *AJS* editorial begins by quoting a *Post* editorial, and the table of contents of this volume of *AJS* erroneously lists the *Post* as the author. If Small was not the author—and the writing style is less clearly his own than is the case with certain other, earlier unsigned editorials in *AJS*—his editorship of the *Journal* implies his approval of an unsigned editorial.

30. For the source of this phrase see n. 36, below.

31. Small, "The Meaning of the Social Movement," *AJS* 3:3 (November 1897): 340-54.

32. For example, ibid., p. 350. "The individual laboring man today ... is haunted by the thought that he may any day lose his job. He feels that he has less certainty of keeping himself and family from starvation or pauperism than the average American slave had of living in comfort through old age."

33. For example, in his bad, bad, bad novel, *Between Eras: From Capitalism to Democracy* (Kansas City, Missouri: Intercollegiate Press, 1913). In "Scholarship and Social Agitation," *AJS* 1:5 (March 1896): 564-82, Small distinguishes between "ownership," a form of property in which (p. 574) "claims [of the owner] ... are practically absolute" and "proprietorship" in which "claims ... have institutionalized limits." Ownership should apply (p. 575) to "the fruits of one's labor," and proprietorship, holding or managing property under restrictions laid down in the general public interest, should apply to, among other things, accumulated capital.

34. The phrase "ameliorative drift" was used by E. A. Ross to take a slap at Spencer. Quoted in Wilson, p. 104.

35. Small's review of Lester Ward, *Dynamic Sociology*, second edition, in *AJS* 3:1 (July 1897): 110-11. The quotation is from p. 110. As Small wrote, he was referring not to 1897, but to 1883, when *Dynamic Sociology* was first published. This review is not listed in the "Book-Review Index" of the *Index to Volumes I-LII, 1895-1947* of the *AJS*.

36. Small, "The Dynamics of Social Progress: An Address," cited above in chap. 2, n. 1, p. 15. As quoted in Morrione, p. 70.

37. Letter of Small to Harper, typewritten on departmental stationery, dated 25 April 1895. (University of Chicago Archives: The President's Papers, "Small, A. W.")

38. Small, handwritten "Report of Albion W. Small. *History. June 1882*," addressed "To the Trustees of Colby University," Colby College Archives, pp. 2-3. The quotation that follows is from the same source, p. 3. The underlinings in the title of the report are in the original.

39. *Colby University Bulletin* (1884), p. 26. As quoted in Morrione, p. 49.

40. Published in *Johns Hopkins University Studies*, Eighth Series, I-II (Baltimore: Johns Hopkins University Press, 1890), pp. 1-77.

41. Small, handwritten report addressed "To the President and Trustees of Colby University," dated 29 June 1885. (Colby College Archives.) The quotation if from p. 4. Small begins this report (p. 1) as follows: "In the department of History, the year just closed has been the most laborious and apparently the least profitable since the department was established.... The work of the class has degenerated into a school boy learning of lessons, with little interest in study of a higher order." Then, he goes on to justify himself. "Since I have succeeded in leading previous classes into more advanced study, I cannot admit that the deficiency this year has been in myself."

42. Small, *Adam Smith and Modern Sociology* (Chicago: University of Chicago Press, 1907), pp. 16-17.

43. Ibid., p. 77.

44. The description is as follows. "Economic questions control to a greater degree than ever before the legislation and general policy of states: hence the pressing importance of giving to the student a knowledge of the fundamental laws which determine the material prosperity of a people. It is maintained that any stable system of economics must find its foundation in Ethical principles. During the time given exclusively to this Science, its principal questions are brought clearly before the minds of the students and its fundamental principles established, while the subsequent studies in History and Ethics at once confirm and complete the expositon." *Colby University Bulletin* (1884), p. 27. As quoted in Morrione, p. 50.

45. Edward Cary Hayes, "Albion Woodbury Small," in Howard W. Odum, ed., *American Masters of Social Science: An Approach to the Study of the Social Sciences Through a Neglected Field of Biography* (New York: Henry Holt and Co., 1927), pp. 149-87 (reissued by Kennikat Press, Port Washington, N.Y.). All of the preceding quotes in this paragraph are from Hayes, pp. 155-56. Hayes does not give any sources for the statement quoted here, and there are very few sources noted throughout the entire essay. It is therefore necessary to consider some reasons why Hayes, writing in the mid 1920s, might have known about Small's readings and about Small's reactions to his readings in the 1880s. First, according to the unpublished "Listing of Ph.D. Degrees: Department of Sociology, 1895 to Present," University of Chicago, dated 1 July 1968, and compiled under the direction of Morris Janowitz, Hayes received a Ph.D. in sociology from the University of Chicago in 1902. Second, excluding articles published in *AJS* after vol. 31 (1926-27), since Small died in 1926, his twelve articles in *AJS*, vols. 10 through 31, imply continuing contact with the editor, Albion Small. (See *Index* to *AJS*, 1895-1947, p. 21.) Third, Hayes writes with an air of personal familiarity about Small's voice, bearing, attire, and traits. Fourth, Hayes notes that the essay is in the present tense because it was completed shortly before Small died, and he quotes a letter from Small to himself (p. 184) that is almost certainly about the essay in question. That is, Hayes corresponded with Small about the essay. In short, Hayes had ample opportunity to know Small's later recollections of Small's readings in the 1880s. As for the accuracy of Small's recollections, we can at least say that they are quite consistent with the contemporary Colby documents quoted above.

46. Small, "Course of Study in Sociology," a handwritten four-page document in the manuscript collection of Johns Hopkins University. Neither the date, nor the context, nor the purpose of this document is clear. An unknown hand has written "1892?" in the upper left corner of the first page. It is possible, however, that Small wrote it during his year at Johns Hopkins, 1888-89, in connection with his requirements for the Ph.D. The document lists "sociology" courses he had taken, beginning (p. 1) with "The Relations of the Church to Practical Philanthropy (2 hours weekly)" in Newton Theological School (from which Small graduated in 1879), and including (p. 1) a course in Berlin and (p. 3) "Lectures on Social Science" by President Gilman and by three other members of the Johns Hopkins faculty. This "Course of Study in Sociology" also includes (p. 1) "an independent study of the theories of 'dynamic sociology'" and "study of one or more representations of the leading systems," such as (p. 2) the "Fatalistic" (e.g., Augustine), the "Pessimistic" (e.g., Schopenhauer), and the "Positivistic" (Buckle and Hegel). Then, on p. 3 comes

the heading, "On Systematic Sociology," under which Small lists Comte, Spencer, Schäffle, and Ward. The last sentence of the document (p. 4) reads, "Works on Pol. Econ. [illegible] approach Sociol. from the economic standpoint have been purposely omitted from this list." This sentence suggests that Small was not writing a general reminiscence about his intellectual development, but, rather, wrote the document in response to some specific assignment or request, perhaps in connection with his Ph.D. at Johns Hopkins. That it was addressed to someone, or to some body, at Johns Hopkins is suggested by the fact that he identified his course at Newton as being a course at that institution, and his course at Berlin as being at Berlin, but does not identify the institutional affiliation of President Gilman and of the three other members of the Johns Hopkins faculty whom he lists. Everybody at Hopkins knew who these people were. On balance, it seems most likely, then, that this document was written during 1888–89, and that Small read Comte, Spencer, and Schäffle in the late winter or spring of 1889, at the very latest, but probably some time before.

47. Ratzenhofer was included, along with Comte, Spencer, Ward, Schäffle, and others in the subtitle of the 1890 syllabus to Small's course at Colby.

48. See n. 18, above, on the apparent timing of Small's first reading of Ward.

49. Small, "Lester Frank Ward, in Memoriam," *AJS* 19:1 (July 1913): 75–78. The quotations are from pp. 76 and 77.

50. See n. 18, above.

51. Morrione, pp. 64–65.

52. See the quotation from Small's *President's Report* of 10 June 1890 to the Colby trustees in n. 18, above.

53. Bryson, "The Emergence of the Social Sciences from Moral Philosophy" cited above in chap. 1, n. 2, p. 307. (Yale in late eighteenth century); p. 309 (Princeton before the Revolution); p. 309 (Brown in 1827 and after); p. 311 (Brown in 1830s); p. 312 (Horace Mann at Antioch, 1854 and after); p. 312 (Yale in the 1820s); p. 313 (Yale in the 1840s and 1850s.) See also Bryson, "Comparable Interests of the Old Moral Philosophy and the Modern Social Sciences," also cited in chap. 1, n. 2, p. 21 (Yale in the eighteenth century); p. 22 (King's College in the middle of the eighteenth century); p. 22 (Dickinson College in the late eighteenth century).

54. In the University of Chicago Archives: The President's Papers, "Small, A. W.," there is a typed letter from Harper to Small, dated 19 January 1892, obviously not the first correspondence about Small's going to Chicago, in which Harper wrote, "Personally I want you." In the same source there is the official offer, a handwritten letter from T. W. Goodspeed, secretary of the Board of Trustees to Small, dated 30 January 1892, notifying Small that the trustees had, on the previous day, elected him "Head Professor in the department of Social Science" at an annual salary of $7,000. That letter was enclosed with a handwritten letter from Harper to Small dated 31 January 1892 in which Harper asks for Small's help "in the Executive work" and prophesies, "A glorious future awaits us." There seems to be no single, definitive letter of acceptance by Small, because he and Harper spent the next few weeks corresponding about the position of anthropology in the sociology department, and about the relationship between sociology and political economy in the proposed departmental organization of the university. Harper accepted certain objections that Small set forth on these matters and, in a typewritten letter to Small dated 8 February 1892 he told Small that he had "taken the liberty of announcing officially your acceptance." The correspondence about departmental jurisdictions continued at some length, but Small did not object to Harper's announcement of his acceptance.

55. Small, "Outline of Course in Sociology: Privately Printed for the Use of the Class of '93 in Colby University," p. 10.

56. Ibid., p. 4.

57. Small and Vincent, p. 373. Emphasis in original omitted.

58. Ibid., p. 374.

4. OBJECTIVITY, THEORY, AND THE UNITY OF KNOWLEDGE

1. *Origins of Sociology*, p. 29. This is but one of many passages and phrases throughout Small's work in which Small paraphrased or plagiarized Small. One of the most striking examples is the following. In 1892, while Small was still at Colby but after he had accepted the Chicago appointment, he objected to Harper's suggestion that his department at Chicago be called "Department of Social Science and Anthropology" by saying that such a title is like "Mathematics and Arithmetic" (letter of Small to "My dear Prst. Harper," handwritten on stationery of the President's Office, Colby University, dated 26 February 1892, in University of Chicago Archives: The President's Papers, "Small, A. W."). In 1922 Small wrote, "In a recent official publication one of our leading universities perpetrates the collocation—'history and social science.' If the science of people had cut its wisdom teeth, that monstrosity would be as impossible as 'algebra and mathematics' " (p. 649 of Small, "Technique as Approach to Science—A Methodological Note," *AJS* 27:5 [March 1922]: 646-51). Such echoes in the 1920s of phrases from the 1890s, even a phrase from an unpublished letter of which Small may have had no copy, tend to reinforce the impression that Small's basic intellectual stance was pretty much set by the early 1890s and that it is not necessary in this book to give more than passing attention to the changes he underwent after the 1880s.

2. P. 296 of Small's review of Franklin H. Giddings, *The Principles of Sociology: An Analysis of the Phenomena of Association and of Organization*, in *AJS* 2:2 (September 1896): 288-305. Small wrote further (p. 302) that in contrast to Giddings's deductive method, "Positive sociology is an attempt to set in order the facts so that inductions may some day be sanctioned."

3. P. 112 of Small's review of Franklin H. Giddings, *The Theory of Socialization: A Syllabus of Sociological Principles for the Use of College and University Classes*, in *AJS* 3:1 (July 1897): 111-13.

4. Lester F. Ward, quoted by Small on p. 196 of Small, "Static and Dynamic Sociology," *AJS* 1:2 (September 1895): 195-209.

5. Ibid., p. 201.

6. Ibid., p. 197.

7. Ibid., p. 196.

8. For example, see chap. 2, p. 18 and n. 36.

9. Small, "The Scope of Sociology: III," *AJS* 5:6: 794-95.

10. For example, of Giddings's attempts to understand all social relationships in terms of "consciousness of kind," Small wrote, "He no more expresses the social truth than he would express the physical truth if he said 'Gravitation is the cause of all physical phenomena.'" (Small's review of *Principles of Sociology*, cited in n. 2, above.) On Tarde, Small wrote as follows. Tarde holds "that this fact of imitation is the pass-key to the social mystery. It will furnish the formulas which will reduce the apparent chaos of history and of human life to orderly expression. But Tarde's weakness is just at this point. The play of imitation in human affairs is beyond question. But that imitation tells the whole story is preposterous.... I suppose he

would say that the first soldiers who used powder and shot instead of pikes and arrows, simply imitated former soldiers in using *weapons*.... The inventors of armor-clad vessels imitated all the sea fighters in *protecting themselves* against other sea fighters.... No one will be satisfied a great while with this stretching of the truth" (p. 397 of Small's review of Tarde, *Les Lois Sociales: Esquisse d'une Sociologie*, in *AJS* 4:3 [November 1899]: 395-400). Emphasis in original.

11. P. 354 of Small's review of A. Eleutheropulos, *Soziologie: Untersuchung des menschlichen sozialen Lebens*, third edition, in *AJS* 30:3 (November 1924): 353-54.

12. Small, review of Carroll D. Wright, *Outline of Practical Sociology: With Special Reference to American Conditions*, in *AJS* 5:1 (July 1899): 116-22.

13. See chap. 3, p. 22 and n. 9.

14. Small, "Some Researches into Research," typed, with handwritten corrections, additions, and insertions. (University of Chicago Archives: "The Papers of Albion Small," Box 2, Folder 12, p. 9. Emphasis in original.) This talk was published in the *Journal of Applied Sociology* 9 (1924-25), but the references here are to the manuscript version. The manuscript itself bears no date. The approximate date, the setting, and the audience are indicated in the following note (p. 1): "This was an informal address to the Research Society connected with the Department of Sociology in the University of Chicago. A long introduction has been omitted. In view of his approaching retirement, the speaker was strongly affected by the prospect that he would not again have a conference with an equal number of graduate students. His remarks were accordingly addressed to them, not to his colleagues in the faculty, and were in the nature of paternal suggestion rather than didactic formulas. With the consent of the editors, the colloquial form has been retained. A. W. S." This version of the document was apparently prepared for publication, after Small had given the talk. By the time of this talk, Small had been calling himself a "methodologist" for at least twenty-five years. On p. 856 of his review of J. H. W. Stuckenberg, *Introduction to the Study of Sociology*, in *AJS* 3:6 (May 1898): 855-59, Small wrote, "...my primary interest is in methodology."

15. Ibid., p. 17 and p. 19, respectively. In context, these quotations are less despairing than they might appear to be, quoted out of context here. For the full context see Appendix F.

16. Ibid., pp. 21-22.

17. Ibid., p. 23.

18. Ibid., p. 9, p. 10, and p. 9, respectively.

19. Ibid., pp. 14-15.

20. Robert K. Merton, "The Bearing of Sociological Theory on Empirical Research" and "The Bearing of Empirical Research on Sociological Theory," in Merton, *Social Theory and Social Structure* (New York: Free Press, enlarged edition, 1968), pp. 139-55 and pp. 156-71, respectively. First published in 1945 and in 1948, respectively.

21. Small, "Immoral Morality," *The Independent* 55 (1903): 710-19. The quotation is from p. 713.

22. *Origins of Sociology*, p. 80. Emphasis in original omitted.

23. Ibid., p. 93. Emphasis in original omitted.

24. Ibid., p. 80.

25. Ibid., pp. 40-41.

26. Ibid., p. 64.

27. Ibid., p. 64.

28. Ibid., p. 66.

29. Ibid., p. 76.

30. Small, "The Scope of Sociology: III," p. 779.

31. Small, "Scholarship and Social Agitation," *AJS* 1:5 (March 1896): 564–82. The quotation is from p. 570.

32. Small, "William Rainey Harper as University President," *The Biblical World* 27 (1906): 216–19. The quotation is from p. 216. Small goes on, following the sentence quoted here, to praise Harper for having had "a respect for the past that often seemed to verge upon ritualism" while, "At the same time his insight into the provisional character of men's achievements prompted an independence of the past frequently branded as iconoclasm."

33. Small's review of James Harvey Robinson, *The Mind in the Making: The Relations of Intelligence to Social Reform*, in *AJS* 27:4 (January 1922): 520–21.

34. *Origins of Sociology*, p. 36. Emphasis in original omitted.

35. Small, "Technique as Approach to Science—A Methodological Note," *AJS* 27:5 (March 1922): 646–51. The quotations are from p. 646. Emphasis in original omitted.

36. Vladimir Ilyich Lenin, *Materialism and Empirio-Criticism: Critical Notes Concerning a Reactionary Philosophy* (New York: International Publishers, 1927, and many other editions).

37. Small, handwritten report addressed "To the President and Trustees of Colby University," 29 June 1885, p. 15. (Colby College Archives.) The full context (pp. 4–5) is as follows: "I do not regard History as a subject belonging in a cramped corner of a College course without relation to other studies, hence without right to concern itself with them. On the contrary, Dr. Anderson has unquestionably been right in trying to realize at Rochester his principle that *all College study should be historical study*. I do not know how he qualifies this obviously hyperbolical formula but its general truth is plain if we concede that a 'liberal' education should afford the student at least a superficial acquaintance with the world he lives in." Emphasis in original.

38. Small, "Scope of Sociology: I," p. 507. (In vol. 5 of *AJS*, not p. 507 of the continuation in vol. 6.)

39. Small, *General Sociology*, p. 283.

40. Ibid., p. 438.

41. Ibid., pp. 438–40.

42. Ibid., p. 442. Emphasis in original omitted.

43. Small, "The Methodology of the Social Problem," *AJS* 4:1 (July 1898): 113–44; 4:2 (September 1898): 235–56; 4:3 (November 1898): 380–94.

44. Ibid., p. 380.

45. Ibid., p. 382 and figure facing p. 382.

46. Ibid., p. 384.

47. Amy Hewes, "Social Institutions and the Riemann Surface," *AJS* 5:3 (November 1899): 372–403.

48. There is a note by Small to ibid., p. 392, which reads as follows: "When the figure, *Journal Of Sociology*, November, 1898, p. 382, was explained to the class of which the writer of this paper was a member, Miss Hewes suggested that the thought could be more fully indicated by the symbolism of the Riemann doctrine. She was requested to elaborate the suggestion, and the paper may accordingly be read as an appendix to the chapter above cited. As its two closing paragraphs clearly indicate, it is not an attempt to give final formulation to social combinations. It tries to make the

fact of *complexity* in all social reactions more evident, and to give an approximate notion of the degree of that complexity. Miss Hewes' contribution to the subject is certainly commendable."

49. Ibid., pp. 396-97. Hewes's concluding paragraph, p. 403, is as follows: "The tedious, but very essential, sort of analysis, indicated in this paper is the kind of work before ... [the sociologist]. Having gained some idea of the interplay of the different forces, some comprehension of the structural interdependence existing between social institutions and human desires, and the functional activity continually at play, he gains also a knowledge of the obstacles which must be removed for his further progress. Before he is able to furnish even skeleton formulae, in which may be substituted approximate values for the meaning terms of desire, he must have a more complete, a more perfect, classification than has yet been made of the various forms of institutions and desires manifest in actual conditions, the data for which are not yet at hand."

50. Amy Hewes, *The Part of Invention in the Social Process* (Ph.D. dissertation, Department of Sociology, University of Chicago, 1903). Hewes, "A Note on Racial and Educational Factors in the Declining Birth Rate," *AJS* 22 (1916): 178-87.

51. This statement is made on the basis of (a) the absence of any more publications of this kind in *AJS* throughout Small's editorship, (b) the absence of any references to mathematical models, or any similar topic, in the course announcements of the department throughout the same period, and (c) the absence of any indication or hint of such works in the titles of the 81 dissertations completed in the department, 1900 through 1930. (See "Listing of Ph.D. Degrees: Department of Sociology, 1895 to Present," University of Chicago, Department of Sociology, 1 July 1968, compiled under the supervision of Morris Janowitz, p. 36.) Such arguments from silence are always weak, and the third one is especially weak. But if there was any work of this sort going on, it must have been isolated and individualized. It did not become part of a shared enterprise and a shared tradition.

52. See n. 48, above.

53. Small, "The Scope of Sociology," pp. 793-95. Note that the term "association" in this passage is virutally synonymous with "system of social interaction." It is a generic term. A wide variety of types or systems of social interaction falls under it.

54. Ibid., p. 795. Small had published Simmel in *AJS* before he wrote these lines. "The Persistence of Social Groups" began in vol. 3 and continued in vol. 4. Simmel's "The Number of Members as Determining the Sociological Form of the Group" (vol. 8) did not appear until some time after these lines by Small were published. It seems likely, however, that Small, an admirer of Simmel, who published nine of Simmel's papers in the *AJS*, took over this question from him.

55. Ibid., pp. 794-95. In writing of schedules of "traits common to associations of men," Small seems to have in mind work such as Merton's "Classification of Types of Membership Groups" and "Provisional List of Group Properties," sections 4:1 and 4:2, respectively, of "The Problematics of Reference Group Theory" in Merton, pp. 335-440. These sections catalogue a number of variables, and discuss some of the significance of each, preparatory to propositional theory. Or, again, Merton's discussion of "mechanisms" for articulating the role set in ibid., pp. 425-33. This discussion identifies conceptually, and illustrates, a number of "mechanisms." The next step from these "things that we see in human associations in general" to Small's "more intimate laws ... contained in these data" would presumably be the specification of the conditions under which one or the other of these mechanisms, or none, comes into play.

5. Professors as Moral Leaders; Sociology and Ethics

1. Small, "The Significance of Sociology for Ethics," in the *Decennial Publications of the University of Chicago: Investigations Representing the Departments: Political Economy, Political Science, History, Sociology and Anthropology* (Chicago: University of Chicago Press, 1903), first series, vol. 4, pp. 111–49. The quotation is from p. 146. There are two different paginations in this volume. Each paper is paginated separately, and there is also a pagination of the entire volume. My references to this work will always use the volume pagination.

2. Ibid., p. 134.

3. Ibid., p. 133.

4. Small, *The Meaning of Social Science* (Chicago: University of Chicago Press, 1910), pp. 10–11. In the quotation here I have corrected an obvious misprint. As printed, the third sentence begins, "Of the role," which I have changed to "Or the role . . . ."

5. Ibid., p. 277.

6. Small, "Research Ideals," *The University of Chicago Record* 10 (1905): 87.

7. The phrase, "a paramount standard of right," is from "The Significance of Sociology for Ethics," p. 117. The other phrases quoted in this paragraph are from "Significance," p. 116.

8. Ibid., p. 131.

9. Ibid., p. 131.

10. Ibid., p. 132.

11. Ibid., p. 140.

12. Ibid., p. 123.

13. Lester Ward, *Dynamic Sociology: Or Applied Social Science as Based Upon Statical Sociology and the Less Complex Sciences* (New York: D. Appleton and Company, 1883), 1, vii.

14. R. Jackson Wilson, *In Quest of Community: Social Philosophy in the United States, 1860–1920* (New York: John Wiley and Sons, 1968). A general statement of the "double challenge" and of the communitarian response is on pp. 29–31.

15. Ibid., p. 104.

16. E. A. Ross, "The New Foe of Thought" quoted in ibid., p. 92. Wilson notes that this paper is in Ross's college composition book in the university archives of the University of Wisconsin.

17. See, for example, the last paragraph of the autobiographical letter of 1915 reproduced as Appendix E below, and the sermons cited below in n. 20 and n. 24. An additional bit of evidence for the liberal or nonfundamentalist nature of Small's religious beliefs, and for the statement that he remained religious throughout his life is a one-page statement entitled "My Religion" that Small wrote in 1924. A copy of this document is in the University of Chicago Archives (The President's Papers, Small, A. W.") (He had apparently sent it to Ernest D. Burton, who was president of the University, 1923–25. In the same source there is an unsigned, typed carbon of a letter to Small, initialed "EDB:CB" in the lower left corner, dated 18 March 1924, in which the writer acknowledges receipt of "My Religion.") The document reads as follows:

Mar 19 1924

MY RELIGION

My Religion:—Is my attempt to make Jesus Christ the Pattern and Power of my life:—

It is my attempt by all the means at my command to find out what the Pattern and Power of Jesus Christ mean in terms of my own daily work:—
It is my attempt to frustrate the tendency of my theology to displace my religion:—
It is my attempt to cooperate with all men of like mind everywhere in trying to make this the religion of every individual and of every group of men of good will throughout the world.

When I want to distinguish this religion from any and all predominantly intellectual schemes of belief, I call it *Christianism*, and all men who hold it as their faith *Christianists*.

———

The above is my quota toward solution of the problem of forming a solid front against Fundamentalist theologizing, and of symbolizing it. I am submitting it to one hundred men interested in the problem. For service during the present stage of transition in religious thought would not agreement upon some such non-theological confession of faith be feasible; and would it not be wise and useful, *in all controversial discussion*, to employ the terms *Christianist* and *Christianism* in place of the meaningless label "Liberalism" or "Modernism"?

Albion W. Small
The University of Chicago.

18. Hayes, p. 150.

19. Although this statement does apply to Small, as compared with Ross, the reactions to Darwinism in the late-nineteenth century, both among religious and among secular people, were so various that simple statements of this sort are hardly valid as generalizations. See Paul A. Carter, *The Spiritual Crisis of The Gilded Age* (DeKalb, Illinois: Northern Illinois University Press, 1971).

20. Published in E. Benjamin Andrews, ed., *History, Prophecy and Gospel: Expository Sermons on the International Sunday-School Lessons for 1891* (Boston: Silver, Burdett and Company, 1891), pp. 380-88.

21. Ibid., pp. 382-83.

22. Ibid., pp. 384-85.

23. Small, "The Annual Phi Beta Kappa Address: The Social Value of the Academic Career," *The University of Chicago Record* 11 (1906): 21-31. The quotation about the church is from p. 27. The quotations about universities are cited below in n. 39.

24. In a volume entitled *University of Chicago Sermons* (Newton, Mass.: Newton Theological School), pp. 181-99. The reference here is to p. 186.

25. Small, Review of Arthur J. Penty, *Towards a Christian Sociology*, in *AJS* 30:2 (September 1924): 225-26.

26. Wilson, *In Quest of Community*, p. 90.

27. Quoted in ibid., p. 91.

28. Cited above in chap. 3, notes 15 and 16.

29. Cited in Morrione, p. 36.

30. *Historical Addresses, Delivered at the Newton Centennial* (Newton, Mass.: Newton Theological School, 1926), pp. 43-44, p. 55, p. 12.

31. In the University of Chicago Archives ("The Papers of Albion W. Small," Box 1, Folder 10), there is a letter to Small from Francis W. Parker, a member of the Illinois legislature, dated 5 October 1904 and typed on the stationery of the legislature. Parker asks Small, as a fellow Republican, to help defeat a prohibitionist

candidate for the legislature by allowing the Republican candidate's committee to use his name. The wording of the letter suggests that Small had previously allowed the use of his name for such purposes. In Small's reply of 8 October 1904 he declines this request, and writes that if he splits his vote he will vote for the prohibitionist. In The President's Papers, "Small, A. W." there is a three-page, unsigned, handwritten document that seems to be written by someone who knew Small fairly well, but was not a member of his family, probably to provide the president of the University with material for use in a eulogy. For example, it begins, "A few snatches of conversation which may be useful," reports that Small registered to vote on the last day of his life, and tells about the painful attacks he experienced during the last months of his life. One paragraph reads as follows: "We often discussed prohibition. We were both for it last fall. During the winter however I had more of an opportunity to see the operations of the law than previously, as I had been out of the country a great deal in recent years, and became an advocate of the repeal of prohibition. Too, Small clung to his ideas and I to mine, so we had many exchanges of ideas. Finally, he saw some where the statement that perhaps after all, many crimes that are now committed in fact used to be committed only in conversation over a glass or two of beer. This made a great impression on him as being perhaps a clue to the so called crime wave. He had not, however, come to any definite conclusion on the subject."

32. Charles Horton Cooley, *Social Organization* (New York: Scribner, 1909), pp. 411–12.

33. On American intellectuals in power and on the "clerisy" tradition in the United States see Marcus Cunliffe, "The Intellectuals: the United States," *Encounter* 4:5 (May 1955): 23. On the Transcendentalists see Wilson, chap. 1, "The Plight of the Transcendent Individual," and Stanley Elkins, *Slavery: A Problem in American Institutional and Intellectual Life* (Chicago: University of Chicago Press, 1959), chap. 4, "Slavery and the Intellectual." On the emergence of University scholars see Richard J. Storr, *The Beginnings of Graduate Education in America* (Chicago: University of Chicago Press, 1953).

34. This is the title of the last chapter of Giddings, *The Mighty Medicine: Superstition and its Antidote: A New Liberal Education* (New York: Macmillan, 1929).

35. In his "Preface to Workingmen," *The American Labor Movement* (New York, 1883) as quoted in Jurgen Herbst, *The German Historical School in American Scholarship: A Study in the Transfer of Culture* (Ithaca: Cornell University Press, 1965), p. 182.

36. Wilson notes, p. 64, "Like dozens of other American intellectuals who chose academic careers during the period, Baldwin thought of the university as only a new institution, more effective than churches, for promoting morality."

37. Small's answers to the question on the place and date of ordination in questionnaires sent to Newton alumni. He answers "Never ordained" (1898), or "Not ordained" (1910), or leaves the space blank (circa 1925). Ellis E. O'Neal, Jr., librarian of the Andover-Newton Theological School, kindly provided me with Xerox copies of these questionnaires and of the questionnaires referred to in the following note.

38. Dating based on mention of three grandchildren, of whom one was one year old in 1915 and of wife, who died in 1916.

39. Small, "The Social Value of the Academic Career," p. 24 and p. 28.

40. Ibid., p. 25.

41. Ibid., p. 25.

42. Ibid., p. 26.

43. Ibid., p. 27.

44. Small, *Meaning of Social Science*, pp. 268-69.

45. Ibid., p. 156.

46. Ibid., p. 177.

47. Ibid., p. 178.

48. Ibid., pp. 236-37. Emphasis in original.

49. Ibid., p. 239.

50. Ibid., p. 242.

51. Ibid., pp. 280-81.

52. Quoted in ibid., pp. 298-99. Emphasis in Small's quotations.

53. Durkheim makes this equation only in some contexts. For example: "Man's characteristic privilege is that the bond he accepts is not physical but moral; that is, social. He is governed not by a material environment brutally imposed on him, but by a conscience superior to his own, the superiority of which he feels." Emile Durkheim, *Suicide*, translated by John A. Spaulding and George Simpson (Glencoe, Ill.: Free Press, 1951), p. 252. (I have changed this translation slightly.)

54. Wilson, 117-18.

55. Albion W. Small and George E. Vincent, *An Introduction to the Science of Society* (New York: American Book Company, 1894), p. 140.

56. Ibid., p. 164.

57. Small, "The Significance of Sociology for Ethics," p. 113.

58. Ibid., p. 119.

59. Ibid., p. 119.

60. Ibid., p. 119.

61. Ibid., p. 113.

62. Ibid., p. 118.

63. Small, *General Sociology*, pp. 94-95. Emphasis in original.

64. Ibid., p. 95.

65. Ibid., p. 95.

66. "The Life," pp. 186-87. Emphasis in original.

67. "Significance," p. 115.

68. Ibid., p. 115.

69. Ibid., p. 121.

70. Ibid., p. 118.

71. Ibid., pp. 125-26.

72. Ibid., p. 122.

73. Ibid., p. 123. Small was aware of the similarites between "telecism" and pragmatism, and he cites his Chicago colleague, John Dewey, in the context of his assertion that all moral judgments are telic, on p. 141.

74. Ibid., p. 123.

75. Ibid., p. 124.

76. Ibid., p. 124. Emphasis in original omitted.

77. Ibid., p. 125.

78. Ibid., p. 125. Emphasis in original omitted.

79. Ibid., p. 125.

80. Ibid., p. 126. Emphasis in original omitted.

81. Ibid., p. 126.

82. Ibid., p. 131.

83. Ibid., p. 128.

84. Ibid., p. 131.

85. These quotations are from hymns 68, 66, 63, and 291, respectively, in *The Methodist Hymnal*, 1939 ed. The authors are, respectively, William Cowper (1731-1800), Joseph Addison (1672-1719), Isaac Watts (1674-1748), and John Greenleaf Whittier (1807-1892).

86. Small, "Significance," p. 132. Emphasis added.

87. Lon Fuller, *The Morality of Law* (New Haven: Yale University Press, 1964). See especially the section on "Eight Ways to Fail to Make Law," pp. 33-38.

88. Small, "Significance," p. 137.

89. Ibid., p. 140. Emphasis in original.

90. Ibid., p. 140. Emphasis in original.

91. Karl Mannheim, *Ideology and Utopia*, translated by Louis Wirth and Edward Shils (New York: Harcourt, Brace, n.d.). Mannheim defines "perspective" as (p. 266) "the subject's whole mode of conceiving things as determined by his historical and social setting" and he, too, associates holistic visions of the social origins of diverse "subjects" views with the overcoming of perspective thinking.

92. Robert K. Merton, "Insiders and Outsiders: A Chapter in the Sociology of Knowledge," in Tom Bottomore et al., *Varieties of Political Expression in Sociology* (Chicago and London: University of Chicago Press, 1972), pp. 9-47.

93. Merton makes essentially this same point in ibid., pp. 24-25.

94. Jean Piaget, *The Moral Judgment of the Child*, translated by Marjorie Gabain (New York: Free Press, 1965). See also Lawrence Kohlberg, "Moral Development," *International Encyclopedia of the Social Sciences* 10: 483-93.

6. HUMAN NATURE AND THE SOCIAL PROCESS

1. Albion W. Small, *General Sociology: An Exposition of the Main Development in Sociological Theory from Spencer to Ratzenhofer* (Chicago: University of Chicago Press, 1905).

2. Small denied that *General Sociology* was a treatise. He called it a "conspectus" (p. v) and, since it grew out of a graduate course at Chicago, a "working syllabus" in "rough, fragmentary, unsymmetrical" form (p. vi).

3. Small refers to the concept of social process as "central" on p. 519.

4. Harry Elmer Barnes, "The Place of Albion Woodbury Small in Modern Sociology," *AJS* 32:1 (May 1926): 15-44. The quotation is from p. 40.

5. The quotation is from Small letter of 26 May 1915 to the Reverend M. F. Johnson, reproduced above as Appendix E. The original is in the archives of the Andover-Newton Theological Seminary.

6. The similarity between this idea and the work of Small's Chicago colleague, George Herbert Mead, is, of course, not coincidental. In a note on p. 472 of *General Sociology*, Small acknowledges his debt to Mead. Small writes that Mead "urged that I started my theory of society without accounting for the individual, the working unit of society. I have never felt that this was the business of the sociologist. It belongs rather to the psychologist. Mr. Mead insisted, however, that it is impossible to draw such a sharp line between psychology and sociology. With that I quite agree. I do not think it is worth while to debate about division of labor so long as it is clear that a piece of work ought to be done. I have always taken this process of individual-building for granted, and have preferred to leave it to the psychologists for analysis,

because they are presumably so much better fitted for it than the sociologists. This state of human development is fundamental, however, and must be kept in mind by everyone who wants to understand society. I am glad that Mr. Mead called attention to it as he did, and hope the psychologists will carry the analysis farther than I can."

7. Adam Smith's hypothetical tribe is in chap. 2, book 1, vol. 1, of *An Inquiry into the Nature and Causes of the Wealth of Nations* (Oxford: Clarendon Press, 1880), pp. 14–18 (first published in 1776).

8. See, for example, Kenneth Dolbeare, *Trial Courts in Urban Politics: State Court Policy Impact and Functions in a Local Political System* (New York: John Wiley and Sons, 1967), p. 25. Dolbeare writes as follows: "There appear to be two recurring motivations evident in County politics: economic self-interest and striving for status in all its intangible dimensions. The economic motivation appears as the great integrator, the primary factor felt by all participants and serving as the means toward consensus and a basis for organizing otherwise disparate forces. The free enterprise system seems to harmonize and direct the actions of this collection of autonomous and self-interested profit-seekers with only a minimum of conflict, at least as long as opportunities for all to profit are so openly available. Status striving takes the home as its focus and seeks to surround it with protections and enhancements to guard its prestige, and subsequently to add to the amenities of life there by beautification or additional recreational facilities, but above all to keep out the danger of lower-class elements and to avoid contamination from unattractive business or commercial development. On occasion these two great motivators bring powerful forces into collision, and it is then that the politics of the County spark and flash into open conflict, widening as the immediate cause links up with preexisting divisions along religious, ethnic, or other situational lines until a substantial segment of the population may be engaged."

9. L. T. Hobhouse, *Liberalism* (London: Oxford University Press, 1945), pp. 125–26. The quotation that follows is from pp. 127–28.

10. Herman Schwendinger and Julia R. Schwendinger in *The Sociologists of the Chair: A Radical Analysis of the Formative Years of North American Sociology, 1883–1922* (New York: Basic Books, 1974) write (p. 249) that "Small ... considered the interest in private property (wealth) a natural and universal property of social groups." This equation of Small's highly general "interest" in wealth with a particular, historically variable institution, private property, is erroneous. Further, private property (or any kind of institution of property) is a certain kind of relationship between people while Small's notion of the interest in wealth refers to the relation of human beings to "things," i.e., to nature.

11. Ernest Jones, "Mother Right and the Sexual Ignorance of Savages," *International Journal of Psycho-Analysis* 6:2 (April 1925): 109–31. The quotation is from p. 120. Punctuation is in the original.

12. In the Marxian view, the essential difference between human labor and animal labor is that human labor is planned, premeditated, and carried out for the sake of previously known goals. See Vernon Venable, *Human Nature: The Marxian View* (New York: Alfred Knopf, 1945).

13. Small, "Sociology," *Encyclopedia Americana* (1918), vol. 25 as quoted in Ernest Becker, *The Lost Science of Man* (New York: Braziller, 1971), p. 24.

7. THE SOCIAL PROCESS AND PROGRESSIVE POLITICS

1. For example, "the cataclysmic destruction of the capitalist system" would leave

"simply a world full of wholly unrestrained greedy people, in place of a world full of partially restrained greedy people" (p. 452 of Small, "The Sociology of Profits," *AJS* 30:3 [January 1925]: 439-61). It is necessary, therefore, to pose "a problem in social psychology, viz. how may the service motive be substituted for the profits motive as the ruling passion in industrial groups?" ("Sociology of Profits," p. 454). It is necessary to see "the shallowness of any schemes or visions of social regeneration by machinery which do not deal with the fundamental actuation of the machinery"; that is, which do not go beyond the "problem of organizing men as they are" to "the problem of getting men as they are to be different sorts of men" ("Sociology of Profits," p. 455). This argument is a special case of Small's general view of "association" as the objectification of the subjectivities of persons in interaction with one another. Similarly, the following passage on "the social movement" reflects Small's ideas that the goal inherent in the "social process" is the maximum satisfaction of the "maximum combination of interests". It alludes to the interests in wealth, knowledge, rightness, and apparently, sociability. But nowhere in this passage, or in the article from which it comes, does Small make any explicit use of these concepts. "The men who are most sincerely struggling for security want it as the passport to more complete living. They feel, if they do not expressly say, that man's life is not realized when he is a well-greased cog in the industrial machine. He is not a man who is merely a well-fed drudge. Manhood is properly many-sided.

"Cultivating man is as proper a pursuit as amassing riches. Therefore let us have security in order that we may become men. There is latent in every man, not merely power to toil, but to toil intelligently. Every man is a possible economist, i.e., an organizer of effort upon rational principles. Every man has it in him to become in some degree a scientist, i.e., one who knows reality. Every man is a potential statesman, i.e., a maker of social life, if not of the highest rank, of some rank. Every man is of necessity at last his own priest. Men today instinctively assert the personal importance that belongs with partial consciousness of their latent powers. They want security in order that as workers and thinkers and citizens and worshipers they may realize their larger selves" (p. 353 of Small, "The Meaning of the Social Movement," *AJS* 3:3 [November 1897]: 340-54). In short, Small's general theory enforms his political writings, though he did not always make that fact explicit, or was perhaps not always aware of it.

2. "Sociology of Profits," pp. 459-60.

3. "Meaning of the Social Movement," p. 354.

4. Ernest Becker, "The Tragic Paradox of Albion Small and American Social Science" in Becker, *The Lost Science of Man* (New York: George Braziller, 1971) pp. 3-70. The first quote is from p. 9 and the second is from p. 13.

5. Harry Elmer Barnes, "The Place of Albion Woodbury Small in Modern Sociology," *AJS* 32:1 (July 1926): 25.

6. "Sociology of Profits," p. 446.

7. Dusky Lee Smith, "Sociology and the Rise of Corporate Capitalism," *Science and Society* 29:4 (Fall 1965): 401-18. Smith relies almost exclusively on "The Sociology of Profits," as against Barnes and Ernest Becker, cited in n. 4 and n. 5 above, both of whom point to Small's novel, *Between Eras*.

8. Herman Schwendinger and Julia R. Schwendinger, *The Sociologists of the Chair: A Radical Analysis of the Formative Years of North American Sociology, 1883-1922* (New York: Basic Books, 1974), chap. 31, pp. 247-53, entitled "Small's Syndicalist Vision," and numerous other passages.

9. Small, "Socialism in the Light of Social Science," *AJS* 17:6 (May 1912):

804-19. The quotations are from p. 808 and p. 809, respectively. Emphasis in original omitted.

10. Ibid., p. 810.

11. Small, "The Social Gradations of Capital," *AJS* 19:6 (May 1914): 721-52. The quotations are from p. 740.

12. "Sociology of Profits," p. 447.

13. Ibid., p. 442. Schwendinger and Schwendinger slur over this point when (p. 248) they write that Small's "syndicalist" view "defined the capitalist's profit as a well-earned wage." Small's view was that some profit was a well-earned wage and some was not.

14. "Socialism in the Light of Social Science," p. 13.

15. Ibid., p. 812.

16. Ibid., pp. 811-12.

17. Ibid., pp. 814-15, 816. Emphasis in original omitted.

18. Ibid., p. 815.

19. Ibid., p. 816.

20. Ibid., p. 816.

21. "Social Gradations of Capital," p. 726.

22. Ibid., p. 728. Emphasis in original omitted.

23. Ibid., p. 740.

24. Ibid., p. 742.

25. Ibid., p. 723.

26. Ibid., p. 733. Emphasis in original omitted.

27. Ibid., p. 752.

28. Ibid., p. 730.

29. Ibid., p. 732.

30. Ibid., p. 746.

31. "Sociology of Profits," p. 460 and, for the five points of Small's plan, p. 461.

32. Ibid., p. 460.

33. *General Sociology*, p. 208.

34. Ibid., p. 300.

35. Ibid., pp. 300, 301. Emphasis in original omitted.

36. Ibid., p. 300.

37. Ibid., p. 203.

38. Ibid., p. 204.

39. Ibid., pp. 204-5.

40. Ibid., p. 227. Schwendinger and Schwendinger seem to miss this point in their discussions of Small's view of the state. For example, they read Small's description of the state (i.e., *Staat*) as "a union of disunions, a conciliation of conflicts, a harmony of discords," as indicating a belief that the state is, in their words, "an impartial arbiter or referee" (Schwendinger and Schwendinger, p. 251). Similarly, they fail to see that when Small writes, "the modern State is both a political organization and an economic system, but it is much more. The State is a microcosm of the whole human process," he is defining the broad German sense of "state" in which he is using the term. Instead, they read these words as a call to broaden the functions of the state beyond laissez-faire definitions (p. 467 and p. 469). To be sure, the broad German sense lends itself more readily than the narrow English sense to the ideology of interventionist capitalism, and if the Schwendingers had caught this point, their argument would have been strengthened rather than weakened.

41. Ibid., p. 242.
42. Ibid., p. 242.
43. Ibid., p. 243.
44. Ibid., p. 244.
45. Ibid., p. 242.
46. Ibid., p. 245.
47. Ibid., p. 228.
48. Ibid., p. 231.
49. Ibid., p. 230.
50. Ibid., p. 233.
51. Small, "Christianity and Industry," *AJS* 25:6 (May 1920): 673–94. The quotation is from pp. 692–93.
52. *General Sociology*, p. 303.
53. Ibid., p. 386.
54. Ibid., p. 388.
55. Ibid., p. 387.
56. "Sociology of Profits," p. 459.
57. *General Sociology*, p. 603. Emphasis in original omitted.
58. Small, "Abraham Lincoln—The Prophet of Democracy," an address given at Temple Adath Israel, Louisville, Kentucky, in 1907. I am grateful to Nancy Taylor, secretary of the temple, for tracking down for me a printed copy of this address in the Louisville Public Library. The quotation is from p. 34 of the printed version.
59. Small, "The Church and Class Conflicts," *AJS* 24:5 (March 1919): 481–501. The quotation is from p. 499.
60. *General Sociology*, p. 279. Emphasis in original omitted.
61. Ibid., p. 280.
62. Ibid., p. 280.

8. Conclusion

1. Small's passing remarks on American blacks are scattered throughout his writings, and are not very numerous. The total impression they make, when judged by the standards prevailing in the 1970s, is that he had certain racist tendencies, but moderately and inconsistently, and that his intentions (as he saw them) were paternalistically benign. In a passing remark in "Abraham Lincoln—The Prophet of Democracy" he suggests that blacks have to learn the discipline of work. In order to make an abstract point in *General Sociology* he refers to a "black fiend" in the south, to the lynch mob, and to the higher type of whites who restrain the mob. Elsewhere in *General Sociology* (p. 485), however, he notes that the "southern man lives in an environment of race-distinctions" while "the northern man lives in an environment of merely personal distinctions" such that "personal likes and dislikes, social inclusion or exclusion, will depend on the individual." "His being a negro makes no more difference than his being a Spaniard or Italian or Russian or Englishman. To the southern man the idea of a socially acceptable negro is a contradiction in terms." See also the letter of the Chicago banker, William H. Underwood to President Harper, 28 April 1904 and the accompanying reply to Harper by Small, dated 11 May 1904 in the University of Chicago Archives: The President's Papers, "Small, A. W." Underwood asked Harper for advice on his daughter's engagement to "a physician, a Christian gentleman and scholar," who was

"40 years of age, a graduate of the University of Illinois," "who deports himself . . . in a very upright way, and seems to have ideals of a high and noble order" and who "was born a *full-blooded* Indian of Apache parents" (emphasis in letter). On the first page of this letter someone, presumably Harper, writes in longhand "Ask Department of Sociology to decide." In an apparently different hand, signed by indecipherable initials which are not "W. R. H.," someone else, perhaps a secretary or assistant wrote "Prof. Small, what is the scientific answer?" Small replied to Harper that he consulted with other members of the department and that their response is not expert opinion but "is the result of such reflection as our poor human nature, assisted by such departmental knowledge as we possess, can bring to bear on the subject." Small advises against the woman's marrying the man. "Other things being equal there is a greater antecedent likelihood of compatibility and marriage in the case of a marriage between two persons of the same race." Interracial marriages "are likely to lead to embarassment" that interferes with marital happiness. However, "this is a matter of sentiment on the basis of very largely artifical conventionalities, there are no known anthropological or physiological reasons why persons of the two races in question should not marry. On the other hand, it is quite probable that the offspring of such a marriage would show decided benefits from such a crossing of blood." In the end, then, although Small writes that the girl "should certainly be advised not to marry the man in question"; nonetheless "her judgment ought to be considered the final criterion." For, "The objections to be urged against her inclination amount really to sentimental prejudices rather than to substantial obstacles."

2. Small apparently believed that ethnicity was dying out in American society and he seems to have favored that goal. In *General Sociology* (p. 256) he quotes Ratzenhofer's prediction that when the United States becomes more densely populated and "the struggle for existence" has to be "more carefully planned," Americans will have a greater "need of attaching themselves to the several political groups into which their individual interests naturally divide them" and that "the memory of racial extraction may at last be reawakend," and "for the first time will America confront decisively the problem of its national existence." (Phrases in quotes above are from Ratzenhofer, as quoted by Small.) Small judges this prediction to be "a typical case of European failure to sense the trend of American tendencies." See also his letter to Mr. George F. Burech 28 September 1904, of which a typed carbon is in the University of Chicago Archives, "The Papers of Albion W. Small," Box 1, Folder 2, refusing to help with a school which the recipient hoped to found because the would-be founder hoped that his school would transmit Bohemian traditions and language to young people of Bohemian background, and in the words of Burech's letter to Small of 14 May 1904 "help preserve our language and our race." Small replied that "immigrants of all nationalities who propose to cast in their lot with Americans . . . should as soon as possible become assimilated with the whole of the population. Anything that tends to keep them a group by themselves is unfortunate both for themselves and their children." If immigrants "are so situated that it is possible for them to cultivate the language, literature and traditions of their native land, this is a luxury which each must support for himself" without help from other Americans. For, "The fundamental necessity is that of providing means of culture which will unite them with other elements of the population."

3. In "The Social Mission of College Women," Small asserts the mental equality of the sexes, favors women's suffrage, and the right of women to hold public office, and writes that if women are (exceptionally) breadwinners, then (p. 263) "No different principles should guide the college woman who depends upon her own earnings from

those that ought to govern the college man." However (p. 204), "The distinctive social mission of college women is the counterpoise of business. . . . They must be the stewards of the mysteries of appropriate human life. They must cherish the ideals, they must uphold the standards, they must protect the programs of thoroughly worthy living. They must take the lead in life itself, while business men and women take the lead in securing the means and equipment of life." See also "Coeducation at the University of Chicago." Both articles are cited above in chap. 3, n. 24. In short, from the perspective of the 1970s, Small was a paternalistic sexist; among his contemporary males he was relatively advanced in this regard.

4. For example, in the University of Chicago Archives, "The Papers of Albion W. Small," Box 3, Folder 6, is a typed copy of what was to have been, or was, a story in the *Chicago Sunday Tribune*, 10 January 1915 with the headline "GERMAN PROFESSORS INSULT AMERICAN INTELLIGENCE says Albion W. Small." The item took the form of an open letter to the secretary of the German University League in New York City, who had asked Small to reply to a statement by two University of Jena professors who had addressed American universities on Germany's position in the war. In his reply, Small refers to "my long time friend, Prof. Simmel of Strassburg," who had written to Small "a long letter, which was in substance an amplification of the statement that all the world had been lying about the Germans, but the Germans have the whole truth about themselves and the rest of the world." He attacks German professors for "an utter collapse of an objective attitude" after a century during which objectivity had been the "fundamental requirement of German scientific methodology," and for "special pleading" in their attempts to influence American opinion. Numerous documents of various sorts in the University of Chicago Archives show that Small was anticipating a possible military clash between Germany and the United States at least as early as 1904, and favored a strong American navy in order to prevent such a conflict.

5. See pp. 649-67 of Small, "The Bonds of Nationality," *AJS* 20:5 (March 1915): 629-83. In the section entitled "A Coherent Family Type" Small attacks adultery, lauds heroic self-sacrificing for one's children, deplores the desire to pursue individual interests that erodes the "coherence" of American middle-class families, equates the drudgery of the homemaker with the drudgery in life in general, and argues (p. 659) that "it is doubtful if there is any relation in which under normal conditions of mutual fidelity and loyalty on the part of all the members, the burdens from one end of life to the other are so well worth carrying and the compensations are so abundant, as in the standard family."

6. Mead and Dewey were Small's colleagues at Chicago. He knew both, and sometimes referred to both in his writings. (E.g., see chap. 6, n. 6, of this volume.) A full analysis of the relationship between these three, of their mutual influences, and of their similarities and differences would be an important contribution to American intellectual history. On Small's relationship to Ward see Bernard J. Stern, ed., "The Letters of Albion W. Small to Lester F. Ward," *Social Forces* 12 (1933-34): 163-73 and 13 (1934-35): 323-40.

7. Ernest Becker, "The Tragic Paradox of Albion Small and American Social Science" in *The Lost Science of Man* (New York: George Braziller, 1971), pp. 3-70. The quotations are from p. 20.

8. Ibid., p. 7.

9. Ibid., p. 10.

10. Ibid., p. 19.

11. Ibid., p. 20. The deletions from the Small quotes are in Becker.

12. Jurgen Herbst, *The German Historical School in American Scholarship: A Study in the Transfer of Culture* (Ithaca: Cornell University Press, 1965), p. 156.

13. Benjamin G. Rader, *The Academic Mind and Reform: The Influence of Richard T. Ely in American Life* (Lexington: University of Kentucky Press, 1966).

14. Vernon K. Dibble, "Political Judgments and the Perception of Social Relationships: An Analysis of Some Applied Social Research in Late 19th-Century Germany," *AJS* 78:1 (July 1972): 155-72.

15. Becker, p. 3.

16. See, for example, Philip Selznick, "Natural Law and Sociology," in John Cogley, ed., *Natural Law and the Modern World* (Cleveland: World, 1962). Selznick writes (p. 171), "In framing a general concept of law it is indeed difficult to avoid terms that suggest normative standards. This is so because the phenomenon itself is defined by—it does not exist apart from—values to be realized."

Index